MORO WARRIOR

Library of Congress Control Number: 2021948328

ISBN (hardcover): 978-1-956450-07-1
        (paperback):978-1-956450-08-8
        (eBook): 978-1-956450-09-5

Armin Lear Press Inc
215 W Riverside Drive, #4362
Estes Park, CO 80517

MORO WARRIOR

A Philippine Chieftain,
an American Schoolmaster,
and The Untold Story of the
Most Remarkable Resistance Fighters
of World War II in the Pacific

THOMAS MCKENNA

For Patti

CONTENTS

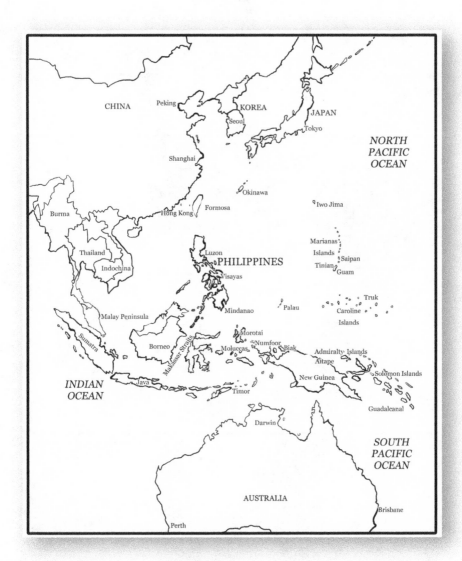

Asia–Pacific Region, 1942

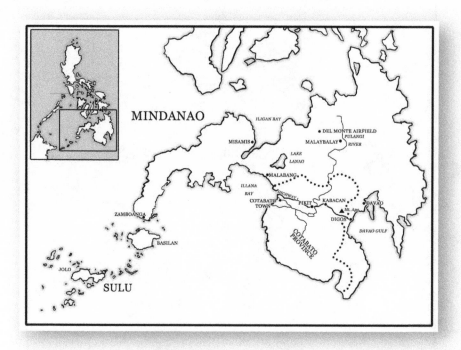

Mindanao and Sulu, 1942

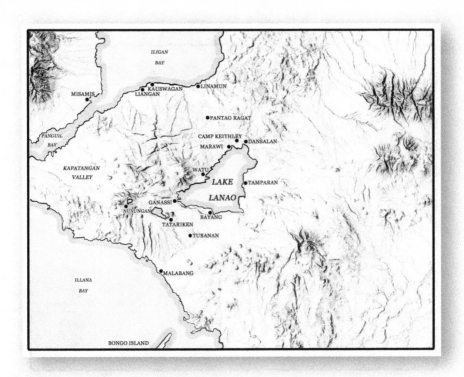

Lake Lanao and Environs, 1942

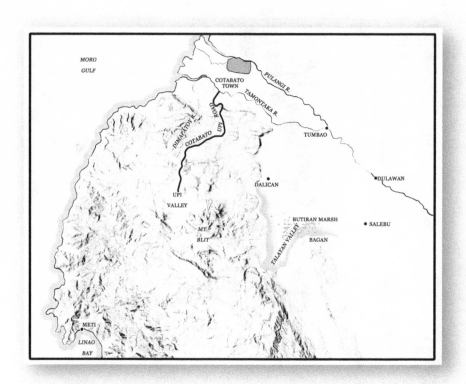

The Cotabato Delta and Cordillera, 1942

When he heard the message of the omen bird
Datu Mayatin readied himself, moving as quickly as thunder
and lightning
to defend his brother from the sea dragon that assailed him.
He took his shield in his left hand and his long-sword in his right,
carrying them like the warrior he was.
Walking thus armed was what he most loved;
so that his shield rang as he strode, first with
a shrill clash and then with a low roar,
and the words it spoke so loudly were these:
"Stay strong, my brother, I am coming for you."

— From *Lagiya sa Madaya*, a Magindanaon oral epic (author's translation)

* * *

He had an exulting eagerness for endeavor; when he talked, his aspect was warlike, chivalrous, and uplifting. No wonder his people admired him. We saw him once walking in daylight amongst the houses of the settlement. At the doors of huts groups of women turned to look after him, warbling softly, and with gleaming eyes; armed men stood out of the way, submissive and erect; others approached from the side, bending their backs to address him humbly…Karain walked fast, and with firm long strides; he answered greetings right and left by quick piercing glances.

— Joseph Conrad, *Karain: A Memory*

PROLOGUE

January 1942, Digos, Mindanao, Philippines

Each night as the sun slipped behind the dark crown of Mount Apo, the barefoot men followed their chieftain into the highland jungle, moving silently through the gold-flecked forest, raucous at dusk with the calls of hornbills and the squabbling of macaques. They spoke no English, wore no uniforms, and carried no guns, yet they were soldiers of an American army. In late December 1941, while ruined U.S. warships still smoldered in Pearl Harbor, they had sworn an oath of service to America and walked from their villages on the wide Cotabato plain to the eastern mountains of Mindanao to fight.

They were Moros—Philippine Muslims—and the first U.S. soldiers of the Pacific War to challenge Japanese troops in jungle warfare. At Digos, between the sea and Mount Apo, a dormant volcano that soared nearly 10,000 feet above the Davao Gulf and towered over the jungle canopy, they stopped the Imperial Japanese Army in its tracks. On December 20th, 1941, a Japanese invasion force of 5000 troops had landed at Davao, on the southeast coast of

Mindanao, intent on cutting the island in half and seizing its two main ports. It also had the task of securing the American airfield at the Del Monte pineapple plantation in the Mindanao interior. The Davao airfield was small with limited capacity, but Del Monte's airfield was large enough to land B17 Flying Fortress bombers. [1]

The defenders of Mindanao, four regular infantry battalions and two Moro battalions—termed "Bolo Battalions" because of the bladed weapons they carried instead of guns—made their stand at a jungled mountain pass, straddling the only highway leading to the interior. Facing a Japanese assault force supported by artillery, armor, and aircraft, none of which they possessed, the four regular battalions fought well but were hamstrung by weapons and ammunition that failed with alarming regularity. The deteriorated bolts on their World War I vintage Lee-Enfield rifles jammed consistently, and their mortar rounds rarely exploded. The sharp blades of the Bolo Battalions never failed.

In the dense rainforest between the opposing lines, the Moros probed the enemy flanks, ambushing Japanese patrols and isolated outposts. They waited beside jungle trails for approaching foot patrols and dropped like evil spirits from banyan trees to kill soundlessly with slashing krises, leaving headless bodies in their wake. Their silent attacks so terrified the Japanese invaders that soon they ventured beyond their lines only in platoon-sized patrols, rarely straying far from the highway.

The chieftain leading the Bolo Battalion on the north flank of the Digos line was Pindililang Piang, the son of Datu Piang, who from the turn of the twentieth century until his death in 1933 was the wealthiest and most powerful man in all of Mindanao. The Americans, with whom Datu Piang was strategically aligned, had called him the King of Mindanao. Like his father, Pindililang

Piang (known to the Americans as "Pindi") was proud, fearless, and plain-spoken. He was thus deeply offended when, one day in late January, he received a directive from division headquarters to collect unit insignia from enemy dead, interpreting the order as expressing doubt that his men were killing Japanese soldiers. The following day, Piang, fine-featured and handsome in crisp khakis and a white turban, strode to the command post with one of his men carrying a gunny sack. In front of his seated commander, Colonel John H. McGee, he ordered the man to tip up his gunny sack and out bounced a Japanese head, which rolled to a stop at the colonel's feet.[2] McGee had commanded Moro troops before the war in the Philippine Scouts and was one of the few American officers who clearly understood their military value. He was convinced, even before his encounter with the gunny sack, that the Moros had "done fine work, without pay" and "made a deep impression on the Japanese," and he considered Pindililang Piang to be "one of the finest fighters he had ever known."[3]

The night attacks of the Bolo Battalions continued to drain Japanese morale to such a degree that the commander of the assault force, Lt. Colonel Toshio Miura, fearing similar attacks from thousands more Moros in the interior, decided that his soldiers would not attempt to advance further. He then succeeded in convincing his superiors that a much stronger force would be needed to conquer the island. The full invasion of Mindanao was delayed until late April and, for the time being at least, Del Monte Airfield remained in American hands.[4]

It was mid-January of 1942, and at that moment, Japanese soldiers were racing down the Malay Peninsula toward Singapore while British commanders, outfought and outmaneuvered at every turn, marveled at an enemy they had begun to call "the superman of the jungle."[5] At Digos, it was the Japanese who were digging in to hold defensive positions and learning to fear a bewildering enemy. The Moros who played such a crucial role in stopping their advance were farmers and fishermen, husbands and fathers—not supermen—but they and their ancestors had been repelling foreign invaders for more than 300 years.

None of the Moros defending Digos had chosen to fight without guns. American military commanders in Mindanao sought Moro volunteers but refused to provide them with scarce firearms, not because they were unskilled with guns but because they could use them so well. By 1941, relations between the Moros and their American colonizers were generally peaceful, but they had only been fully "pacified" for a little more than two decades, and old fears remained. The prospect of large numbers of Moros armed with modern weapons still alarmed American and Filipino officers old enough to remember the Moro Wars.

* * *

Moros—the original inhabitants of the southern Philippines—are famous for their seafaring skills, their 300-year defiance of attempted Spanish rule, and for the fact that they are the only Muslim population ever formally colonized by the United States. Moros and Filipinos (the Philippine population colonized and Christianized by Spain) have shared the same archipelago and much of the same culture for thousands of years. It is colonial history that separates them. The conquered inhabitants of the northern two-thirds of the Philippines maintained their rich variety of local languages through three centuries of Spanish colonialism but lost almost everything else: dress, local religions, music, dance, mythologies, and social organization—especially the central role of the chieftain, or *datu*. In

1942, Christian Filipinos were the most Westernized people in all of Asia, whereas the Moros, despite 40 years of nominal American rule, still lived in a world filled with colorful costumes, oral epics, traditional music, soothsayers, sword duels, and magic; a world inhabited by warriors and ruled by local chieftains.[6]

The homeland of the Moros is the southern Philippines, consisting of the great winged island of Mindanao, abutting the deep Pacific, and the island chain of Sulu, strewn across the western sea. The Moros, who make up less than six percent of the population of the present-day Philippines, are actually a collection of distinct ethnic groups, including three main ones. Two of the three are found on Mindanao. The Magindanaons inhabit the broad Cotabato basin of central Mindanao and, just to the north, the Maranaos occupy the high valley surrounding Lake Lanao, an ancient lake formed by volcanic collapse. The territory of the Tausugs is centered on the island of Jolo, the largest island of the Sulu archipelago. Moros are thus not a single people. They are lowland people, highland people, and far-flung island people; river people, lake people, and people of the sea. They speak different languages, and they have never been united in a single political system. It is Islam and their evasion of Spanish colonialism that unites them.

For 300 years, the Moros fought the Spaniards every time they attempted to invade the southern Philippines. They then stubbornly fought the Americans who replaced the Spaniards before finally succumbing to overwhelming force and becoming America's only Muslim colonial subjects. At the dawn of the twentieth century, the United States defeated Spain in a ten-week war that the U.S. Congress had reluctantly declared over dubious grievances. In early 1899, the victorious U.S. acquired Spain's island possessions as its first overseas colonies. The jewel in the crown of that instant overseas empire was the Philippines, the largest, most populous, and most strategically-situated of the new colonies.

Surveying their new Pacific archipelago, the Americans were especially intrigued by Mindanao, the great southern Philippine island never fully subdued by the Spaniards. It was a land of super-latives; it had the highest mountain in the Philippines, the longest river system, the largest timber reserves, and the richest mineral deposits. It also had the Moros, colorful warriors utterly unlike the uniformed soldiers of the Philippine independence forces who had opposed them in the northern Philippines. With their fighting spirit, individual acts of bravery, and vibrant battle garb, the Moros appeared familiar to the U.S. soldiers (many of them former Indian fighters) tasked with seizing the new colony, and invited compari-sons to Sioux and Apache warriors.

Americans in general, were fascinated by the Moros. They flocked to see them when they were put on display at the St. Louis World's Fair of 1904 with other inhabitants of the new Pacific colony, exhibited like zoo animals in the "Philippine Reservation," which was, in essence, the first American theme park. The Moros, it was asserted by fair organizers, "were the most aggressive and at the same time the most civilized...of the non-Christian inhabitants of the Philippines." A sign posted in front of the Moro Village warned: "Persons Photographing the Moros Do so at Their Peril."[7] In the first decades of the twentieth century, scores of popular books and articles were written about the Moros by Western authors, including Joseph Conrad and Mark Twain. Most often depicting their subjects as noble, haughty, and appealingly exotic, they included memoirs, travelogues, histories, novels, and even children's books.

But when the Moros, like the Sioux and Apache before them, opposed the occupation of their lands, U.S. military commanders responded with well-practiced severity. They called them hostiles and renegades, hunted them down across rugged wilderness tracks, and massacred them—men, women, and children—by the hundreds using the most advanced weapons available. The veterans of the Indian Wars began calling these new armed encounters the Moro Wars.

In 1903, Captain John J. Pershing hauled field guns and mortars up a newly-built wagon road to Lake Lanao and began a campaign against the Sultan of Bacolod and the datus of Taraka, who were resisting American rule. Before it was over, nearly 400 Maranaos had been slain, almost all by artillery fire, while only three American soldiers died in the fighting. The Lake Lanao campaign made Pershing a war hero back home, gaining him a promotion to Brigadier General and launching him on the path to become General Blackjack Pershing, the commander of the American Expeditionary Force of more than two million soldiers in World War I.[8]

Three years later, on the island of Jolo in the Sulu Archipelago, more than 800 Tausug men, women, and children gathered in the crater of a large extinct volcano, Bud Dajo, a few miles outside of Jolo town, in an attempt to escape the American occupation and protest the imposition of a colonial head tax. Major General Leonard Wood, the first military governor of what the Americans had designated the Moro Province, decided that the gathering of Moros on Bud Dajo was a provocation that could not be tolerated. Convinced that decisive action was necessary to remove them, he dispatched a large contingent of Army troops to the mountain base.

On the morning of March 6, 1906, American troops under the command of Colonel J.W. Duncan, began the assault of Bud Dajo, fighting off Moro defenders as they went. That night they used block and tackle to haul mountain artillery and a machine gun up the thickly forested slopes to the rim of the volcano and, as dawn broke the next day, they began firing furiously and indiscriminately into the crater. A hailstorm of shrapnel and machine-gun bullets scythed down the men, women, and children on the crater floor like the stalks of rice they had planted there to sustain themselves in their place of refuge. As they fell, their bodies interlaced until they lay five deep in death. Of the 800 or more defenders, only a handful survived to be captured alive. The Americans lost a total of 21 soldiers killed. It was the largest massacre in all of the U.S. military's counterinsurgency wars in North America or overseas. General Wood, a medical doctor, publicly regretted the carnage and especially the mangled corpses of so many Moro women and children reported by journalists on the scene. But the bloodshed was unavoidable, he said, and added in his final report as Governor of the Moro Province that, since the massacre, "the people were pliable and plastic...and anxious for schools."[9]

Wood's claims notwithstanding, Moro resistance to American rule continued. Reviewing the first decade of American occupation, colonial official and scholar Joseph Ralston Hayden noted that armed encounters between Moro fighters and American troops had been more frequent and more intense than at any time during America's Indian wars.[10] In 1910, John J. Pershing, now a brigadier general, returned to the Philippines as Governor of the Moro Province and declared that the only solution to continued Moro armed resistance was their complete disarmament.

The Moros had long made small, beautifully ornamented bronze cannons and obtained muskets and rifles in trade, but the American occupation provided new opportunities to obtain modern weapons. The Moros transported to the 1904 World's Fair in Saint Louis for display had enthusiastically purchased firearms while there and secreted them back to Mindanao. Lieutenant Jesse Gaston, the acting military governor of Lanao, reported with frustration that "the Moros who attended the St. Louis Exposition bought and brought in, apparently without question, no less than fifty rifles and revolvers of the very latest models."[11]

Now Pershing required that the Moros surrender all their guns, and some of their bladed weapons, in exchange for cash payments. Some Moros responded by turning in decrepit muskets, and rusted blades, and others went back to war. In Sulu in 1913, Datu Jami and Datu Sahipa gathered about 500 warriors in another mountaintop crater—Bud Bagsak—and declared that they would never surrender their arms. Pershing called them "outlaws" and "desperados" and, once more, field guns were hauled up a mountain. This time, the warriors made several rushes to escape but were repulsed. As with Pershing's previous battles, the casualties were brutally one-sided. The Americans lost 14 killed while almost none of the 500 Moro fighters at Bug Bagsak survived the battle. Pershing, who reported that "a very severe, though well-deserved, punishment was administered," was recommended for the Congressional Medal of Honor for his actions at Bud Bagsak. It was the last major engagement of the American occupation. After 14 years, America's Moro colony had finally been secured.[12] With the end of military rule in the Moro South, the disarmament policy was replaced in 1920 by a set of regulations, already in force in the rest of the Philippines, that required firearms to be registered and taxed—rules that were still much stricter than existed at the time on the U.S. mainland.

* * *

Hadji Adil Tambis was part of the first generation of Moros to grow up under American colonial rule. His father, Datu Pangilamen (whose name meant "Fearsome"), had fought both the Spaniards and the Americans, but as the child of a newly conquered people, Hadji Adil did not want to be a warrior nor did he look like one. In 1941 he was about 40 and possessed the face of a man wise beyond his years who had seen the world's sorrows too soon.

After his father's death, his mother had sent Hadji Adil to the new American school. With his seven years of English-language education, he took advantage of the economic opportunities presented by American colonialism. First he tried commercial farming, an occupation previously shunned by datus. Later he became the only licensed seller of firearms in the vast province of Cotabato, both selling guns and providing the bonds that the colonial government required for firearms possession.

He must have appreciated the irony, then, as he enrolled Moro volunteers in late December 1941 to fight the Japanese without guns as part of an American army. Still, he was one of the few Moros of his generation who could read and write English well, and his good friend, Gumbay Piang, another son of Datu Piang, had asked for his help. Hadji Adil Tambis had brought along his eldest son, Mohammad, who had recently turned 17 and had just been sent home from his high school in Lanao because of the Japanese invasion. That day, young Mohammad Adil sat dejected on the Tamontaka dock because his father, refusing to send his son into battle against Japanese machine guns and tanks without modern weapons, had forbidden him to sign his name to the roster. The boy could only watch forlornly as his kinsmen and friends went off to war without him.

Despite not sending his son to fight in their army, Hadji Adil Tambis *was* an ally of the Americans and a friend to some of them. It was not that he had forgotten the Moro Wars and the massacres, but the intervening years had brought new considerations. For all the death they rained down on the Moros in their pacification efforts, the Americans had never conducted brutal scorched earth campaigns against them, as the Spaniards and their Filipino foot soldiers had so often done, burning homes, fields, and granaries. And when they were finally able to crush the last organized resistance, the Americans had tread relatively lightly in their new Muslim colony. They brought roads and schools and a Pax Americana, but they also had strictly limited plantations and settlers in the territory.

Most important to the Moros, they had not brought their religion. The Spaniards who tried for so long to colonize them had made religious conversion the leading rationale for their attempted conquest. The Americans placed it last; although they did not prohibit proselytizing missions outright, colonial officials gave the missions so little support or encouragement that they quickly failed.

Colonial education policy was carried out by young, generally idealistic, American men, and a few women, who had answered the call to "uplift and civilize" the people of the Philippines, including the Moros, through English-language education.[13] Among them was Edward Kuder, a young man craving the exotic and aiming to fulfill the prediction in his college yearbook that he would "win fame as a teacher in the orient." The staunchly secular son of proselytizing missionary parents, Kuder possessed a pragmatic idealism well-suited to his particular colonial profession.

When he stepped onto the dock at Manila Bay in 1922, Kuder was following in the footsteps of thousands of young American teachers who had dispersed throughout the Philippines over the previous twenty years, each of them intent on a mission to educate their colonial charges in American values. The U.S. colonial endeavor to transplant American values among the Moros was an experiment in "civilizing" without Christianizing, and no one approached that experiment more seriously than Edward Kuder.

Even as a younger man, Kuder was the personification of American colonial governance in the Philippines—paternalistic, imposing, and determined. And as provincial Superintendent of Schools, he oversaw the most significant official activity of America's imperial rule in the Philippines—ensuring the educational progress of its colonial charges; for the United States (whose citizens were of two minds about possessing overseas colonies) had promised to grant the Philippines some form of independence as soon as its inhabitants had achieved "American standards" of democratic values and institutions. In Mindanao at least, it was far from a desk-bound job. In the line of duty, Kuder traversed jungles, crossed storm-battered straits in tiny boats, and survived outlaw attacks.

Unlike most of his American colleagues, Kuder was a colonial official in the European mold. With his full college education, he was better educated than many of his fellow teachers and administrators. Most of them also served relatively short tours, while Kuder's colonial service lasted twenty years. Although he never learned a Philippine language, he was consistently curious about the culture and history of the Moros. Partly due to this interest, he was more determined than his colleagues to transfer American values to the Moros without Christianizing them. He also personally fostered a significant number of Moro students, paying for their high school (and sometimes college) tuition. Some of those students—all boys—lived with him in his house if they were studying away from their homes. One of those boys was Mohammad Adil.

Mohammad's father, Hadji Adil Tambis, agreed to register Moro volunteers at the end of 1941 because he strongly favored the American colonizers over the Japanese invaders. The atrocities of the latter in their occupation of China had filled Philippine newspapers. He was willing to support the Americans in their war, but not to send his eldest son off to fight in a battalion without guns. He must have known, however that his adventure-seeking son would eventually find a way to join the American war.

* * *

Moro Warrior tells the story of the extraordinary wartime adventures of young Mohammad Adil and, through him, of the remarkable and mostly unrecognized contributions of the Moros to the defense of the Philippines and the American war effort in the Pacific. It is also the story of America's Muslim colony in its last days and of its American colonialists in the person of Edward Kuder. Their shared story puts the Moros, at last, in their proper place in the history of the Japanese-occupied Philippines—fighting heroically and with exceptional success in their homeland of Mindanao from the very first days of the Pacific War to the very last.

I first met Mohammad Adil as a young anthropologist conducting field research in Mindanao in 1986. Many steps had led me there but I may have taken the first one at age nine when I used the gift money from my First Communion to buy my first book—an illustrated story about the Eskimos of the Arctic Circle. Their traditional life in the frozen waste felt immediately brighter and more exciting than my own. In college, I majored in cultural anthropology, which seemed to have been invented for me, and, unsurprisingly, it became my profession. When I needed a research subject for my dissertation, my first impulse was to avoid the Philippines because, ironically, it seemed too close to home. In my childhood's multi-ethnic San Francisco neighborhood, my Filipino friends and neighbors, despite their exotic origins, shared a religious culture with my Irish Catholic family. They attended Mass regularly, sent their children to parochial schools, and were pleased when one of those children decided to become a priest or nun.

But when I discovered that in Mindanao, there were Moros, who had shamans instead of priests and Sufi saints instead of Catholic ones, I was intrigued. And when I learned that the Moros had held fast to a glorious cultural heritage in the face of more than 350 years of assaults from the West, I knew I had to go to Mindanao. In 1985, the Moros were a small Muslim minority struggling to determine their fate in the most Westernized country in Asia. It was a predicament that resonated with me, and I wanted to learn as much as I could about them to tell their story to the world.

I arrived in Manila in the spring of 1985, the thirteenth year of the dictatorship of Ferdinand Marcos, the man who had destroyed Philippine democracy because he refused to relinquish the office of President. The national capital felt tense and exhausted, like the regime itself. Everyone I met in Manila told me that I was going to a very dangerous place, although none of them had ever been to Mindanao. When I arrived in Mindanao and took up residence in a Moro shantytown in a riverside marsh on the edge of Cotabato City, I found generous, welcoming people who taught me and protected me as though I were a child of the community.

In that community I tried to live in the same way as everyone else; eating, fasting and celebrating with them. I stayed with a large family and became an honorary brother and son. Within a year, I spoke passable Magindanaon (the language of the Moros of Cotabato), I had become known in the community, and I had learned a tremendous amount about Moro culture and history with still much left to discover. And as the year ended, I found Mohammad Adil.

The day before I first saw him speak, everything had changed in an instant for the people of the Philippines when, in a sudden rush of rotor blades, Ferdinand Marcos fled the country in a U.S. government helicopter. Nonviolent mass demonstrations had defeated the dictator and restored democracy, and in every city in the country, the next day, February 26th, 1986, was a day of jubilation. In Cotabato City, a People's Victory rally brought thousands of people—Muslims and Christians—to the central plaza to celebrate.

One of the featured speakers at the rally was a man I had never seen but whose name I had heard more than once. He was known then as Major Adil, a man in his 60s, vigorous and handsome, with salt and pepper hair brush cut in the military style. He was 5'6," squarely built, with a ramrod-straight back and a forceful voice that filled the large plaza and occasionally rose to a roar. As he spoke scathingly about the corruption of the Marcos regime, the crowd roared back its approval. Forty-five years after sitting disheartened on the Tamontaka dock, he had become a legendary figure. A former Philippine military officer, he had reluctantly fought against his former army comrades when the dictator attacked the Moro homeland.

The more I learned about Major Adil, the more I knew I had to interview him. A few months later, I visited him for the first time at his home near Cotabato City. The very first story he told me on that day in 1986 was about his exploits as a teenage guerrilla officer in World War II. The next story was about how he had met his American foster father, Edward Kuder. From that first day, his stories entranced me with their richness and detail—their warriors and princesses, magic and menace.

Most surprising were his memories of the Japanese occupation. These were his favorite stories and the ones he came back to most often; stories of his adventures, and those of other Moros, during that time. In the postwar decades, Western authors wrote popular books about the war in Mindanao, but they rarely mentioned Moros, who, when they were portrayed at all, were usually disparaged as villains rather than admired as noble. Mohammad Adil's stories painted an entirely different picture of anti-Japanese resistance in the Philippines—one in which the Moros not only played crucial roles but were, in many cases, the leading actors.

His stories, and the documents that accompanied them, eventually led me to enough evidence in scattered sources to weave together, for the first time, a full depiction of the contribution of the Moros—one that includes remarkable achievements (such as those of the Bolo Battalions at Digos) as well as exceptional sacrifices. The story of Mohammad Adil's wartime adventure begins, like so many of the best stories, with disappointment and defeat.

1
INVITATION TO WAR

The first time the guerrilla courier appeared in the night at his father's door, Mohammad Adil was not there to receive his message. He was 30 miles upriver courting a princess. Adil, recently turned 17, was the grandson of two renowned warriors whose exploits were still celebrated in song. A warrior was all he wanted to be, but by February 1943, he was sure he had missed his best chance. The greatest war in anyone's memory had swept past before he could join the fight. The battle for the Philippines had ended with the Americans surrendering their colony to the Empire of Japan, and the Pacific War had moved on. In his upriver refuge in Tumbao, he consoled himself with cockfighting, although lately, it was a courtship that occupied his thoughts.

With time on his hands and the war out of reach, the young man had turned his attention to the game of love—an entirely new undertaking for him and one, he was beginning to realize, not entirely within his grasp. The object of his attention, Umbus a Bai, the Flower of the Princesses, was lovely, haughty, and disturbingly self-assured, having never in her 17 years been denied anything she desired. At the moment, she desired Adil. Newly marriageable, she told everyone in Tumbao who would listen that her first choice for a husband was the conceited but handsome son of Hadji Adil Tambis, the boy who had defeated the magnificent rooster of her uncle, the sultan, with a bird that looked fit only for the frying pan.

Mohammad Adil had never known a girl who so unsettled him. The Flower of the Princesses, sultry and soft, was also so imperious that he felt outmatched for the first time in his life. Adil knew nothing of courtship, but compelled to act on these new feelings, he devised a plan.

One cloudless morning in Tumbao, he watched from the window of his father's rice mill as a procession left the house of the sultan. Umbus a Bai and four of her handmaidens were going to bathe. Upstream from the mill, on the opposite bank of the river, a spit of fine black sand appeared at every low tide, forming a quiet pool perfect for bathing.

Adil grabbed his .22 and crept up the near bank for a better view. Crouched behind a narra tree, he watched the princess and her attendants lift their *malongs* an inch at a time as they waded into the waist-deep water, then lower themselves into the pool until the water touched their shoulders. They tossed their knotted *malongs* onto the riverbank. Umbus a Bai was unclothed in the water, her attendants, surrounding her in a circle of shining hair and bright laughter. This was his chance. He desperately desired to see her naked and wanted nearly as much to see her unnerved. And one small part of him, he realized as he put the rifle to his cheek, was hoping to scare her off.

The .22 cracked three times in quick succession as the bullets zipped through the water not far from the bathers. Umbus Bai's maids, raced naked from the river, but she remained right where she was. Slowly the princess stood to her full height in the pool, her hands covering her breasts, the water reaching just below her navel. She glared across the river, her eyes searching for him on the opposite bank, and shouted her outrage.

"You pig! You idiot! You coward! Show yourself! Look, you didn't even hit me! If you were a real man, you would come here now and get me!"

Adil laughed loudly, attempting to sound triumphant, but he stayed hidden behind his tree because his plan hadn't anticipated this reaction.

Umbus a Bai cast one more fiery glance across the river, searching for the infuriating young man who had started a game he didn't know how to finish, then turned sharply and started up the bank where her attendants waited nervously with her *malong*. She pulled her long wet hair back past her shoulders as she walked, and Adil, now entranced, watched the water roll over her perfectly curved hips on its way back to the river.

Before noon, a delegation of her aunts came to him at the rice mill, carrying gifts of food. Addressing him by his ancestral title, chieftain, the eldest of them, said, "*Datu*, it is time that you married this girl." It would be an ideal match between two noble families, she went on, and his father would surely approve. Adil was not so certain, which was why he had told his father nothing about Umbus a Bai.

At his farm downriver in Pagalamatan, Mohammad Adil's father greeted his nocturnal visitor—an itinerant trader named Gandamasir, whose wizened face drew no attention from the Japanese sentries who manned the river checkpoints—and took a crumpled envelope of coarse brown paper from his wrinkled hand. On the front of the sealed envelope was written one word—Mokamad—but Hadji Adil, recognizing the handwriting, knew who had sent the message and what it meant. The writer was Edward Kuder, most recently the American superintendent of schools in neighboring Lanao province. Five years earlier, he had held the same post on Jolo Island in the Philippines' Sulu Archipelago. Unhappy at the agricultural boarding school his father had chosen for him, thirteen-year-old Mohammad Adil had run away from home and appeared on Kuder's doorstep, accompanying his distant relative Alun, one of the boys that Kuder was sponsoring through high school.

It was a Moro custom to lend a child for a time to a friend or relative if their fostering would advantage the child, although it was rarely a foster parent of the child's own choosing. Edward Kuder had accepted the young runaway into his household pending his father's permission for him to stay. Hadji Adil eventually consented to the arrangement, because he knew of Edward Kuder and wanted his headstrong eldest son to have the American high school education that had not been available to him.

Mohammad had lived with Edward Kuder for most of every year since then, at first on Jolo and later in Lanao, on his home island of Mindanao, after the American transferred there. In late December of 1941, Japanese planes attacked Camp Keithley, the U.S. military base at the edge of Lake Lanao where Kuder lived with the five Moro boys he was sponsoring through high school. Awakened by the drone of heavy aircraft, Adil walked out into the predawn gloom just as Japanese bombs gouged a straight line of brilliantly-lit destruction across the middle of the camp's airfield. Fully awake now, he looked up, transfixed, as a Japanese Zero made a strafing run at the airfield's guardhouse. As the aircraft's 20mm cannon demolished the wooden shack, Edward Kuder grabbed him by the arm and shoved him into one of the foxholes they had dug under their house. The next day he sent the boy home to his father for his safety.

* * *

Japanese twin-engine bombers and Zeros had first struck the center of American air power in the Philippines, Clark Field outside Manila, shortly after noon on December 8th. Despite 12 hours having passed since the attack on Pearl Harbor (on the other side of the international dateline), their attack was a replay of that disaster. The Japanese pilots were astonished to find much of the U.S. air fleet still on the ground and, meeting little opposition, quickly destroyed or damaged every one of the B-17 bombers and P-40 fighter planes parked wingtip to wingtip, fully armed and fueled, beneath them on the tarmac. The airfield itself was also left in ruins, with 55 of its defenders slain. Other airfields were attacked with similar results and, by the end of the day, half of American air power in the Philippines was gone and much of the rest damaged. Within a week, the soldiers of Imperial Japan were landing across the archipelago, crushing resistance and moving rapidly inland.

It was a scenario that American war planners had often imagined and one that Edward Kuder, already an old hand in the Philippine colony, had long feared. A decade earlier, he had written to his parents that "the future of the Philippines is in the hands of Japan...the world's foremost imperialist nation" because the United States was wholly unprepared and possibly unwilling to defend its colony. Kuder was expressing a fear shared by nearly all U.S. military strategists. Japan's victory in the Sino-Japanese War of 1894-1895 gave it control of Formosa (now Taiwan), a large island to the north of the Philippines and so close to it that it might have been part of its archipelago. Three years later, Spain ceded the Philippines to the United States after losing the Spanish-American War. From then on, the two new imperial and industrial powers from opposite edges of the Pacific eyed one another warily across the narrow strait that separated their neighboring possessions. When Japan seized Germany's North Pacific colonies—including Truk, Saipan, and Palau—in World War I, the Philippines was effectively surrounded by Japanese outposts. By 1920, American military planners generally agreed (though not for public consumption) that no realistic means existed to defend their Philippine colony from Japanese invasion and occupation.

One military man disagreed. Douglas MacArthur, known to combine unwarranted optimism with an unshakeable belief in his infallibility, was convinced that the Philippines could be defended. He pressed that case with Filipino leader Manuel L. Quezon in 1935 when the United States modified the status of the Philippines under American rule from colony to commonwealth, and Quezon won election as the commonwealth's first president. In response, Quezon appointed him head of the Philippine Army, a new military force subject to ultimate American authority and dependent on American funding. MacArthur, who had recently retired as Chief of Staff of the U.S. Army, came at a cost, requiring an exorbitant salary and an air-conditioned Manila penthouse for himself and his new wife. He took the Field Marshal title, a rank that did not exist in the U.S. Army, and fitted himself out in a heavily filigreed uniform to match.

As the threat of Japanese aggression against the Philippines heightened in July of 1941, General George C. Marshall, the U.S. Army Chief of Staff, recalled Douglas MacArthur to active duty, at his request, and absorbed the Philippine Army into the U.S. Army. MacArthur, a field marshal no more, returned to the U.S. Army as a lieutenant general to head a new command known as the United States Army Forces in the Far East (USAFFE). MacArthur's newly-formed American army, composed of the Philippine Army and

U.S. army units stationed in the islands, was even more poorly supplied and trained than the mainland U.S. military.

* * *

By early January 1942, the Moro volunteers of the Bolo Battalions
were in place at Digos, on the opposite end of the Philippine archipelago. Each man carried either a kris—a short sword—or a *panabas*.
Despite the battalion's name, a *panabas* was not a bolo, or Philippine machete. The *panabas*, which like the machete, was also a farm
implement, was a far more effective weapon than any machete. With
a rattan-wrapped hardwood handle just as long its two to three-foot
curved blade, it was a formidable two-handed cleaver—both a long
sword and a battle-axe.

Edward Kuder knew the Moros well enough to realize that
steel blades were not their preferred weapons in the fight to come.
In a 1943 classified briefing, he reported that "one of the chief incen-
tives of the Moros in joining the Bolo Battalion[s] was the possibility that firearms would be issued to them," while at the same
time noting that "some of them realized the hopelessness of blade
weapons against firearms and feared a scheme by Christian Filipinos
to get them killed off."[1]

The Japanese battle plan had anticipated it would take 50 days
to conquer the Philippines. Instead, it took five months due mostly
to MacArthur's ordered retreat to the highly defensible Bataan Peninsula that bordered Manila Bay and the successful stand far away
at Digos. From his headquarters on the fortress island of Corregidor
in Manila Bay, MacArthur awaited the reinforcements that never
arrived while watching the steady deterioration of his Bataan defensive position.

A man whose exceptional physical bravery and devotion to duty complemented his towering vanity, MacArthur had pledged to his superiors to go down fighting in the Philippines. But he was also a man of intense ambition and a soldier who obeyed orders for the most part. In February 1942, President Roosevelt appointed him supreme army chief for the Pacific, ordered him to evacuate to Australia, and, as a consolation, awarded him the Medal of Honor, which MacArthur had long coveted.

MacArthur wavered for more than two weeks but finally obeyed Roosevelt's order. On the night of March 12th, he and his party, including his wife, his young son, and the boy's Cantonese *amah*, boarded a PT boat in Manila Bay and made the hazardous journey south to Mindanao, weaving their way in the dark through a Japanese blockade. MacArthur, who may have suffered from claustrophobia and hated traveling in confined spaces, spent much of the 36 hour trip on deck.[2]

Because of the stand at Digos, the Del Monte Airfield was still in USAFFE's hands. MacArthur's party landed on the Mindanao coast and was taken to the airfield, where they boarded a B17 recently dispatched from Darwin for the flight to Australia. Neither MacArthur nor any of his senior staff evacuating with him seems to have been aware of the key part played by the sword-wielding Moros of the Bolo Battalions in stopping the invasion force at Digos, preventing the loss of the Del Monte Airfield, and saving MacArthur from a slower, more dangerous, and far more claustrophobic submarine evacuation.

For their crucial role in halting the Japanese invasion of Mindanao, the Moro volunteers received nothing—no firearms, none of their promised pay, and no quinine for the rainforest malaria that was decimating their ranks. Not for the first time were they being mistreated by the Americans and their Filipino counterparts. Gradually, in twos and threes, Moro men slipped again into the rainforest, this time to walk home, and by the time the Japanese commenced their second invasion of Mindanao on April 29, 1942, the emperor's birthday, most were already gone.[3]

That offensive was a coordinated attack from three directions by three separate assault forces. Lt. Colonel Miura's troops, now reinforced by an additional battalion, set out from Davao. A second force made an amphibious landing at Parang on the west coast, and a third landed in the north at Macajalar Bay. Their goal was to meet in the island's interior not far from the Del Monte Airfield. USAFFE soldiers on Mindanao fought the advancing Japanese until, to their bewilderment, an order to surrender arrived from USAFFE headquarters on May 10th, carried personally by an American officer flown from Manila in a Japanese military plane.

With Bataan having fallen, the remnants of MacArthur's main force, nearly 11,000 soldiers and civilians, found themselves trapped on Corregidor. On the morning of May 6th, 1942, General Wainwright, MacArthur's replacement as USAFFE commander, considered his options. The tiny, tadpole-shaped island had been under intense artillery bombardment for almost a month, his coastal guns and mortars had been destroyed and, a day earlier, Japanese assault troops with tanks had overrun his forward defensive positions. His last bastion was Malinta Tunnel, dug into the heart of the rocky island, which now held more than one thousand wounded soldiers. Convinced that the next Japanese assault would surely breach the tunnel entrance, he decided to surrender Corregidor. The Japanese commander refused to accept his surrender unless it included all USAFFE forces in the Philippines. In no position to bargain, Wainwright finally agreed to surrender all of the troops under his command, including those in far-off Mindanao. Having lost an entire army as well as its largest overseas colony, the United States surrender marked the worst military defeat in its history.

But the Mindanao defenders had not been defeated, and a number of officers objected to the forced surrender when they had suffered few casualties and still had the means to fight on. In the end, most obeyed the surrender order, and more than a thousand surrendered soldiers on Mindanao marched into Japanese prison camps where they discovered a world of unending deprivation and cruelty. Many Filipino soldiers, and some officers, left their units and returned home rather than become prisoners of the Japanese.

American soldiers and civilians, Edward Kuder among them, disappeared into Japanese prison camps or mountain hideaways with the surrender. For more than seven months, no word of the fate of any of the 150,000 soldiers and 17 million civilians in its captured colony reached the United States from across the Pacific. Then, in mid-December 1942, a listening station south of San Francisco began picking up scattered short-wave radio signals from the Philippines. One of the strongest was in a recognized code. When translated, the message resolved into familiar American slang: WE HAVE THE HOT DOPE ON THE HOT YANKS IN THE HOT PHILIPPINES. The guerrillas of Mindanao had made contact.[4]

* * *

On February 8th, 1943, Edward Kuder arrived at the headquarters of the Mindanao guerrillas, having been invited there by Lt. Colonel Wendell Fertig, recently designated military chief of the Mindanao guerrillas, in a radio message from General Douglas MacArthur. After much trying, Fertig's men had assembled a radio transmitter out of scattered scraps of old radio receivers and movie projector parts and managed to send a coded radio signal to the U.S. mainland. It was weeks before they received a reply from the cautious Americans, who were suspicious of their outdated coding device, but before long, they were communicating directly with General MacArthur, who now held the title Supreme Commander of Allied Forces in the Southwest Pacific Area.

Kuder had been mostly alone on the high Lanao plateau for more than a year, hiding in the jungle with a price on his head. Still recovering from a tropical illness, he rode a horse down off the west slope of the plateau into the Kapatagan Valley, a basin so fertile and empty that it had attracted thousands of Christian settlers from the northern islands in the previous decade. A headquarters physician examined him and informed him he wasn't strong enough to serve as an active guerrilla fighter. Kuder was disappointed, but Fertig had other plans for him.

Even before establishing radio contact with MacArthur, Fertig had managed to gain control over a significant-sized liberated territory. His "free" provincial government printed its own money and included a hospital, a court system, and even a prison for captured Japanese soldiers. Fertig wanted Kuder to be his director of Civil Affairs, and the former superintendent of schools found himself in a new world that looked surprisingly similar to the prewar American colony he knew so well.

That new world included the company of a number of American expatriates, most of whom were men of middle years like himself, men whose settled lives the Japanese invasion and American surrender had violently upended. Unlike Kuder, they were typical American colonialists who, certain of their own cultural and racial superiority, casually denigrated Filipinos and despised Moros. Kuder liked Filipinos and admired the Moros, though he didn't advertise that fact to these men. He would describe the Moros in a 1945 feature article for the Saturday Evening Post as "the most fascinating people I have ever known.⁵" He had taught Moros, employed them, and brought them to live under his roof. As for the Japanese, Kuder felt exactly the same way about them as did his fellow colonialists. He hated them unreservedly for obliterating his well-ordered world.

Although Douglas MacArthur and Edward Kuder inhabited different Philippine worlds, they had much in common with respect to their adopted land. Both had arrived in the Philippines at the age of 24 to launch their careers—Kuder as a first-time high school principal and MacArthur as a West Point graduate on his first overseas posting. Both had spent a good deal of their adult lives in the colony, and both had been happiest when they were there.

Like Kuder, MacArthur was a rare colonialist who rejected racial bigotry. MacArthur socialized with Filipinos (who, in his case, tended to be men of some wealth and prominence) at a time when doing so invited opprobrium from other Americans. He had close Filipino friends and, like Kuder, his relationships went beyond friendship to honorary kinship. Manuel Quezon regarded MacArthur as a brother and was godfather to his only child. In February 1943, both Kuder and MacArthur desperately wanted the Philippines, the land that had shaped them, to return to American control. And both men expected the people of the Philippines, including their friends and honorary kin, to risk their lives in that effort.

On arriving at Fertig's headquarters, Edward Kuder immediately took advantage of guerrilla couriers to send letters to his two Moro foster sons, both of whom had chosen him, rather than the opposite. The oldest, Salipada Pendatun, was fully grown and leading his own guerrilla force in the interior. Kuder was proud of Pendatun's actions against the Japanese but wanted to bring him under

American command. The other, Mohammad Adil, was on the cusp of manhood, living in safety with his father. He, too, could soon have a role to play in restoring the Philippines to America.

* * *

Hadji Adil pondered the unopened letter for his son from Edward Kuder. Kuder was clearly with the guerrillas. Did he want his foster son to join him? Hadji Adil was not eager to send his son to fight in an uncertain cause. The rapid surrender of the Americans nine months earlier had left him perplexed. He could not understand surrender without defeat—no Moro could.

For over 300 years, the Moros had fought the Spaniards who conquered the northern islands, forging occasional truces with them but never surrendering. His father and father-in-law had both fought the Spaniards and, after them, the Americans. Moros across the southern islands shared, in addition to a religion, a cultural ideal, *maratabat*—a term rich with meaning but most generally translated as a profound individual sense of dignity or self-worth. One's sense of dignity was more meaningful than anything else in life, including, in some cases, life itself. There was no shame in slipping away to fight another day, but surrendering to one's enemy without having been vanquished was dishonorable, a violation of *maratabat*. Tens of thousands of American and Filipino soldiers had laid down their arms and marched into Japanese prison camps. Not one Moro soldier (and only one Moro officer) had joined them.

Moro chieftains were adept at surviving foreign invaders—the Spaniards, the Americans, and now the Japanese. They knew how to come to terms with external rulers and wait for the right moment to fight. For Hadji Adil, that moment had not arrived. The Americans would eventually defeat the Japanese, of that he was certain, but given how quickly they surrendered the Philippines, he did not expect them to return anytime soon. After the American surrender, he had collected guns from USAFFE soldiers who had been issued the rifles denied to Moro volunteers but now were anxious to relieve themselves of evidence they had fought the Japanese. He gathered scores of rifles, which he buried along with his firearms for when the time came again to fight. He was not yet ready to dig up his guns or send his son into danger. But he also knew that when his son's American foster father called him to the war, *maratabat*, as well as his thirst for adventure, would speed him on his way. Perhaps he should let Mohammad remain upriver for the present.

News of his son's courtship reached Hadji Adil a few days later, forcing him to act. He sent his senior servant, Kadungan, to his rice mill in Tumbao, telling him to bring the boy back one way or another. Hadji Adil's rice mill was his pride and joy, and it was a sign of his confidence in his eldest son that he let him run the mill without him. Hadji Adil was the first Moro to own a rice mill, and he would not let anything—not even a war and an enemy occupation—shut it down. Diesel fuel had disappeared many months ago, but the mill's engine—a 12 horsepower Blackstone—was modified to run on coconut oil.

When the younger Adil was milling rice, a few villagers always gathered to watch the flywheel spin round and enjoy the sweet smell of the coconut exhaust. Adil loved the freedom of managing the upriver mill, with one of his father's servants on hand to cook his meals and plenty of time to travel to nearby villages to fight his gamecocks, which grew strong on the rice bran and kernels scattered on the ground about the mill.

* * *

It was at a cockfight that Adil had first encountered Umbus a Bai. Traditional entertainments had become popular again, and for the first time in years, there was a *bulangan*, a dedicated cockpit, in Tumbao, near the public market and across the river from the rice mill.

The Sultan of Tumbao, Muluk, was a cruel and jealous ruler who mistreated his subordinates. He was also known to be a man of extraordinary power. He possessed a potent form of *ilemu*—protective magic—an incantation that could paralyze anyone who opposed him. The sultan kept a magnificent black rooster that he displayed in an ornate cage hung at the corner of his great house, which stood along the river, next to the marketplace and the new cockpit. It was said that all within the sound of the rooster's crowing were magically drawn to the sultan. The rooster was also a champion fighter, and young Adil, having had success in all the surrounding villages with his unlikely looking gamecock—a dirty-white Leghorn rooster with a sickly pink comb that drooped over its eyes—decided to challenge the sultan's rooster.

On the next market day, Adil appeared at the cockpit with his rooster and surveyed the scene. On the veranda of the sultan's great house, which overlooked the cockpit, women were playing the *kulintang*, the ringing melody from the bronze gongs creating a celebratory mood. Next to them sat the old sultan in a red silk Chinese jacket and embroidered fez, leaning on his staff of office with his sword-bearer standing behind him. Beside him sat his niece, Umbus a Bai, a striking young woman, splendid in a green silk blouse with a brooch fashioned from a five-dollar gold piece; her uncovered hair, lustrous with coconut oil, was tied loosely in a low bun on her neck and on her cheeks the lightest dusting of rice powder set off the deep red of her lips. Her father was Datu Sinsuat Balabaran, patriarch of the Sinsuat clan, a friend of the Japanese, and, at that moment, the most powerful Moro in the entire province of Cotabato. As Adil approached, she raised her voice, and the *kulintang* fell silent.

"I have been observing you, and I see that you are very arrogant. Now you want to challenge our rooster, so let us bet." A crowd had already gathered. "Witness, everyone, our wager. If his rooster defeats our rooster, he can take me as his servant, and I am willing to go with him. But if he loses, he will be my servant, and he will stay here in this house." The crowd laughed and cheered. "Agreed," Adil replied, "I accept the wager."

Samal Mangulamas, the cockfighter of the sultan, approached the far side of the pit, facing directly east, the winning direction. He squatted, holding his rooster, waiting. Everyone at the market had by now gathered to watch and comment on Adil's rooster's pathetic appearance. Adil brought his bird to the center of the ring and removed the sheath from its knife while Samal did the same. Adil glanced at the veranda as he held his rooster and noticed the sultan muttering intently and pointing his finger toward him. At the signal, the fighters released their birds.

Within seconds, the rooster of the sultan had spurred Adil's unmoving bird repeatedly. His feathers flew, and he squawked imploringly. The crowd screamed. Umbus a Bai laughed and exclaimed, "So now I will have a servant who is a real man!" Adil's rooster neither moved nor kicked, but lay on his back with his legs in the air, behavior so passive that the sultan's rooster decided that he was a hen and tried to mount him. But as he leaned in, Adil's rooster suddenly pumped his legs as if trying to run away, and the five-inch blade on his left spur punched into his attacker's belly. In his excitement to mount, the sultan's rooster kept pushing forward, slicing himself open on the long curved blade. Finally, he pulled away and slid to the ground, dead. Adil's bird struggled to his feet and pecked at the intestines of the dead rooster, then spread his wings and crowed exultantly while the crowd roared its amazement. Above the din, Umbus a Bai called to him, "Come and get me! I am ready to be your servant!" The Flower of the Princesses, waited upon from childhood, was not in truth ready to be anyone's servant. Still, she *was* prepared to be courted, and the young cockfighter had obliged after a fashion and become her uncertain suitor.

* * *

On Kadungan's arrival in Tumbao, he learned that the young datu had taken his rooster to a cockfight in an upriver village. Kadungan gathered up Adil's things, stowed them in his dugout, and told the servants, "Tell the young datu his father has ordered him home."

When Adil returned and discovered that all his possessions were missing, he was furious, firing his rifle in the air and demanding to know who had stolen his things. One of the servants finally told him hesitantly about Kadungan's visit and message. Angry at this affront to his independence, Adil jumped into his dugout and paddled fast downstream to Pagalamatan.

An hour of paddling on the wide river turned his anger to resentment, then apprehension. What did his father want of him? As soon as he saw his father, he began to protest Kadungan's actions, but Hadji Adil cut him off: "Quiet! I forbid you to marry those people!"

Despite their kinship ties, there was bad blood between his father and the Sinsuats, and he was not yet ready to cure that condition with a marriage. Furthermore, the Sinsuats, unlike most Moros, had sided wholeheartedly with the Japanese. Datu Sinsuat had met the Japanese commander of the Mindanao invasion force at the Cotabato pier, and he had recently sent one of his sons to Japan to study. Hadji Adil remained a friend of the absent Americans.

His father told Adil that he needed, in any case, to continue his studies. "Mr. Kuder will be angry with you if you marry this young."

His son looked at him curiously, and he continued more gently, "There is a letter."

The boy opened the envelope, unfolded the creased paper, and read that his American foster father was safe with the guerrillas, who had recently contacted General MacArthur by radio. Kuder added that his other foster son, Salipada Pendatun, had "submitted" to Colonel Fertig and would be recognized by MacArthur. The letter asked nothing of him, but Mohammad Adil felt his world suddenly expand. The war was *not* over, and his foster father was with the guerrillas. It might not be too late for him after all.

Within days Hadji Adil noticed a change in his son. For the eight years before 1942, the young datu had lived a life little different from any Philippine schoolboy because his father, a modern man, wanted him to become an American-educated lawyer, not a warrior. After the American surrender, however, with no schoolwork to occupy him and no modern attractions to divert him, he had slipped easily into the pastimes that young datus had pursued for centuries. He raced sailboats, hunted deer, and raised his fighting cocks. He practiced swordplay with his sinuous-bladed kris, and he wooed a princess.

His day-to-day life had become more isolated and elemental than that of any Cotabato datu of the previous four decades as signs of American rule faded by the day. There were no longer any buses to ride or cinemas to attend, or newspapers to read. Radios were allowed only for Japanese propaganda broadcasts. Schools and government offices remained closed, and stores shuttered as their stocks of cloth, shoes, soap, medicine, and gasoline were depleted and never replaced. The province's main highway gradually reverted to a nameless, overgrown footpath as its asphalt crumbled from neglect and its road signs found better use as firewood.

Isolation was what his father wanted for him. In 1942, isolation meant safety—from the Japanese soldiers thinly spread in garrisons across the vast Cotabato river basin, but even more from the chaotic violence that descended on Mindanao with the collapse of American rule. Robber bands, some Moro, some Filipino, roved the ruined highways by foot or on horseback, stealing goods and sometimes people, for slave-raiders were once more on the hunt in Mindanao.

As in the past, Moros turned to powerful datus for protection, and the most powerful datu of all was Datu Sinsuat, the father of Umbus a Bai, and at least 20 other children by his seven current wives. Already in his seventies, Datu Sinsuat was a former protégé of Datu Piang who had come into prominence only after his death eight years earlier but since that time had worked quickly to consolidate his power. He made Cotabato town his seat of power and, through his friendship with Manuel Quezon, soon to be the first president of the Philippine Commonwealth, he was appointed in 1934 to the Philippine Senate. Despite his relationship with Quezon and his previous cooperation with the Americans, Datu Sinsuat decided in 1942 to collaborate fully with the Japanese occupiers. That collaboration benefitted his clan, but also had the effect of shielding the Magindanaons—the Moros of Cotabato—from some of the savage treatment experienced by civilians elsewhere in Mindanao and in the rest of the Philippines at the hands of the Japanese military.

Young Mohammad Adil began to shed his isolation from the war like an outworn skin. He asked more questions about the war and read the secret newsletters—transcribed broadcasts from illegal radio receivers—that Mr. Monte de Ramos carried to his father rolled up inside his bamboo walking stick. When he read about American landings at a place called Guadalcanal, he understood it to mean that the American push across the Pacific to take back the Philippines had begun.

* * *

Hadji Adil knew there would be another letter. It was time to provide his son with a man's weapons. He chose a pearl-handled .38 revolver from his cache given to him by a USAFFE officer and a reliable Springfield bolt-action rifle. Mohammad Adil was elated, but his father told him that the guns weren't all he needed. It was time to provide him with another sort of protection.

He sent Kadungan on a second mission, this time far upriver to Talitay, on the edge of the marshlands, to find Ama ni Sulay, a master of *ilemu*, protective magic. Some days later, Ama ni Sulay stood before him, an old man in handspun cotton clothes and a woven conical hat, its braided rattan cord, varnished by sweat and sun, looped under his chin. He had a gaunt face made longer by a wispy beard and, beneath his wide brim, remarkably bright eyes. Hadji Adil greeted him warmly and pressed a purse filled with 40 silver dollars into his palm. It was the traditional payment for teaching the secret knowledge to a young datu, and would support the old man's family for a year.

On seven consecutive Friday nights—for Friday was the sacred day and night was the time for sharing secrets—they met at midnight, sitting side by side with legs crossed on a woven mat with candles burning at each corner. They were protected by a diaphanous mosquito netting and shrouded in the fragrant smoke of incense mixed from sandalwood and the dried husks of rare fruits.

Throughout each night, Ama ni Sulay softly spoke the secret knowledge into his ear, sometimes drawing diagrams in the dirt in front of them. The older man was a guest of his father for those seven weeks, sitting with the elders in the village during the day and talking of past warriors and the wonders he had seen. Adil often joined them, as he had since he was a young child, but Ama ni Sulay never spoke of the secret knowledge until they were alone on Friday night.

On the first Friday night, he told him of the four elements that make up man—fire, water, earth, and air—and about the fifth element, soul. On the second and third nights, he told him how to prepare himself for any endeavor by calling for his six protective angels. He taught him to summon them silently and arrange them about him in a particular order: at his front, the angel Artan Nurallah; on his left, Mukharabin; at his back, Sagala, the guardian of the universe; and at his right hand, Raja Mangala, the ever powerful. Below him, he should place Muna sa Lalan, to guide and protect him on the path ahead. And directly above him, he was to put Markaimout, the Angel of Death, who released the soul from the body.

On the fourth, fifth, and sixth Friday nights, Ama ni Sulay taught him the twelve incantations to disable or beguile his enemies: The Verse of Thunder ("Make his tongue stiffen, make his eyes dim, make his spirit falter, make his body fail"), the Verse of Mother's Milk, and the Verse of the Stone among them. He told him the power and the purpose of each spell. And on the seventh Friday night, he took the boy's smooth wrist in his gnarled hand and, with a surprisingly strong grip, turned his palm upward and held it fast. He then produced a small shiny ball of what looked like molten metal and rubbed it, pressing hard, into the boy's palm. As he worked, he told him about the powers of *lasa*— mercury. As a mirrored substance, it could repel blades. As a liquid metal, it could turn bullets into water. He taught him the words that would command the mercury to rush to wherever it was needed in his body.

As the sky lightened in the last hour of the final Friday night and Ama ni Sulay was satisfied that his pupil had correctly memorized everything he had taught him, he told Adil to pull his .38 revolver from its holster. The teacher took the gun from him, held it by its barrel, and pointed it at his own forehead, his hand relaxed and steady.

"Datu, shoot me in the head," he said.

Adil stared at the old man, uncomprehending and speechless.

"Datu, shoot me!"

This time the boy understood what he was supposed to do and why. Slowly, tentatively, Adil reached toward his gun, which Ama ni Sulay held pressed to his head. He wrapped his hand lightly around the grip and bent his index finger toward the trigger, trying not to look into his teacher's eyes. He wanted to obey the order and prove to himself the power of the secret knowledge. But his finger froze and would bend no further. Try as he might, he could not will himself to shoot the old man. Sunlight lit the leaves of the tallest palms. The night was gone, and the final lesson was over. He would have to test the power of the magic on his own.

* * *

In late May of 1943, Edward Kuder wrote a second letter to his foster son Mohammad. Much had changed in the intervening months. Most importantly, General MacArthur, now in Australia, had taken control of the Mindanao guerrilla movement, sending his agent, U.S. Navy commander Charles "Chick" Parsons, by submarine to review Fertig's operation. Parsons brought supplies—including precious rifles, ammunition, and radios—and the supplies continued to arrive regularly by submarine rendezvous, but the deliveries came with conditions. MacArthur, in exile, was leery of Fertig's "audacious" establishment of a Free Philippine Government, and he attempted to limit the reach of Fertig's authority. MacArthur also wanted more intelligence from the guerrillas and an end to offensive actions against the Japanese, which he felt would invite reprisals and imperil the coast-watching network he wanted to build.

MacArthur controlled the resources the guerrillas wanted most, including official recognition and military promotions, but MacArthur was also far away. Fertig set up the coast-watching network and made the proper responses to Parsons and MacArthur, but he did not slow his offensive operations or his civil affairs organizing. In a mission statement to his guerrillas in the fall of 1943, he told them that their first priority was to provide MacArthur with intelligence and their second priority was to "defeat the Japanese on Mindanao by means of guerrilla warfare."[6] And despite MacArthur's misgivings, Fertig had already decided to expand his area of operation south into the vast Cotabato delta.

In 1943, Wendell Fertig was 42 years old, with bright blue eyes and leading-man looks accentuated by a well-trimmed goatee grown to make himself look older. Fertig was a child of the American West, raised with his younger brother in a small ranching community on the high plains of eastern Colorado. He attended the Colorado School of Mines and, in 1936, struggling to support his wife and two daughters in the midst of the Depression, used his meager savings to buy four tickets on a passenger liner bound for Manila after reading about opportunities for mining engineers in the Philippines. He worked first as an engineer and then as an executive in a mining company and, by 1940, the man who had fled the Depression and the dusty plains had acquired a lifestyle unimaginable in eastern

Colorado; his house was filled with servants, his weekends were spent at the country club, and his children were being educated at an elite private school.

Then the dream ended. By the early summer of 1941, the increasing prospect of war with Japan was depressing the Philippine mining business. Noticing the winds of war, Fertig met with MacArthur's chief engineer, General Hugh J. Casey, and soon after dusted off his reserve commission from the Colorado School of Mines and volunteered for active duty with the rank of major. Casey quickly promoted him to lieutenant colonel, and that same summer, Fertig sent his wife and daughters back to the U.S. on the last regularly-scheduled passenger ship to leave Manila.[7]

Less than a year later, he found himself, in April 1942, in the Malinta Tunnel, trapped like so many others under constant artillery bombardment on the besieged island of Corregidor. But Fertig was confident that he was on his way to Australia. General Casey, now his commanding officer, had flown to Australia with MacArthur eight weeks earlier and had given Fertig orders to join him there to command his construction division. On the night of April 29th, on his sixth attempt to leave Corregidor, Fertig saw his name on the evacuation manifest. Just before midnight, he joined the sixty passengers, including twenty army nurses, boarding two Catalina Flying Boats. They would be the last two aircraft to leave Corregidor, flying first to Mindanao for refueling, then on to Australia. None of the passengers sitting crowded together on the floor of the seaplane's narrow aluminum hull was aware that the full invasion of Mindanao by Japanese forces had begun that same day.

The seaplanes landed on Lake Lanao and hid until sunset, but when trying to take off for Australia that evening, Fertig's plane struck a submerged rock and tore open its hull. The crew worked all night and through the next day to patch the fuselage, and by the following evening, the seaplane was repaired enough to fly but could not take a full complement of passengers. Ten army nurses, three civilian dependents, a naval officer, and Lt. Colonel Wendell Fertig were left to wait for the next evacuation flight to arrive from Australia. He reported to General Sharp at Camp Keithley, who told him there would be no more evacuation flights because Japanese forces were advancing too quickly. Fertig's luck had run out, and he would be staying on Mindanao.

He was off inspecting road demolition sites when the order to surrender arrived. Deciding that his detached status exempted him from the surrender order, he became a fugitive and spent months in hiding until slowly, from a small core of fugitive USAFFE officers and enlisted men, he began to build a guerrilla force. The army nurses, who had made their escape from the hell of Bataan and Corregidor only to be stranded on Mindanao, surrendered with the other USAFFE troops and were eventually transported back north to the civilian internment camp at Santo Tomas University in Manila. They rejoined the 65 American nurses who had not made it off Corregidor before the island fell to the Japanese. [8]

Fertig, a self-described eccentric, possessed some MacArthuresque tendencies. His detractors pointed to his egotism, his pettiness, and his grandiosity (he had given himself the rank of brigadier general), but no one could deny his entrepreneurial flair or his organizational skills, which allowed him to lead an extraordinarily diverse group of guerrillas—men (and some women) divided by ethnicity, religion, nationality, and armed service. To no one's surprise, MacArthur disliked Fertig despite investing him with his authority. MacArthur's most prominent biographer, William Manchester, has suggested that MacArthur was jealous of Fertig's accomplishments and wanted no one else to share credit with him for liberating the Philippines.[9]

Fertig was the rare guerrilla leader who preferred a briefcase to a bandolier. Surprisingly deskbound, he travelled infrequently and seldom even ventured beyond his headquarters office. But sedentary as he was, he was able to consolidate and maintain control of the largest guerrilla organization in the Philippines, one that eventually covered all of Mindanao. Fertig's efforts in Mindanao also provided a blueprint for unconventional warfare that the United States military would utilize for decades to come. From his post-war Pentagon office in the early-1950s, Fertig helped to found the U.S. Army Special Forces.

Edward Kuder, when he wasn't laid low by his mysterious recurring illness, was busy in his role as Director of Civil Affairs. After setting up the civil affairs administration and establishing the mint, he spent most of his time countering Japanese propaganda. When, in late February of 1943, reports reached Mindanao of an American victory at Guadalcanal, the Japanese garrison commander for western Mindanao dismissed the news, telling local civilians that Japan would never surrender and America could never prevail. When asked by the same civilians for his comment, Kuder told them that the American soldiers hoped the Japanese would fight to the very last, "so they can kill them all, and …never be bothered by them again." Kuder's remarks so enraged the Japanese commander that he raised the price on Kuder's head, already a tempting sum of 2000 pesos, by "two rifles, two revolvers, and 500 rounds of ammunition," a reward intended to entice Moros in particular to try to collect it.[10]

Fertig was anxious to add Cotabato to his territory but knew nothing about the province. Kuder had lived and worked there for years and had Moro protégés still in Cotabato. The war had cut him off from all but one of them. He wrote again to his young foster son, this time to ask a favor.

* * *

One evening in June 1943, a second guerrilla courier arrived at the farm of Hadji Adil with a letter addressed to his son. The courier on this occasion was Abuk Juanday, the brother of an old friend. Abuk knew the intricate network of estuaries and creeks in the delta and used them to avoid the Japanese checkpoints. He had paddled the last miles up Kakar Creek to Pagalamatan—the Praying Place— where travelers paused before fording the stream in whose shaded pools great crocodiles were known to wait. This time Mohammad Adil was there to receive the letter and read his foster father's famil- iar handwriting. Edward Kuder wrote that the guerrilla movement in the north had grown. He reported that the boys from Jolo, Adil's classmates, who had stayed with Kuder in hiding because they could not safely cross the Sulu Sea, had recently returned to their families. And there, in the last paragraph, Adil read with rising excitement the words he had been hoping to find. Kuder asked him to travel north to join him at guerrilla headquarters in Lanao. He was finally going to war.

With his father's reluctant blessing and with the courier, Abuk Juanday, as his guide, Adil was on his way in a few days. The last time he had made the journey from his father's house to the high Lanao plateau, it had been on a transport bus that headed up the coastal highway, then turned inland to climb the winding mountain road cut through the jungle by the Americans in 1902, at the outset of their occupation.

In late May of 1941, sixteen-year-old Adil had ridden the bus with his father and stepmother, traveling to start his senior year at a new high school—the school year cut short by the Japanese invasion. This trip would be different. In Mindanao in 1943, journeys that had been made in hours now required days or weeks of difficult and dangerous travel. Eighteen-year-old Adil, craving adventure, wanted it no other way, fearing only that he would not be equal to the challenges of the journey.

Hadji Adil saw them off at the river's edge, telling Abuk to look out for the boy, who was undeniably edging toward manhood. He still wore the short pants and wide smile of a schoolboy, but he had the eager eyes of a hunter and he carried his new revolver with confidence. Standing there at the praying place, his father may have recited a silent prayer for his son's safety. Shouting their goodbyes, the travelers steered Abuk's two-man sailboat into the current. It was a sleek-sided racing craft composed of thin wooden planks and woven bamboo made watertight with coconut fiber and forest resin. With double outriggers and a pale lateen sail, it flew over the water like a graceful shorebird skimming down the wide river.

2
THE JOURNEY NORTH

It was the details in his stories I noticed first; not only names and dates but initials and hours, makes and models, kinship connections and weather conditions, and a wealth of other invaluable minutiae of a marvelously well-remembered life. His attention to details of events 45 years in the past was so acute that often he would interrupt himself minutes later to correct a name or date in a story. We sometimes spoke in Magindanaon, but he preferred English, which he spoke and wrote flawlessly. In conversation, he was remarkably animated—pounding the table to punctuate a point, shooting out an arm to point his finger at some faraway person or place.

In my journal, after our first meeting in 1986, I wrote that he was a "wonderful man" who was "immediately warm and friendly" to me and that he had "lived an incredible life." I also naively noted that I would "have to be a bit more firm about keeping him on the topic." No matter my preference, Mohammad Adil did not tell stories to order. He followed the traditional Magindanaon conversational directive, "Babasal tanu" or "Let us plant squash." I soon learned that I was welcome to plant a single seed by asking a question, but, like the wandering vines of a squash plant, his response would branch and spread in often surprising directions.

* * *

By afternoon, they had reached Cotabato town, not far from the river's mouth. They tied up at Punul, a mangrove island in the middle of the river opposite the waterfront, and Adil, ignoring Abuk's objections, hailed one of the dugout canoes that served as water taxis to take him to town. He had not been there in many months, and he wanted to visit his father's favorite coffee house in the public market. When he arrived, it was filled with men discussing the current war rumors, including a recent occupation radio broadcast claiming that the Japanese had bombed Washington D.C. One of the men repeated a favorite saying of the Sinsuat clan: "The Americans will return only when the crow turns white, and the white heron turns black."[1] Unable to restrain himself, Adil raised his voice to proclaim to the group what his father had told him quietly at home. "The Sinsuats are lying! No nation in the world can defeat the Americans."

A short while later, as he left the coffee house, he saw another patron, a Filipino, talking to a Japanese soldier stationed at the market and pointing in his direction. Before he reached the river, the soldier and a companion intercepted him and quickly relieved him of his .38 revolver. Then, with their long bayonets urging him along, they marched him to the stockade attached to the market. He sat slumped on the ground in the bamboo enclosure, so deeply ashamed that he hardly cared about his fate. Away from home for less than a day, he had failed his first test. He had violated *maratabat* by letting the enemy disarm him. He was no warrior. He lowered his head to avoid the eyes of the other prisoners.

Adil had been sitting about two hours when Datu Usman Baraguir, who had heard of the boy's detention from one of his men, arrived with a Japanese officer he addressed as Lieutenant Miyaki. Datu Usman was chief of the new police force of Cotabato town, which had been organized by the Sinsuats under the Japanese. He pointed at Adil and told Miyaki, through words and gestures, that this was his nephew, a foolish but harmless boy, and that he guaranteed there would be no further trouble from him.

When the lieutenant reluctantly agreed to hand the boy over to him, Datu Usman walked Adil quickly out of the stockade and, with his large hand on Adil's elbow, guided him down the main street toward the river. They were in fact, distant cousins, and as they passed more Japanese soldiers, Datu Usman inquired politely about Adil's father. At the river's edge, he discreetly handed him his pearl-handled .38, telling him curtly, "I won't be able to protect you again. The next time the Japanese catch you with a gun they will kill you. Now go home to your father and stay there." By the time a water taxi returned Adil to Punul and Abuk's boat, the herons were settled in the mangrove tops, white ornaments by the hundreds against a darkened sky. Abuk reclined against the side of the beached boat with eyes closed, having fallen asleep watching for his return. Adil woke him and told him of his arrest. As the boy excitedly recounted the story of his imprisonment and his salvation at the hands of Datu Usman, Abuk shook his head slowly and then said, "I thought I would have to go back and tell your father I had failed him. From now on, you *listen* to me!"

They slept uneasily until they felt a breeze from the east signaling the approach of dawn and set off downriver, following the Pulangi's last wide curves past rice fields and sandbanks to the sea. By full dawn, they could see the mouth of the river ahead of them. In the first shimmering light off the water they also noticed a dugout canoe pushing off from the southern bank, its narrow prow pointed on a course to intersect theirs. The two men paddling the canoe wore headscarves that marked them as Moros and the red and white armbands that identified them as members of KALIBAPI, the pro-Japanese political party that provided civilian employees for the occupation forces.

As the canoe sped toward them, Adil, sensing an opportunity for redemption, reached for the Springfield rifle he had tucked under a woven nipa mat. He told Abuk, "I can kill them both with two shots."

"No!," Abuk replied. "Those are Sinsuat men. Let me talk to them."

The boats converged, and the paddler in front, an older man in a dirty white *tubao*, hooked his right leg over their outrigger and raised his right arm. Adil stared, for the first time, into the barrel of a .45 revolver, which looked, from inches away, like a small cannon.

"Where are you going? What are you carrying?" the man demanded.

Abuk replied, "We are rushing up to Lusayin to bring rice for the funeral feast of our kinsman."

The man's face softened slightly. He relaxed his arm, and the barrel of the pistol drifted down to Adil's midsection. He said, "The next time you pass through here, you better have papers from the Japanese. Now go on."

The silt-laden flow from the great river painted the sparkling sea a dull brown where the two met, but before long they were sailing in the blue expanse of the Moro Gulf. With a favorable wind, they steered north toward Lanao, hugging the coast with the dark shape of Bongo Island on their left. In a few hours, they had cleared the rocky point that marked the southern boundary of Sugud Bay and the entrance to Polloc Harbor, the Cotabato headquarters of the Japanese Navy. As they started across the bay with the Lanao coast already in sight, they heard a distinctive bup-bup-bup and saw a Japanese patrol launch motoring straight toward them from Polloc

Harbor. There were six men aboard, four uniformed Japanese and two Filipinos.

Abuk stared at the launch and, without turning said, "Datu, who will tell our kinsmen that we died here today?"

Try as he might, Adil could not recall a single incantation but only the words of Ama ni Sulay, "No one can kill you unless Allah wills it."

He was reaching again for his rifle when one of the Filipinos on the launch hailed them in Chavacano, the Spanish-based trade language of the southern coasts: "*Tienes piscao?*" Do you have fish?

Abuk answered, "*No hay piscao.*"

Without slowing, the launch veered away, leaving them rolling and trembling in its wake. They continued across the deep bay toward the headland on its northern rim.

At the very tip of the long slender headland, a group of young men, long-haired and carrying rifles, who had watched their encounter with the Japanese launch, stepped out of the trees to hail them. They had found the guerrillas they were seeking. When Adil showed Edward Kuder's letter to Lieutenant Erich, the leader of the guerrillas, Erich told him that the guerrilla headquarters where he was to meet Kuder no longer existed. It had just been overrun by the Japanese.

* * *

MacArthur's concern had been well-founded. Fertig had established his headquarters in Misamis, an out-of-the-way location on Iligan Bay that the Japanese had never fully garrisoned because they did not consider it of strategic value. By early 1943, Misamis under Fertig and Kuder had electric lights, plentiful food, and a working telephone system, in addition to its hospital, money-printing operation, and POW camp. Only the schools remained closed. As painful as it was for him, Kuder refused to open them because he feared the Japanese would target them with air attacks.

The extraordinary prosperity and stability of the town—Fertig's Capital of the Free Philippines—attracted people and, eventually, the attention of the Japanese military. But MacArthur's initiatives also attracted some Japanese attention. American submarines had been reported in the waters around Mindanao, and signals from the new radios provided by MacArthur to Fertig had been detected.

General Morimoto, the Japanese commander of garrison troops in Mindanao, had determined that the fast-growing guerrilla movement needed to be crushed and Fertig captured. At dawn on June 26th, 1943, Wendell Fertig woke to the sound of bombs falling on Misamis. Looking to the bay he saw several landing craft churning their way toward the beach. Within minutes, 2000 Japanese troops were streaming ashore. As reports came in, it became clear that the Japanese knew exactly where to attack for maximum damage. There had been a spy. Fertig sent messages to his commanders ordering them to scatter, and they disappeared into the jungled hills to make their way south to the shore of the narrow Panguil Bay and across it to reach the relative safety of the Moro territory of Lanao.

Fertig then packed the briefcase that was never out of his sight. It was a gift from Parsons cleverly designed to ignite an intense magnesium fire if not opened correctly. But he had waited too long to make his escape. Along with his headquarters staff, he was cut off from his escape route and marooned in Misamis surrounded by Japanese troops. In a daring move, Fertig's second-in-command, Lt. Colonel Charles Hedges, led an elite group of Maranao fighters on a night mission to rescue them. The Moro guerrillas silently paddled small dugouts across the bay and, avoiding Japanese outposts, made their way into the interior, following a jungle trail that paralleled a road that the Japanese assault troops were feeling their way along in the dark, a stone's throw away. The next morning, they found Fertig and his staff, gathered up their baggage, and, that night, guided them back through Japanese lines and recrossed Panguil Bay to reach Lanao.

Edward Kuder, who recounted the rescue mission in a 1945 magazine article, remembered that "it called for extreme courage, determination and clever guerrilla tactics."[2] Wendell Fertig, who like MacArthur always preferred the hero's role and rarely credited his junior officers with accomplishments he could claim for himself, never mentioned the rescue mission in his autobiography. Nevertheless, as Kuder makes clear, it was the Moros—those for whom Fertig rarely had a good word—who saved him from being captured or killed by the Japanese.

Fertig's Mindanao force weathered the Japanese attack, but the guerrillas had lost Misamis. The Capital of the Free Philippines was gone, never to be recovered or replaced. Fertig's command posts from now on would be more temporary affairs, as pressure from the Japanese forced him to move frequently. For the time being, he made his headquarters in a Maranao village on the Lanao coast— Liangan—where Hedges brought him after his rescue. Fertig, the former mining executive and current briefcase-wielding guerrilla chief, excelled at the entrepreneurial and administrative tasks required to set up and run Misamis. He had even financed guerrilla operations by hiring the best dance band in Mindanao and selling tickets to their performances. He was less adept at, or attentive to, the defense of the "Free Philippines." Navy commander Frederick Worcester, trained in naval intelligence and Fertig's first intelligence officer, had disagreed with him on the importance of good defensive positions. He felt that Fertig had neglected the defense of his headquarters, and Fertig, in a rare moment, admitted as much after the Japanese attack of June 1943. Worcester eventually resigned as a result of their disagreements.[3]

* * *

Mohammad Adil, young and impatient, was learning that warfare required waiting. The guerrillas had escorted them a short distance up the coast, and there they waited for news of what had become of guerrilla headquarters and waited again for a break in the heavy rains that had made the forest trails impassable. Finally, the rains lightened, and they set out in different directions, with Abuk and a few guerrilla companions continuing up the coast to rejoin his relatives in Malabang. Adil joined Lt. Erich's party, which turned inland to begin their trek to the new guerrilla headquarters in Lanao.

They headed north along the coast, avoiding the road, but soon turned east to climb the forested slopes of the Lanao Plateau, following an old trail along the Mataling River through an untouched upland rainforest of hardwoods two hundred feet tall. Beneath the forest's towering canopy, they were enveloped in a gently-lit world of bamboo groves and ferns and branches decorated with beautiful flowering vines, and everywhere there were orchids in brilliant hues. The forest was lively with birds and butterflies, chattering monkeys, and wild pigs. Less enchanting were the mud and the thorns, the leeches and biting insects. They climbed steadily upward on the narrow river trail, Adil shouldering his canvas rucksack and his Springfield rifle, with his pistol in its holster and his kris tucked in his belt. As he walked, he searched his bare legs for leeches and winced when his worn shoes reminded him that he was outgrowing them. After more than a day in the shadowed rainforest, they emerged onto the rocky rim of the plateau and, squinting against the bright afternoon sun, Adil looked down again upon the stunning Lanao basin rimmed with pines, a deep blue lake twenty miles long shimmering at its center. To the north, barely discernable through the heat haze, lay the town of Marawi and his former high school, a place of fond memories now shuttered, a relic from another age.

In Tubaran, in the hills overlooking the southern shore of the lake, the guerrillas rested in the house of a Maranao datu. Lieutenant Erich had orders to escort an elderly American teacher, Mr. Doherty, from Tubaran to the new guerrilla headquarters. Doherty, who had been in hiding for more than a year, was too sick to travel for at least two weeks.

Adil was impatient for action and wanted to keep moving. He found two high school friends in Tubaran, one the younger brother of Captain Manalao Mindalano, who was already famous among the Maranao as a resistance fighter. They were on their way to his camp in Tatariken, and Adil obtained Lieutenant Erich's permission to accompany them. They followed a trail west into the mountains to an old *kota*, its wooded palisades dug into the smooth slope of a dormant volcano.

The Lanao plateau, elevated more than 2000 feet above the coastal plains and surrounded by high, rugged country, was a world of its own. The 100,000 Maranaos who lived there called themselves People of the Lake, but were also mountaineers. Like highlanders elsewhere, they were proudly independent, fractious, and prone to violence. They had fought the Spaniards and the Americans; they regularly fought the Magindanaons, their lowland Moro neighbors to the south, and, when outsiders weren't available, they readily fought one another. They certainly made no exception for the Japanese, and there was no Maranao more defiant of the Japanese than Captain Mindalano. Before the war, he had attended an American agricultural school and worked as a school inspector employed by Edward Kuder. Now, he focused on killing Japanese soldiers.

Captain Mindalano, who had a personal score to settle, was the first Maranao to attack the Japanese after the American surrender. Japanese soldiers had killed his father, Datu Mindalano, on the first day of their invasion of Lanao. Despite his advanced age, Datu Mindalano had led a Bolo Battalion in defense of Ganassi, the town on the southwestern corner of the lake. When the first Japanese tank reached Ganassi after rumbling up Pershing's road, the defenders attacked. Seeing a helmeted head protruding from the top of the turret, Datu Mindalano charged the tank armed with only his kris. His blade had almost found its target when another member of the tank crew shot him dead. Seeking vengeance, his son found his opportunity a few weeks later when, late one evening, he and his men happened upon two Japanese tanks with their turrets swung open to catch the slightest breeze in the steamy dark. Gasoline poured into the hatches, followed by lit torches were the only weapons they needed to destroy both tank crews.[4]

Mohammad Adil was taken to the commander as soon as he arrived at the guerrilla camp. Captain Mindalano was a powerful man with fierce, deep-set eyes and a thick beard that, according to his younger brother, he had vowed not to cut until the Japanese were defeated. Adil showed him Edward Kuder's letter and Mindalano welcomed him heartily, telling him of his plans to attack the Japanese garrison at Ganassi once again. Adil begged the captain to let him join the attackers, but Mindalano cut him short.

"No, no, the old man would be angry with me. You're too young. Stay here."

Dejected, Adil remained behind but eventually consoled himself with the distractions to be found in the Moro guerrilla camp,

which was, in fact, more village than encampment. When Mindalano had moved up to his mountain redoubt and dared the Japanese
to come after him, all of his kinspeople went with him. After a few
days at the camp, Adil began to notice one pretty young woman who
was paying him special attention. She would bring him his meal on
a decorated brass tray and stay to whisk the flies away while he ate.
Like the other women, she was barefoot and dressed, in a simple
cotton *malong*, but her hair was shorter, and she spoke Maranao with
an accent. She was nursing a toddler and looked to be four or five
months pregnant.

One day he walked to the nearby stream to bathe and wash his
clothes, still infested with fat yellow body lice from hiking through
the forest. As he scrubbed his shirt on a rock, rubbing hard with
lye soap, he was startled to hear her voice behind him, speaking
in English, "Datu, how are your mother and father? How is your
cousin, Datu Sema, and his wife, Bai Supia?"

"How do you know them? Who are you?"

"Don't you remember me? I was Dr. Tan's attendant."

He recognized her then. She and her sister were nurses who
worked for the most prominent physician in Cotabato town, whose
office was just across the street from his father's. Adil asked her how
she came to be in this remote Lanao outpost. She told him that
when the war came, her family had evacuated with others to Bongo
Island because they were afraid of what the Japanese would do to
them. Instead, a few weeks after the American surrender, it was slave
raiders who attacked them. The raiders killed all the men, including
her father and older brother, and brought the women and children
to Lanao to sell them to the Maranaos. She was sold to a man older
than her father, who took her as a wife. She had not seen her mother
or sister since that day.

She was crying softly now, tears starting down her sunburned cheeks. Adil tried but could not find any words to offer her. At Mindalano's camp, he had begun to feel like a guerrilla. Suddenly, he was a homesick schoolboy far from home and surrounded by scores of armed men. There was nothing he could do for this young woman, and he felt that fact as keenly as a bayonet jabbed between his shoulder blades.

He managed to stammer that he was sorry that he could not stay longer in the camp, but he had to find his American foster father. She smiled sadly and said, "Datu, when you return to Cotabato, please just tell someone that you saw me here." As she walked quickly away, he realized that he hadn't even asked her name.

By the time Adil returned to Tubaran, Lt. Erich was ready to move out again. They hiked down from the mountains to the shore and found two boats to carry them across the wide lake, waiting until nightfall to cast off to avoid Japanese patrol boats. Steering by moonlight, they made their way to the far north shore by dawn. Now they hiked away from the lake, back into the mountains, heading north. By early evening they had reached the hamlet of Mamaan on the lip of the Lanao plateau.

Adil had been sick with dysentery and wanted badly to wash. At the edge of the hamlet, the plateau dropped off sharply into the deep forest. Looking for privacy, he saw a game trail wandering into a lush ravine with a stream at its bottom. He asked Lieutenant Erich for permission to explore it, then skidded down the steep slope to the secluded stream. He soothed himself in its water, but as he started his climb back up the wall of the ravine, a sudden downpour began that quickly accelerated to a deluge, the rain slicing down in great sheets. The scant trail was instantly obliterated as the slope liquefied into streaming mud. He turned back around and, as the rain slackened somewhat, walked uncertainly through the dripping forest, following the now-swollen stream, looking for another way out of the valley. This far below the plateau, the light had nearly gone, and, squinting through the rain and pushing through the wet, tangled undergrowth, he sometimes lost sight of the ravine wall itself.

He could find no other trail leading out of the dim, sodden valley, and he was beginning to lose track of how far he had walked down the stream when he chanced upon a small clearing and a dimly-lit stilted house with water falling from the eaves of its palm-thatched roof.

Over the sound of the flowing water, Adil announced himself in Maranao, and an old man appeared silhouetted in the open doorway cradling a homemade 12 gauge shotgun in his arms. Adil identified himself, and the man invited him to climb the notched-log ladder and enter. He shared the house with his wife and their teenaged granddaughter, a beautiful girl, Adil noticed, of fourteen or fifteen. She was boiling sweet potatoes for their dinner and asked him to eat with them. He happily accepted as the rain beat its rustling staccato on the roof.

They ate together and, when the rain tapped less vigorously on the palm thatch, he said his thanks and stood to leave. The old man answered, "Datu, it is already dark. Stay the night with us." Still weak from dysentery and tired from travelling through the previous night, he thought of remaining in that dry refuge near the girl with the soft voice and pretty smile, but he replied that he needed to return to his companions. While they were talking, the girl, who had been outside washing the dinner dishes, hurried back in and said quietly but urgently to her grandfather, "Apo, two young men are waiting outside with machetes."

The old man told Adil that they must have followed him there in the storm and were after his guns. "Come with me," he said. "No one will harm my guest!"

Shotgun at the ready, the old man stepped down from the house, calling a challenge to the hidden attackers, "Do you think you can kill this Magindanaon datu? Come and try!"

As Adil followed close behind, gripping his rifle, they heard the rustle of the two men retreating quickly through the forest. The old man told him he should be safe now. He escorted Adil to the edge of his rice field and pointed out a narrow trail that would be an easier way out of the valley—longer but less steep.

Adil lost the trail more than once in the wet darkness, requiring him to zigzag back down the slope until he re-crossed it, then start up again. He held his rifle tightly the entire time, listening intently for footsteps behind him. After walking for what seemed like hours through the night forest, he finally climbed back onto the edge of the plateau not far from the hamlet and his companions. Only the sentry remained awake, and he offered him the remains of dinner—corn and *carabao* meat.

"We were worried," the sentry said. "Lieutenant Erich was going to send someone to look for you in the morning. He didn't want to have to tell Mr. Kuder that we lost you."

In the morning, Lt. Erich was happy to see him back in camp—so happy that he decided to let him move ahead more quickly to the coast, sending two of his men along as guides. They walked north off the Lanao plateau toward the bay and guerrilla headquarters. Adil was back in the rainforest, but this time on a well-traveled jungle trail along the rushing Matengao River that was, judging by the number of armed travelers they passed as they descended, a veritable guerrilla highway.

About halfway to the coast, they stopped at the hamlet of Pantao Ragat and made their way to an old wooden schoolhouse that his guides told him was the headquarters of the guerrilla leader Lt. William Tait. They were met by sentries who disarmed them, then took them to meet the lieutenant. On the way, Adil saw two bodies laid out beneath the schoolhouse awaiting burial. The sentry, dressed in a ragged tunic of handwoven burlap, told them they had died of malaria. Although American submarines had been arriving on the Mindanao coast for months, no quinine or uniforms had yet reached these guerrillas.

Lieutenant Tait was tall, with a handsome face marred only by a badly swollen right eye. Adil introduced himself and told him that he had been a classmate of Tait's younger sister, Victoria, at Lanao High School. Surprised and pleased, Lieutenant Tait embraced him and began conversing rapidly with him in perfect Magindanaon. He told him that his mother was from Dulawan in Cotabato and that he had been born there. "I am Magindanaon!"

Tait's father had served as a veterinary surgeon with the all-black U.S. Tenth Cavalry Regiment—the famous Buffalo Soldiers—in the Moro Wars under John J. Pershing, who received the nickname Black Jack from his white fellow officers because of his stated respect for the black soldiers he led. Dr. Tait was a civilian employee of the army and may, like many other army veterinarians in the Philippines, have been on a temporary assignment. When his service was finished, he stayed in Cotabato and married a young Magindanaon woman from Dulawan, then the seat of power of Datu Piang, the "King of Mindanao."

Adil asked him about his swollen eye, and Tait told him that while out that morning hunting hornbills one of his cartridges had exploded. With the American surrender, guns were relatively plentiful in Lanao but ammunition was extremely scarce. Japanese military intelligence had put purposely overloaded cartridges onto the local black market to dissuade the Maranaos from firing at Japanese soldiers. Lieutenant Tait invited them to eat, and they had rice and corn, a special treat for the visitors.

* * *

Of the local guerrillas operating in the orbit of Wendell Fertig, none was more disrespected than Lieutenant William Tait. Fertig's introductory description of him in his autobiography is crassly racist, and, in his diary, he consistently refers to Tait as "Sambo." Other American guerrillas simply called him "N****r Tait." Beneath the crude racial slurs, however, can be found a grudging recognition that William Tait was a cunning and highly capable guerrilla leader. In his most notable action, just after midnight on September 16th, 1942, he sailed with 34 guerrillas (most of them Moros) across Panguil Bay to Misamis Occidental. There, in less than a week, he captured 87 guns, secured control of the capital, Misamis City, and made the entire province a haven for guerrillas. Fertig, who by now had declared himself a brigadier general, crossed into Misamis Occidental in October 1942 and set up his Capital of the Free Philippines there—an achievement made possible only by the military successes of William Tait, both a Moro and a Black American.[5]

In the reports and memoirs of American guerrillas, William Tait is most often mentioned in conjunction with Captain Luis Morgan, his sometime collaborator. Morgan's father was also an American and his mother was a Filipina. He was acknowledged by all to be handsome and brave, but the Americans had decided he was a troublemaker—overly proud and unreliable. Morgan and Tait were rough and ready characters, and neither one was blameless. Morgan in particular, seems to have ordered a massacre of innocent Moro villagers early in the war. But the amount of concern expressed by American chroniclers about these two independent-minded guerrilla leaders was far out of proportion to their effect on the war effort. Wendell Fertig, whose concern with Morgan verged on obsession, devotes more than 50 pages of his autobiography to his interactions with Morgan. Fertig's concern was echoed uncritically by Edward Kuder and others, and seems to have reflected the threat that Morgan and Tait represented, not to the war effort—they were, after all, also fighting the Japanese occupiers—but to the taken-for-granted racial hierarchy that underpinned American colonial rule.

William Tait's father, the 10th Cavalry veterinarian, was not the only black American veteran to remain in Mindanao and make a life among his former Moro enemies. Mohammad Adil himself knew of five such men. One was a close friend of his father known only by his last name, Boswell, which the Moros pronounced as "Baswil." A veteran of the Philippine Constabulary who had stayed on in Cotabato after his service, he owned the first outboard motor anyone had ever seen. He was also the first American to establish a rice mill in Cotabato. Boswell, who never married and spoke very little Magindanaon, became friends with Adil's English-speaking father and convinced him, over many nights of conversation, to start his own rice mill.

When the Japanese invaded, Boswell refused to abandon everything he had worked for and escape to the hills, deciding instead to stand and fight. As Japanese soldiers entered his house to arrest him, he emptied both barrels of his shotgun at them, killing two soldiers before he was shot and killed himself. One of Adil's cousins, Baswil Pangilan, was named in honor of Boswell, who in the eyes of the Magindanaons had demonstrated true *maratabat*. The four other black Americans who had settled in Cotabato were also veterans of colonial military forces. Two owned rice mills, and three married Moro women. There are Moros today in Cotabato who are descendants of those men who chose to remain on the wild frontier of a strange land rather than return to American hometowns with more perils and fewer opportunities.

* * *

William Tait sent them on their way with one of his men to accompany them to the coast. In a few hours they had reached Linamun on Iligan Bay. At the guerrilla outpost there he showed his letter to a first lieutenant, who told his companions, "You take this boy to Kauswagan." But they were anxious to get back to the hills, so they pointed him west and he walked the coast road alone. He was in guerrilla-held territory, and there was plenty of foot traffic, but there were few vehicles of any kind on the road, which was pitted with large, fresh craters from Japanese bombing.

As he approached Kauswagan he was overtaken by two young men on horseback. He recognized his Lanao High School classmates, Pedro Maibituin and Gregorio Cabili, and yelled to them, "Pete, Greg!" Both wore sergeant's stripes.

"Where are you going?" they asked.

"I am going to see Mr. Kuder! Is he here?" They told him he had been there until a few weeks ago but that he had recently evacuated inland because of the Japanese attacks up and down the coast. They offered to accompany him to guerrilla headquarters where someone would know Kuder's whereabouts.

Adil jumped up behind Pedro on his horse, and they continued down the coast road. Just west of Kauswagan they heard the throb of a ship's engine around a point of land, and the riders hurried the horses off the road into a stand of coconut palms. They told him it was a Japanese cruiser that had been patrolling slowly up and down the bay since the Japanese attacks of the previous month. It was watching for guerrilla activity and would occasionally send a salvo into suspected guerrilla locations. When the cruiser passed, they continued their journey.

Further along the coast, they heard the sound of an engine approaching around a bend in the road accompanied by a loud thumping and slapping. A cargo truck bumped down the road and stopped in front of them. Each wheel of the truck had several old tire treads lashed to it with thick wire. Adil dismounted and saw a middle-aged American in short pants and khaki shirt, wearing a pith helmet and a .38 revolver strapped to his leg. It was Lt. Colonel Charles Hedges, Fertig's second-in-command. He returned the salutes of Pedro and Gregorio and, pointing to Adil, asked, "Who's this?"

Adil identified himself and handed Hedges his letter.

"Ah, so you're the one he's been waiting for. How many guns do you have, son?"

Adil showed him his .38 and his Springfield rifle. Hedges clapped him on the back and said, "Good boy, good boy. We always need more guns." He told Pedro and Gregorio that Kuder was staying in the schoolhouse in Panguiyawan. Then he turned back to Adil. "The old man will be happy to see you."

Another easy hour on horseback brought them to the new headquarters in Liangan. Pedro and Gregorio, on the way to their quarters in nearby Esperanza, left him after providing directions. Alone again, Adil walked into the late afternoon forest, following a trail inland along the Liangan River. As he walked, he anticipated his reunion with his foster father, "the old man" whom he had not seen in 18 months. Kuder, 16 years younger than MacArthur, was not, in fact old. But even at 47, his deep voice, formal manner, and tropical suit projected an air of mature authority to everyone he encountered. He was "the old man" in the same sense that a high ranking American officer was "the old man" to those under his command. But he was more than that to Adil. He had taken him under his roof, shown him kindness, and paid him attention.

* * *

Five years earlier, Edward Kuder was taking his usual breakfast at his usual place on the veranda of his house overlooking the turquoise waters of the Sulu Sea. He had just started in on the eggs, bacon, and Hills Bros. coffee prepared by his housekeeper, Mrs. Morales, when he heard a whispered commotion on the stairs. An unfamiliar boy was hiding behind Alun, who was standing at the top of the stairs. The boy stared at him wide-eyed as Alun, a student from Cotabato whom Kuder was sponsoring through high school, hissed at him in his native language and attempted to push him forward. The undersized boy was trembling with fear, but in his eyes, Kuder could see curiosity and determination.

When Kuder asked him his name, the boy replied, "Mohammad," pronouncing it "Mokamad" in the Moro way. When he asked him why he was there, the boy answered in his language, with Alun translating, that he wanted to study at Sulu High School. Alun added that Mohammad was his distant relative, a few years younger than him, and had insisted on coming with him when he returned to Sulu from school vacation in Cotabato.

Kuder gruffly asked the new boy, "Does your father know you are here?" The boy began to answer when Alun interjected. After a brief heated exchange between the two in their language, Mohammad said in English, "No." Gradually the full story emerged.

Mohammad had run away using the 15 pesos—a princely sum for a 13-year old boy in 1938—that his father had given him as a present for graduating from middle school.

Kuder already had a house full of boys, but there was something special about this one. Of all the boys he had sponsored in his years as superintendent of schools, only one other, the most talented of them all, had chosen him rather than the opposite. Salipada Pendatun, the son of a sultan, was now a law student in Manila. This new boy, also an aristocrat by birth, reminded Kuder of him. He told Alun to translate a letter to Mohammad's father, requesting his permission to let the boy stay.

* * *

Four miles later, in fading light, Adil arrived at the abandoned schoolhouse in a large clearing. He stepped inside and, peering into the deep shadows, saw a lone figure lying on a bare cot. Adjusting his gaze, he shuddered with recognition as the eyes of his foster father, the most powerful man he had ever known, stared back at him from a shockingly frail and emaciated body. This was not the same man he had been seeking, not the man he had known. The realization struck him like a blow. Despite his reassuring letters, his foster father had not been spared by the war. The sight of the feeble man before him, struggling to sit up, made his heart sink, but he willed himself forward with a brave smile.

Kuder recognized him and smiled weakly, signaling for Adil to sit next to him. He turned to his foster son and tried to speak, but only tears came. Adil, now unable to hold back his tears, hugged his foster father. They sat for a long while there, side by side on the cot, arms around each other, both crying, neither one able to speak, as the last light seeped from the schoolhouse.

3
TOTAL RESISTANCE

When the man and the boy had finally found their voices, they began to tell one another of their adventures since the Japanese invasion. Adil spoke excitedly, and Kuder replied in the deep, measured tones that the boy remembered so well, though now his voice was weaker, echoing the frailty of his body. He talked first of his mysterious illness.

The sickness had started eight months earlier, in November 1942, while he was hiding in the steep green hills above Lake Nunungan, on the southwestern edge of the Lanao plateau. The Japanese had already put a price on his head, but he was living under the protection of Datu Lagindab, a fearless fighter whose son-in-law, Miguel Alug, had worked for Kuder for almost twenty years. Datu Lagindab, had a great many daughters and sons. With 24 wives, he was the most-married Moro of his generation. Not even the Sultan of Sulu had more wives.

The white-bearded Lagindab had led a Bolo Battalion against the Japanese when they marched up the same road Pershing had used to invade Lanao. He and his followers had rushed the invasion force with their blades drawn, but were quickly repulsed and faded back into the forest. Lagindab lost six nephews in that melee and he swore to avenge their deaths.[1] Once again, Moros had paid a terrible price for their lack of modern weapons, although this time those weapons had been withheld by their allies.

In Nunungan, Kuder hid in plain sight. His newly–built bamboo house stood just behind the crest of a hill and was surrounded by trees tall enough to prevent it from being seen easily from the air; camouflaged foxholes and ditches had been dug nearby. A few dozen yards away, at the top of the hill, a hidden observation post overlooked the Japanese garrison far down the steep slope at the edge of Nunungan Lake.

It was in that house that Kuder first fell sick with a cold and fever and soon after with dysentery. He remained ill and mostly bedridden for 47 days but continued to plan attacks on the Japanese with Lagindab and other Maranao datus. By day 30, unable to tolerate food and too weak to walk, he thought he might die, and the prospect struck him as not unwelcome. But his Maranao hosts offered their remedies and coaxed him to eat. Eventually, his health improved enough for him to leave his bed and, at the end of January 1943, to leave his Maranao protectors and make the trip to join Fertig's guerrillas at the coast. He hadn't fully recovered but was well enough to assume his position under Fertig as Civil Affairs Officer. And now, eight months later, the mystery ailment had returned in force, weakening him once again as he steadily lost weight.

For the following days, Adil took over Kuder's care from Lumala, his Maranao former high school classmate who had been staying with Kuder since the two students from Sulu had returned home. In a week or so, his foster father was strong enough to ride a horse down the trail to guerrilla headquarters at Liangan on the coast to see the doctor and collect his allotment of supplies. While Kuder was with the doctor, Adil explored the guerrilla camp and found his way eventually to Colonel Hedges' office. The new guerrilla headquarters, formerly Hedges' satellite camp, was smaller and far less elaborate than Fertig's former headquarters across the bay in Misamis City. It was a small Maranao village lining the coconut-fringed, grey sand shore of Iligan Bay, and Hedges' office was simply the largest bamboo and palm-thatched house in the village.

It was midday, and there were few guerrillas about. Hedges was not in his office, but Adil recognized Datu Lagindab, whom he knew from his time as a student in Lanao, sitting with some other Maranao men on a bamboo bench along the wall. Adil saw that Lagindab carried one of the new M1 Garand semi-automatic rifles recently offloaded from an American submarine, and he asked if he could examine it. Its mechanism was unlike the Springfield rifle he was used to, and as he handled it, the gun went off, its .30 caliber bullet smashing into Hedges' portable typewriter on the nearby desk and flinging it across the room.

The sound of a gunshot from Hedges' office woke the camp, and within seconds the room was filled with men, mostly Americans and Filipinos, with guns drawn and pointed at Adil, standing now with the Garand by his side and beginning to tremble. As shouts of "spy!" rang out, Datu Lagindab and a few other Maranaos stepped in front of Adil. With raised guns and hardened faces, they roared back that the gunshot was an accident and that they would defend this lad. Several tense moments passed until Hedges appeared, recognized the culprit as Edward Kuder's boy, and ordered all the men to stand down. He cursed vigorously at the sight of his punctured typewriter, scowled at Adil, then dismissed him. Burning with shame, the boy went to find Kuder. It was not the sort of first impression he had hoped to make at guerrilla headquarters.

Charles Hedges, in his late forties, was wiry, foul-mouthed, and physically brave. He wore a MacArthur-style crushed cap and an Errol Flynn mustache that civilized his somewhat feral face.

Lt. Col. Charles Hedges and his elite Maranao fighters displaying Browning Automatic Rifles (BARs) recently delivered by an American submarine, circa 1943

Hedges had run a lumber operation in the nearby Kapatagan Valley before the war and had developed a reputation among his fellow Americans for being able to "handle" the Moros. That reputation notwithstanding, Hedges had likely learned by mid-1943 that the Moros were not amenable to handling by himself or anyone else. He certainly knew that were it not for Edward Kuder, he would have had far fewer Moro fighters under his command.

As the only unsurrendered American on the Lanao Plateau, Kuder had spent much of the previous year living under the protection of various Maranao datus, Lagindab being just the most recent.

While Fertig and Hedges and other American holdouts had been on the run from the Japanese in 1942, the Maranaos of the Lanao Plateau had been attacking their occupiers. The Maranao insurgency was both the earliest and the most dramatically successful armed resistance in the entire Philippines, and Edward Kuder was a witness and contributor to its accomplishments.

On May 2, 1942, the day the Japanese army marched into Dansalan, the provincial capital of Lanao, Kuder's was the last civilian car to leave town. His world had collapsed unimaginably fast as American-led troops on the island of Mindanao fell back before the Japanese onslaught. Within a few weeks of the occupation of Dansalan, U.S. forces surrendered unconditionally and 44 years of American rule in the Philippines disintegrated overnight.

All American civilians were required to present themselves to Japanese authorities. When Brigadier General Guy Fort, the American commander of the Lanao forces, wrote to Kuder on the eve of his own surrender, he did not tell Kuder to turn himself in, although he had advised other American civilians to do so. Instead, he sent him his radio receiver for safekeeping "until we should meet again, not too long in the future."[2]

Kuder already knew that a brighter future in the form of a U.S. armada would not arrive anytime soon. An American naval officer had confided in him months earlier about the extent of the devastation at Pearl Harbor. But he had friends among the Maranaos, and he decided that he would rather suffer the hardships of a fugitive than those of a prisoner of war. He sheltered first with an old friend, the Sultan of Ramain, who hid him during the perilous first weeks of the Japanese occupation.

In those early days, Kuder recalled in a 1943 report, Japanese assault troops "slapped, kicked, bayoneted, or even beheaded" Lanao townspeople who offended them.³ Elsewhere in the Philippines, conditions were even worse. Civilians were stunned by the cruelty of the occupiers, who shot them for minor transgressions, such as listening to American radio broadcasts. For every Japanese soldier assassinated, ten Filipinos were randomly chosen and beheaded, and their bodies strung up in town squares as examples. And everywhere else in the Philippines, Japanese soldiers routinely abducted and raped girls and young women, subjecting many of them to weeks or months of sexual slavery.

In Mindanao, however, Japanese commanders and troops were mindful of the depredations of the Bolo Battalions at Digos and elsewhere. Fearful of further attacks by the Moros, the occupiers tempered their behavior in Lanao. In particular, the abuse of Maranao women was rare. Instead, according to Kuder, "prostitutes reported to be Formosan, Chinese and Japanese were imported for the use of the officers and men of the Imperial Japanese Army."⁴

In Lanao, the occupiers' first goal was to defang the Maranaos by depriving them of their weapons, just as the Americans had attempted 30 years earlier. Once again, every household was required to turn in all firearms, while chopping tools were limited to one for every two households. And once again, the Maranaos surrendered a few defective rifles and some old rusty blades. The Japanese then threatened to shoot any Maranao they found with a gun and did so, executing each violator immediately in a public square. Those public executions provided the initial spark for an eventual wildfire of Maranao retaliation.

In June of 1942, the Japanese commander of the Dansalan garrison sent a punitive expedition to Watu, a small village on the western shore of the lake, looking for Manalao Mindalano, the first Maranao leader to launch attacks against them. Mindalano had not stopped with his attacks on the Japanese tanks. He obtained guns from escaping USAFFE soldiers and gathered others from Maranaos who had hidden them. He then began setting ambushes and sending letters in English to the Japanese provincial commander to taunt him.

The surprised villagers of Watu, who had no connection to Mindalano, were trapped against the lakeshore as they tried to escape the soldiers, who methodically bayoneted men and women alike, killing 24 in all. In reprisal, Datu Pantangan, who had been a fifth-grade student of Kuder, attacked a Japanese convoy, firing well-aimed volleys into the drivers and tires of speeding trucks and sending them careening off roads and tumbling from bridges. The Japanese responded by burning scores of houses along the road where the ambush was laid. The cycle of retaliation, one well understood by the long-feuding clans of the Lanao Plateau, was underway.

Some inhabitants of the garrisoned towns around the lake abandoned their homes and fled to the forest to escape the Japanese reprisals. The Sultan of Ramain, a pragmatic and cautious man, was among them. He and his followers had moved from the capital, Dansalan, to an evacuation camp deep in the wooded hills above the lake, taking Kuder with them.

As a senator of the Philippine Commonwealth, the sultan was a symbolically important political figure for the occupiers, and they pressured him hard for his cooperation. Seeing the Japanese burning houses, his followers were afraid that his resistance would cost them dearly. Those of his kinspeople favoring submission were led by his senior wife, who was even wealthier and more pragmatic than her husband.

They finally persuaded the sultan to submit to the Japanese for their sake. With tears in his eyes, he broke the news to Kuder while assuring him that he would honor his vow, sworn on the Holy

Qur'an, to shelter him. Kuder trusted the sultan's word but declined to stay, not wanting his presence to jeopardize the sultan's family. Kuder had also decided that he needed to be with Maranaos who were still resisting the Japanese. He sent a messenger to the southern shore of the lake to find Datu Pagandaman, a trusted friend who had worked for him for many years, and ask him for sanctuary.

Some nights later, in the dark of the moon, Pagandaman appeared at the sultan's forest camp with a retinue of turbaned men, young and old, barefoot and dressed in *malongs*, with ammunition belts slung over their shoulders and rifles in their hands. They gathered Kuder's few remaining possessions—his blankets and clothes, a twenty-gauge shotgun, a few books and a single precious bottle of Bacardi rum. Bidding goodbye to the sultan, he followed them into the misty dark on the most difficult trek of his life.

After leaving the forest, there were miles of rice paddies to traverse before reaching the lakeshore. All Moros were skilled acrobats around water wherever it was found—in seas, rivers, lakes, or flooded rice fields. To this day, Moro children play their games of tag, racing barefoot across impossibly narrow bamboo footbridges or hopping from one bobbing dugout canoe to another. As his companions strode quickly and silently atop the narrow dikes that separated the flooded fields, Edward Kuder floundered. Time and again he slipped off the ice-slick dike and into the water and mud of the rice field. He would then crawl and claw his way back onto the dike and try once more to maintain his footing in the wet blackness before, inevitably, sliding off again.

More than three exhausting hours later, they reached the pebbled shore and the outriggered motor launch waiting to take them south. As they shoved off, the low clouds crowding the sky over the lake released a light but steady rain that chilled them as they gained speed, but which they welcomed because it hid them from Japanese patrol boats. Before morning, they reached a gravel beach, and then hiked again, climbing for hours up an old dry stream bed overhung with bamboo clumps and fruit trees until they reached a tiny glen notched into a ridge and fringed with vegetation so thick that it was completely hidden from view. Tucked against the back wall of the tiny valley was an old outlaw cabin that would be his hideout for the next month. There was no denying now that he was a fugitive on the run.

To his outlaw hideout came daily visitors from the nearby village of Bayang, bringing him the news and asking his advice about potential attacks against the Japanese. There was much to discuss. The Japanese had sent a patrol against Mindalano's stronghold on the slope of Mount Gadungan, where Adil would later visit, and this time the Maranaos were forewarned. Mindalano and his brother-in-law ambushed the Japanese column twice on the way to Gadungan, killing 15 Japanese soldiers.

In response, the Japanese increased their patrols, looking for weapons. Soon after Kuder's arrival at the hideout, a Japanese patrol appeared without warning in Bayang. Just outside of town, the patrol surprised three men with guns. They bound them and brought them to the marketplace in town, where they were blindfolded and made to sit on rocks. Then, with the townspeople watching, the officer leading the patrol unholstered his pistol and shot each man through the skull. From his hiding place, Kuder could hear the shots echo up the slope.

The people of Bayang were convulsed with anger and shame at the Japanese outrage, and some feared worse to come. A few days later, Japanese propaganda leaflets appeared in the village. They were last chance warnings to any Americans still in hiding, threatening death to those who did not immediately surrender as well as to those who were hiding them. A rumor soon spread that a second and even larger Japanese patrol was headed to Bayang, this time looking for the American, Edward Kuder. Some villagers began to grumble that, when the Japanese came, the American would have to take care of himself. They were not ready to sacrifice everything to defend him.

Datu Pagandaman, Kuder's current protector, was away, but his wife, Maruki, hearing the grumbling, picked up a *panabas* in one hand, held her youngest son with the other, and announced, "If there is no man here who will protect Mr. Kuder, then I will."[5] She then climbed the long, steep trail to Kuder's hideout and appeared unannounced—a small woman in a *malong*, silk blouse, and conical hat woven from palm fronds, holding a *panabas* that, with its curved blade resting on the ground, was almost as tall as her. She told him in rudimentary English that the Japanese were on their way and that she, the daughter of a chieftain, would defend him. Seeing the fire in her eyes, Kuder picked up his shotgun and field glasses and selected his best brass shells. Then they sat side by side, waiting for the Japanese patrol to arrive.

It was Maruki's male relatives, shamed into action, who arrived first, heavily armed and pledging to defend Kuder. No Japanese soldiers came that day. The report had been a false alarm. When the Japanese patrol eventually did arrive, days later, it was not searching specifically for Kuder. By then, the villagers had forged a compromise among themselves. They would defend Kuder if he was attacked. Datu Pagandaman had, after all, made a vow, and *maratabat* was at stake. But they would not attack Japanese patrols unless attacked first. There were some who wanted to fight the Japanese on sight, but more who did not want to send their wives and children to the forest to live and to see their homes burned in reprisal for attacks.

It was a custom among the Moros to name one or more of

their children after admired figures, and Maruki had named her youngest son MacArthur. On the day the second Japanese patrol marched through Bayang, little MacArthur, who had just learned to walk, toddled in front of the advancing column and his nanny, rushing to catch him, called out in Maranao, "MacArthur, MacArthur, come here!" Datu Pagandaman, alarmed to hear that name shouted in front of the Japanese, moved to hush her, but his wife, Maruki, turned to him and said the shaming words, "What? Are you not a man?" He remained quiet, and the nanny kept calling for "MacArthur," but the Japanese patrol walked on unheeding. The people of Bayang took the event as a good omen. They had spoken the forbidden name in the face of the enemy and no harm had come of it.

For Kuder, however, these were days of frustration and, not occasionally, despair. He was alone and cut off from the outside world, with almost no news of the war in the Pacific and even less information about other Americans in Mindanao. Japanese propaganda, by contrast, was ubiquitous—broadcast by radio or distributed in pamphlets, magazines, and newspapers. It boasted of steady advances in New Guinea and China, threats against India, and, most worrisome to Kuder, successful landings in the Aleutian Islands.

He burned with hatred for the Japanese, who had attacked his country and destroyed his colonial world. He wanted the Maranaos—all the Moros—to hate them just as fiercely and to fight in his cause. War required sacrifice, and he welcomed theirs. His zeal was tempered only by his concern, shared in his confidential report to MacArthur's team, that should the guerrilla attacks result in "too many slaughtered" in the Moro ranks, it "would undo all the painful, step-by-step morale-building and backbone stiffening I had done."[6] He knew that the Maranaos he was trying to enlist in his cause made their decisions to resist, avoid, or cooperate with the new occupiers based on practical calculations but also on *maratabat*. More often than not, the decision to fight was determined by the requirements of *maratabat*—upholding honor and fulfilling vows. Kuder hoped to use *maratabat* in his favor. It was *maratabat*, after all, that had motivated the Sultan of Ramain and Datu Pagandaman to protect him even at great risk to themselves and their followers.

Yet by early August 1942, he was ready to leave Pagandaman, his second Maranao protector, because Pagandaman's people weren't willing to risk enough in his war. He was dissatisfied with the compromise toward the Japanese arrived at by Pagandaman's villagers and now more afraid that one of them would be tempted to reveal his location to the enemy. Kuder had heard stories of Datu Lagindab's exploits against the Japanese. He sent a messenger to Miguel Alug, Lagindab's son-in-law, asking him to come for him. This time, 18 armed men appeared at his hideout to escort him on a less hazardous daylight trek to Lagindab's redoubt in the hills above Nunungan Lake. There he began planning attacks on the Japanese with Lagindab and other Maranao datus.

Over the next two months, they organized two ambushes of Japanese convoys on Pershing's road between Malabang at the coast and Ganassi on the shore of the lake. Kuder led the logistics planning for both attacks and provided the money to buy ammunition on the black market. Maranaos poured a murderous fire into the Convoy targeted in the first ambush from cliffs overlooking the mountain road, killing 10 Japanese soldiers, including the commander who had first put a price on Kuder's head.

The second was set on a dangerous hairpin turn, where a high bank with good cover commanded both arms of the sharp curve. The attackers reported to Kuder that they had counted 23 dead soldiers and had barely missed killing the notable collaborator, Datu Sinsuat

Balabaran , father of Umbus a Bai. His car at the head of the convoy had passed by just before they opened fire. The ambushers suffered only one casualty a young man shot through the body who survived his wounds. Concerned that the Japanese would retaliate by sending reinforcements up the same road to punish the people of Ganassi, Kuder suggested to Datu Lagindab that his men block the road, and they did so by felling scores of trees across it. The Japanese did not use that road again for at least a year.

In September of 1942, while Kuder was at Nunungan, the Maranaos dealt the Japanese a stunning loss when, in a spontaneous attack, a collection of villagers armed primarily with blades nearly annihilated an entire company of Japanese infantry. The Battle of Tamparan was the gravest defeat inflicted on the Imperial Japanese Army by irregular forces in the Philippines and quite likely their greatest loss at the hands of civilians in the entire course of the Pacific War. For the Japanese infantry, it was a defeat as improbable, shameful, and symbolically charged as that suffered by the U.S. cavalry at the Battle of the Little Bighorn but, unlike that iconic defeat, it has been mostly lost from history. Edward Kuder had no connection to the attack but was told about it immediately afterward and was its only contemporary chronicler.

The patrol, a company of 90 infantrymen, accompanied by support personnel, had arrived in Tamparan at dawn in three launches on the morning of September 12th, the first day of the Muslim holy month of Ramadan. They were looking for Datu Busran Kalaw, a Maranao resistance leader who was no longer at the village. Hoping to take Busran by surprise, the patrol disembarked at the pier and took a side trail to the village, which ran past a traditional *kota*, a palisaded fort constructed of coconut logs. As the patrol neared the *kota*, shots rang out. It is not clear who fired first, but the Japanese patrol withdrew to the main road, set up their mortars, and began shelling the fort.

Attacking a Maranao village on the first morning of the most sacred month of the Muslim calendar was a fatal mistake. The fasting month in Tamparan celebrated selflessness and mutual aid as the highest moral principles of the community. The union of religious selflessness and *maratabat* birthed a terrible resolve for total resistance on that fateful morning. It was the sound of the shelling that brought Maranaos by the hundreds, farmers and fishermen from Tamparan and three surrounding villages, weapons in hand, running to the scene. Those with rifles crawled through the marsh grass and fired on the Japanese ranks from the rear as they shelled the *kota*. Those armed only with blades, the large majority, rushed straight down the road at the invaders and into a cyclone of bullets and shrapnel.

* * *

A Moro frontal attack with bladed weapons, if survived, was never forgotten. Edward Kuder, on a small island in the Sulu Sea in 1935, had witnessed such an attack. There, from the edge of a jungle, three Moro "outlaws," armed only with spears and krises, charged eight Philippine Constabulary soldiers at a dead run from about 30 yards away, throwing their spears at close range then slashing furiously with their krises. "Despite the fact that the soldiers had high-powered rifles, three of them were killed and the three outlaws were killed. The fight lasted about 15 seconds." Kuder wrote to his father that the toll on the soldiers could have been worse. "There were armed Moros with us in the headman's house and it was their firing from the house that helped to kill the outlaws." Kuder was awed by the ferocious attack, telling his father that he had "never seen anything to equal the speed and fury of the outlaws' rush."[7]

* * *

Surrounded on three sides and taking casualties from both bullets and blades, the Japanese soldiers broke and ran for the pier and the launches but were soon mired in the marshlands that edged the lake with their ammunition exhausted. Now they fought without bullets, desperately using their bayonets to parry blades, their boots sucking them into the mud while the barefoot villagers rushed in from all sides.

Some soldiers attempted unsuccessfully to surrender. One of the company's officers, First Lt. Atsuo Takeuchi, made it back to the pier with a few of his men, but the boat crews, who were Filipino forced laborers, had dived overboard when they saw how the battle was going. With no way to escape, he dropped his sword and raised his hands in submission. Takeuchi had been very active in propaganda efforts among the Maranaos and had often bragged that the Japanese never surrendered, unlike the Americans and Filipinos. According to Kuder, one young Maranao remembered those boasts and yelled at him, "No surrender, Takeuchi!," before cutting him down with his *panabas*. [8]

Of the 90 Japanese infantrymen who marched down the Tamparan pier that morning, 85 now lay dead on the muddy lakeshore; their lacerated bodies, sprawled individually or tangled together in clumps of blood-soaked khaki, dotted the trampled grey marshland. But Japanese rifles and mortars had also taken a heavy toll on the defenders of Tamparan. In death, as in life, the Japanese soldiers were surrounded by Moros. In every direction lay the shattered bodies of villagers, more than 200 in all, who had run to the aid of their neighbors on that sacred morning with blades drawn to meet the terrible firepower of the Empire of Japan. The sound of keening soon pierced the air and rose and flew from settlement to settlement along the lakeshore as families discovered the bodies of their loved ones on the field and carried them home to prepare them for burial.

The Japanese bodies lay where they had fallen. For two days afterward, the terrible reek of their corpses bloating in the heat kept villagers from the battlefield. The Japanese commander at Dansalan, Lt. Colonel Yoshinari Tanaka, offered rewards for returning the bodies of his soldiers, and a few enterprising Maranaos stole bodies, despite the stench, and sold them to the Japanese. The body of First Lt. Takeuchi had been mutilated beyond recognition with scores of wounds from blades. In his account, Edward Kuder explained the mutilation by noting that the Maranaos were simply "blooding" their weapons because of their belief that "before a weapon can become fit to use, it must many times taste blood."[9] A Maranao survivor of the battle, Abubakar, recalled differently 52 years later. A farmer from Tamparan, Abubakar was at home that morning when he heard the firing, grabbed his *panabas*, and joined "a great crowd" that had gathered from surrounding villages. He then took part in the fighting, "narrowly escaping death." He remembered that Takeuchi's body was mutilated because "people felt angry seeing so many of their friends injured or dying."[10]

Tamparan buried its dead, but its suffering was not over. The worst fear of Lt. Colonel Miura, the Japanese commander who had first invaded Mindanao and met the Bolo Battalions at Digos, had come true at Tamparan. Ordinary Moro villagers had risen , weapons in hand, to drive the invaders away. How to prevent this total resistance from spreading throughout Lanao? To punish the villagers the Japanese attacked Tamparan and its surrounding settlements for 25 days straight, but only from afar, using aerial and artillery bombardment. Edward Kuder reported that the bombardment was ineffective and killed no Maranao fighting men. Mohammad Adil, however, remembered hearing of one Japanese bomb that struck a mosque where villagers were seeking shelter, killing 80 men, women, and children.

The victory at Tamparan, costly as it was, inspired even more Maranao resistance. In this instance at least, Kuder's concern about "too many slaughtered" was unwarranted. In response to the retaliatory bombings, the Maranaos destroyed Pershing's road, felling trees for miles and obstructing culverts so that rains would wash the roadbed away.

Shocked by the defeat at Tamparan and desperate to regain the upper hand, the Japanese military tried an unusual tactic. In early November of 1942, Maj. General Giichi Morimoto, chief of the Mindanao Military Government, transferred Brigadier General Guy Fort from his prison in Manila back to Dansalan on Lake Lanao. Fort was the USAFFE commander of Lanao forces who had organized the Maranao Bolo Battalions and left his radio with Edward Kuder for safekeeping before surrendering. General Morimoto demanded that Fort order the Maranaos of the Lanao Plateau to stop fighting and surrender their weapons. Fort refused to do any such thing. Lt. Colonel Yoshinari Tanaka, commander of the Japanese forces at Dansalan, and the man who had sent the patrol to Tamparan, was charged with securing Fort's cooperation. In addition to recovering the bodies of those slain at Tamparan, it had been Tanaka's responsibility to write letters to the families of the infantrymen killed there, and he had recently led a memorial service for his slain soldiers at the site of the battle.

On November 11, 1942, Tanaka presented Fort with a typed statement to sign ordering the Maranaos to cease their armed resistance to the Japanese occupation. Fort again refused. His hands were then tied, and he was placed in a truck with "10 Japanese Kempeitai soldiers with fixed bayonets." The truck drove a short way out of Dansalan to a Kempeitai (military police) firing range. There, Fort was blindfolded and tied to a square wooden post. Tanaka read a brief statement, then ordered the soldiers to fire. Fort fell forward, still shivering and gasping for air. Tanaka's second in command, Major Hiramatsu, drew his sword and pushed the point of its blade between the ribs of the dying general, pinning him to the ground until he lay lifeless. It was a noteworthy killing. Guy Fort remains today the only U.S. Army general ever executed by enemy forces. The unauthorized execution of General Fort infuriated Tanaka's superior, Colonel Torao Ikuta, who transferred Tanaka to Korea, calling him "'sick in the brain and afraid of the Moros."[11]

Six years later, at the Tokyo War Crimes Tribunal, Tanaka pleaded guilty to the summary execution of Fort and was sentenced to death by hanging. On his final day he wrote his death poem, prayed with the prison's Buddhist chaplain, and ate a last meal of broiled fish, miso soup, and rice. Then, just after midnight on April 9, 1949, Lt. Colonel Yoshinari Tanaka, still "sick in the brain" with grief and shame for his 85 men cut down by Moro blades in a single morning, was escorted to the brightly lit gallows building at Tokyo's Sugamo Prison where he climbed the thirteen stairs to the execution platform. There he was positioned over a trapdoor and a black hood was placed over his head, followed by a noose of stiff four-ply Manila hemp. Then, with the single order, "Proceed!" the trapdoor sprung open with a sound like a rifle shot, and he fell to his death. He was, it is fair to say, the last Japanese casualty of the Battle of Tamparan.[12]

Word of General Fort's execution spread fast and far along the lakeshore. Fort had only arrived in Lanao a few months before the American surrender and he was neither well-known nor influential among the Maranaos. Had he signed the statement ordering them to end their resistance to the occupation, they would have ignored it. But the Maranaos admired his exceptional bravery, and his murder provided one more provocation. They intensified their resistance further, laying siege to the Japanese garrison at Ganassi. The original plan had been for a frontal assault, but when the leaders brought the plan to Kuder, he argued for a siege instead, mindful of the high Maranao casualties at Tamparan.

As the end of 1942 approached, the three Japanese garrisons around Lake Lanao were cut off from one another with their soldiers confined to base, and one of the three was under active siege. New propaganda measures by the Japanese Mindanao Military Government signaled a sharp turn toward conciliation. The new measures focused on placating the Maranaos, abandoning the demand that they turn in firearms, and avoiding angering them in other ways.[13] Just half a year after the Japanese occupiers of Lanao had set out to pacify the Maranaos, it was they themselves who had been tamed and surrounded. The Maranaos of the Lanao Plateau had effectively won their war of resistance against the Japanese before the American-led guerrillas recognized by MacArthur had fully begun theirs.

In 1965, Wendell Fertig, nine years retired from the military, was asked to write an introduction to the English language translation of Swiss Army Major H. von Dach's 1958 *Total Resistance*, the first-ever field manual for organizing and operating an insurgency. In his brief contribution, he noted that "a resistance that can be organized and sustained early in the occupation has the best chance of surviving." He also offered lessons from his guerrilla organization. He did not acknowledge (in that book or elsewhere) the extraordinary success of the early Maranao resistance, which allowed his nascent organization to survive and grow and which later strengthened it with seasoned Maranao fighters.

Edward Kuder first heard of Wendell Fertig's guerrilla force in late November of 1942. In December, he was able to contact Fertig by courier. He was thrilled to place himself under an American guerrilla commander after so much time spent alone among the Maranaos. Kuder had seen what the Maranaos were capable of, and he knew what Fertig and Hedges needed. He spent January of 1943, his last month on the Lanao Plateau, contacting Maranao resistance leaders, writing them letters of introduction, and sending them to meet Fertig at his headquarters in Misamis. At Fertig's request, he also made the sensitive arrangements to allow Hedges, whom Fertig had placed in charge of the prospective Maranao recruits, to make an "expedition" to the Lanao Plateau to organize the Maranao resistance leaders and their followers into a cohesive force under Fertig's command. Among those new guerrilla recruits were the Maranao fighters who, six months later, would rescue Fertig from the Japanese in Misamis and provide him use of the village of Liangan as his temporary headquarters.

By the end of January 1943, Edward Kuder had convinced every active Moro resistance leader within 100 kilometers of Fertig's headquarters to join his new guerrilla force and accept him as their leader. All except one. In the high plains of Bukidnon to the east, a Moro datu who, like Fertig, called himself "General," led his own highly effective guerrilla force—one that included American officers—and he had no interest in submitting to Wendell Fertig. This datu, Salipada Pendatun, also happened to be the oldest, the most accomplished, and the most beloved foster son of Edward Kuder.

4
"A GOOD MORO BOY"

One midsummer morning in 1943, Adil and his foster father rode again to guerrilla headquarters at the Lanao coast. This time it was the boy who needed a doctor. He was speechless with pain from an inflamed tooth, and Kuder had insisted they go. Back down the rough trail, they rode, Adil wincing with each jarring hoof strike.

At headquarters, Lt. Dumawal, the medical officer, took one look in the boy's mouth and pronounced a severe abscess. He said the tooth had to be extracted immediately, but there were no pain-killers available because the limited morphine supply was reserved for American officers and officials. Kuder told the doctor, "Use my allotment for the boy." Lt. Dumawal had Kuder sign an order, then administered the morphine and extracted the tooth. Compared to the morning's journey, the trip home, swaying up the trail beside the rushing creek, was a ride through paradise. Adil never forgot that kindness, nor any of the others that Kuder had shown him.

* * *

When the written reply from his father finally arrived at Edward Kuder's house in Jolo town in July of 1938, it was addressed to Adil, and it demanded that he return home immediately. The boy was heartsick but unsurprised. He had, after all, run away on the day after his middle school graduation, using the money his father had given him as a graduation present.

Three years earlier, his father had enrolled him in Upi Agricultural School, founded by an American former Philippine Constabulary officer, Captain Irving Edwards, who had been his father's elementary school teacher. It was a boarding school in the forested highlands far from his delta home. Colonial agricultural schools taught modern American farming techniques, which his father wanted him to learn. They were more affordable than ordinary schools because they were also working farms, where students labored to pay for their room and board and their expensive American books. Adil's father, Hadji Adil Tambis, was a relatively prosperous man, but the global depression had not spared him, and it was currently the school he could best afford for his eldest son.

On the day of his seventh-grade graduation, the thought of four more years at the agricultural school—his father had insisted that he finish high school there—weighed on Adil like a wooden yoke. He had already tired of the dark hills, the dreary dormitories, and, most of all, of the tedium of daily farm labor. He missed sea breezes and the freedom of his village childhood, and he craved adventure.

At thirteen, he was still small for his age, but he was solidly built, and in his childhood face it was possible to see early suggestions of the striking features—sculpted brow, sharp cheekbones, and piercing eyes—that would define his adult countenance. At this age, though, his eyes were more likely to sparkle with excitement, as they did when his uncle Alun, a distant relative just a few years older first told him about Jolo. Alun, who was staying at his father's house for

the school holiday, described a beautiful island in the Sulu Archipelago and a house full of boys overlooking the sea. On Jolo, he said, he
lived in that house with an American, Mr. Kuder, the Superintendent of Schools for the Province of Sulu. The American sponsored
Alun and other Moro boys at Sulu High School—paying for their
books and uniforms and tuition, and they lived with him at his seaside house in Jolo town.

Adil listened intently, imagining the possibility of escape. The
school break was ending, and when Alun told him he was returning
to Jolo early the next morning, Adil saw his chance. "I'm coming
with you."

"You can't," Alun objected, "Your father will be furious."

"Then don't tell him."

Adil slipped away from his father's house the following morning before sunrise and followed Alun to the town pier. There they
boarded a local steamer to begin their journey to faraway Jolo. By the
time his father's household was fully awake, the boy had vanished.

Weeks later, sitting in Edward Kuder's house reading his
father's letter calling him home, Adil also knew that *maratabat* was
at stake. Hadji Adil Tambis was an aristocrat and a man of means.
He knew of Edward Kuder from his time spent in Cotabato, and
he knew that Kuder took in promising boys from poorer families
who could not afford the high costs of high school. His son did not
belong among those boys. Hadji Adil was a datu, and he needed no
American to support his son for him.

* * *

Descended from a long line of chieftains, warriors, and holy men,
Hadji Adil had become, to the consternation of his elder kinsmen,
a man of business, the first ever in his clan. The Tampakanens, the

People of the Raised Ground, were the traditional rulers of the lower Cotabato delta—a land surrounded by water, lying between two great rivers flowing their final miles to the sea. Its inhabitants dwelt in graceful stilted houses amid creeks and marshes and estuaries and stood in slender boats on the water as confidently as they did on solid ground.

Toughened by their tidal environment, the Tampakanens were predisposed to go against the flow. They were known as nonconformists who spoke their minds freely and frequently cited the aquatic proverb: "Only rotten fish and feces flow with the current." Adil Tambis was inclined to fight the current. So, for that matter, was his eldest son.

Adil Tambis' father, Datu Pangilamen, was also a nonconformist. He resisted every part of the American occupation and refused to go along with Datu Piang, the acknowledged ruler of Cotabato, when he directed his datus to cooperate with the Americans. When Piang sent his own children to the new American schools and told others to follow his example, Pangilamen travelled to every corner of his territory, telling his followers, "I will kill any man who sends his child to the American school."

Life on the Pulangi River, 1933

Of the five wives of Pangilamen, Bai Tambis was the youngest, and it was not until her husband's death in about 1915 that she defied his orders and, ignoring the warnings of the elders, enrolled her ten-year-old son in the Americans' school. The Americans told her that the boy needed a second name for their records. Fearing her husband's wrath from beyond the grave, she had them enter her own name into the register, and the boy became Adil Tambis. He thrived at school, finishing at the top of his class every year for seven years. And then there was no more schooling to be had. Frontier schools had only seven grades.

His teachers recommended that he be sent to Manila to attend high school; he would be one of the first Moros to do so. The elders forbade it. *"Makapir ka,"* they said. "You will become an unbeliever." He was preparing to leave for Manila despite them when his older brother, in a last attempt to keep him home, arranged his marriage to Bai Atik, the prettiest daughter of all the seven wives of Datu Manguda Ibad. Adil Tambis could have refused the marriage, but he fell immediately in love with her. He wanted Atik; he realized more than he wanted Manila.

Seven years of American education was enough to let him take advantage of the opportunities presented by newly established American rice mills and coconut oil processing plants. He became a commercial farmer growing rice and planting coconut trees. It was an occupation that his father, and most traditional datus, disdained, but it brought him wealth and prominence at a young age, and then it brought him catastrophe.

Five years after marrying Bai Atik, Adil Tambis took her with him on the pilgrimage to Mecca, wanting her to share both the adventure and the blessing of the Haj. Almost no Muslims in the world live farther away from Mecca than do the Moros of the

Philippines. Even with steamship travel, it was a long and expensive journey in 1928 to reach the opposite end of the Asian continent, and only a tiny number of Moros accomplished it. Adil Tambis now had the means, and he would be the first of his clan to make the pilgrimage.

It took more than six months to reach Mecca. They spent much of that time going nowhere, waiting in ports for ships. In Zamboanga, Jolo, and Sandakan they waited, and in Singapore, they sat for months until the white-hulled pilgrim ship that would take them to Arabia finally appeared. They began their last leg then, boarding the great ship with more than 1000 other pilgrims speaking a confusion of languages.

Across the Indian Ocean they sailed, making a final stop in Ceylon before turning northwest into the Arabian Sea. Eventually, they threaded their way through the Gulf of Aden to join other pilgrim ships that had converged there from Calcutta and Mombasa, Karachi and Jakarta. The ships formed an impromptu convoy that made its way up the slender Red Sea to Jeddah, the entry port for Mecca. Every deck was filled with pilgrims dressed in identical haj attire—white cotton robes and white caps or headscarves—and every starboard rail was crowded with passengers buoyant with anticipation as the pilgrim ships, like white clouds scudding over a coral sea, sailed the last few hundred miles to their final port.

It had been an especially arduous journey for Bai Atik, who was now quite pregnant with her fourth child. Had she even known that she was expecting when they bid farewell to the joyous, tearful relatives that had come to see them off at the Cotabato wharf more than six months earlier? She and her husband were on the adventure of their lives, but she had never been so far away from home before or so long separated from her children. She had ridden in many boats but she had never crossed even a single sea, let alone five, nor been seasick, nor had to endure an inescapable sun for weeks on end. Only the very wealthiest passengers could afford cabins; the rest made do on the open deck. Visiting the sacred sites in Mecca and Medina and performing the haj in the month of June, she was confronted by enormous crowds, choking dust, and unimaginable heat.

When they had completed the haj and returned to Jeddah, ready to begin the long journey home, the baby came. The delivery was difficult, then disastrous, and in the end, both mother and child were lost. Bai Atik would never return to her children waiting in Mindanao. Her shattered husband buried her and her stillborn child there in Jeddah, just outside the city walls in the Cemetery of Eve, where, they told him, the First Woman was also interred. On the green metal gate leading to the graveyard, they showed him a small sign that quietly proclaimed "Our Mother Eve."

Adil Tambis, stunned with grief at his wife's death, eventually returned home to his children. His eldest son, just three years old when his mother left, grew up unable to remember "ever tasting the love of a mother." Now he was the one who had sailed away.

* * *

The local steamer with Adil and Alun aboard hugged the curve of the Moro Gulf then cruised down the interior coast of the long Zamboanga peninsula, ragged with bays and inlets; at sea, but still enveloped by Mindanao. They put in at small ports along the way, taking on sacks of rice and copra and boarding passengers, all bound for the market in Zamboanga, the principal seaport of Mindanao.

In Zamboanga, they transferred to the SS Islas Filipinas, an inter-island steamer built for open water. Adil stayed at the rail until the ship had cleared the harbor and pointed her white-banded prow southwest across the Sulu Sea. The night was descending, and the boy peered at the dim outline of the island of Mindanao, all but obscured by the brightening lights of the town. It was the island of his birth, and its coasts had, until that moment, marked the edge of his world. As the ship quieted, he joined Alun and the other third-class passengers who had settled in among the deck cargo amidships.

The Islas Filipinas steamed through the night and arrived at Jolo before daylight, the waterfront already awake, the harbor busy with watercraft. Adil followed Alun along the bustling pier and down the coast road, the peak of Bud Dajo and the walls of the old Spanish town revealing themselves in the lightening day until they arrived at a two-story wood-frame house built over the bay. As they entered on the ground floor, his senses were struck for the first time by the smells and sounds of an American house in the early morning—in the downstairs kitchen, the mingled aromas of brewed coffee and frying bacon and, above his head, heavy footfalls, the unfamiliar sound of shoes worn at home.

As he climbed the stairs behind Alun and peeked around the corner, he saw an American, very tall and pale, in a rumpled white suit and brown brogans. His voice, as he questioned Alun was deep and stern, but his face was soft. He had been frightened when the American first spoke to him directly, but Kuder's cordiality made him quickly lose his fear. He told him about the 15 pesos his father had given him and showed him his five remaining pesos. "Oh, so you have money."

"Yes, sir!"

When Kuder asked him if he had come to be baptized, he answered with a direct "No."

"Oh, very good," Kuder replied and patted his shoulder. "Because if you came here to be baptized, I would not be able to accept you. Remember, just be a good Moro boy, and you can serve God and your people."

The first month had passed quickly. Adil already felt comfortable in the house, and he was finding his place at Sulu High School. Desperate to stay in Jolo, he asked Kuder's permission to write his father to change his mind. He penned a letter begging his father to let him stay and telling him about his new high school and his life in Jolo. He reminded his father that Salipada Pendatun was also being sponsored through school by Edward Kuder. Pendatun, the son of the Sultan of Barongis, the ruler of a small upriver domain in Cotabato, was now finishing law school in Manila.

More weeks passed before a second letter arrived for Adil. His father had relented, requiring him only to return home for the next school holiday in December. Edward Kuder marked the occasion by bringing Adil and Alun to a photography studio in town to have their portrait taken to send to their families in Cotabato. In the photograph, Adil sits on the arm of the studio chair in his best white school uniform, his arm around the older Alun. Alun is relaxed and smiling. Adil's face is serious, his gaze fixed. His eyes blaze with determination, but his frown signals inevitable homesickness. It is the expression of a boy who, having succeeded in running far away from home, now turns to look back.

In its 1945 profile of Edward Kuder, the Saturday Evening Post noted that "an unending parade of dogs, cats, and Philippine youngsters made their home in his bachelor quarters." Mohammad Adil had now officially joined that procession. To the Post, as well as to most others, Kuder depicted those youngsters as houseboys, who "kept house for him and ran errands." Some of them may have done so, although Kuder employed a Filipino couple to cook and clean for him. Adil, as with Pendatun before him, did not. They were born into homes filled with servants and knew nothing of serving. Adil remembered running the occasional errand but spent almost all of his time at school or play.

Alun (left) and Adil, 1938

Kuder's "houseboy" designation served a purpose. In the social system of the American colony, there was only one acceptable arrangement for an American to live with "natives" in the same house, and that was in a master-servant relationship. Writing in 1928, American constabulary officer John R. White noted that, in Cotabato, simply to socialize publicly with Filipinos or Moros risked "social annihilation."[1] Only unusually powerful or popular colonial figures, such as Douglas MacArthur, could afford to flaunt the rules of socializing. According to Florence Horn, an American journalist visiting the islands on the eve of the war, marrying a Filipina and living with her and her children under the same roof was "the one socially unpardonable thing."[2]

Filipina mistresses, on the other hand, were quietly tolerated. While a bachelor, MacArthur kept an exquisitely beautiful Filipina actress, Isabel Rosario Cooper, in an apartment in Manila. Edward Kuder never married and seemed never to have had a mistress. For most of his time in the Philippines, until his death, young Moro men lived with him in his house. In private correspondence, he referred to them as his dependents. They were the closest he ever came to having a family of his own.

Almost immediately, Mohammad Adil became a favored member of Kuder's household. When the Sheum Circus of Singapore came to town and raised its Big Top on the Sulu High School grounds, Kuder took Adil, who had never seen a circus, to the premier performance. The wire walkers and acrobats dazzled him, but more marvelous were the tigers and elephants, passing so close to their ringside seats that he could smell their musty scent and try, despite Kuder's scolding, to grab the long tails that whisked past him. On another occasion, Kuder invited him to the movies, and they walked to the cinema inside the old walled city to see *Dr. Jekyll and Mr. Hyde*. The next night they returned to watch it again. On the walk home, Kuder told him its lesson, "There is good and evil in every man."

At home, Kuder observed him swimming at high tide in the cove behind the house and surprised him with a beautiful laminated springboard he had ordered from the Sulu Trade School. They attached it, pointing out the back door and from then on Adil jumped straight from the house into the sea. Beyond Kuder's seaside home, Jolo town was, to Adil's eyes, a wonderland. His birthplace in the Cotabato delta was a land of muddy rivers and grey-green marshes. Jolo, a coral-fringed island in the Sulu Sea, was a relative paradise of white beaches and blue water. The Cotabato town of Adil's childhood was a nondescript river settlement of bare wood buildings and corrugated iron roofs, fifty years past its prime as the domain of a wealthy and powerful sultan. Jolo town in 1938 was brimming with color and excitement. A bustling trading port at the crossroads of island Southeast Asia, it was the capital of a still vital sultanate and a place of broad boulevards, grand balconied buildings, and trading emporiums.

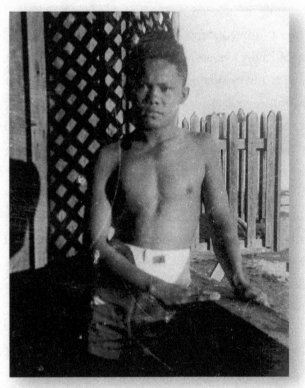

Mohammad Adil, age 13, at Edward Kuder's house in Jolo

Despite more than two decades of nominal American control, Jolo remained the chief smuggling port of the region. Moro trading *prahus,* sleek lateen-rigged sailing ships built of wood, bamboo, and rattan and rigged with brilliantly-colored sails striped in red, orange, blue, and yellow filled the harbor. Those boats and other vessels—junks, schooners, and steamers—brought in opium, silk, guns, and Chinese laborers, among other contraband.

Jolo Harbor with Chinese Pier and, in the background, Bud Dajo, 1933

The Chinese Pier stretched more than a quarter-mile into the Jolo harbor and was lined with the two-story wood-frame warehouses, or godowns, of the Chinese merchants who managed the smuggling economy. Buyers and sellers from ports near and far paraded the boardwalk fronting the godowns in a swirl of colors and languages; Bugis traders from Makassar in gold and green pillbox hats, white-robed Hadhrami Arab traders from Singapore, Chettiar moneylenders from Madras in turbans and dhotis. And among them walked the Moros of Sulu, themselves a colorful mix of dress and dialect: Tausugs, the lords of the Sulu archipelago, in skin-tight embroidered jackets and trousers, with ornate krises tucked in broad sashes; Samals from the outer islands in bright-striped loincloths; and Iranuns, their green and red *tubaos,* cotton kerchiefs, tied high on their heads, who once ruled the Philippine seas as marauders and now specialized as maritime smugglers.

In the nearby market, Moro women in cotton *malongs* and fitted silk blouses in every combination of brilliant red, blue, fuchsia, orange, green, and purple offered the bounty of the islands, an abundance, and variety of seafood and fruit found nowhere else in the Philippines. In a 1926 letter to his wife Elizabeth, Joseph Hayden, on his first trip to Jolo, described with delight the displays of "pink, red, green, blue, spotted fish, fish with great gaping mouths and with long snouts, loathsome looking squibs, and devilfish...crabs, lobsters, snails, clams almost as big as your head and little clams too." The fruit displayed at the outside stalls included durian, madang, langka, lanzones, mangosteens, and a dozen more varieties, all arranged in woven palm-leaf baskets.[3]

Young Adil quickly made the waterfront his playground, paddling his painted dugout canoe, a gift from Edward Kuder, along the waterfront, under the Chinese Pier, and throughout the busy harbor. He paddled to the palace of the Dayang-Dayang—the High Princess of Sulu, the favorite niece and adopted daughter of the Sultan (childless despite his numerous wives), groomed for the throne by her uncle. She had become acting Sultana on the Sultan's recent death, but her claim to the title was challenged by male rivals, so she married a man of her choosing and had him installed as Sultan. She also arranged to have her husband appointed Governor of Sulu Province by the Americans, thus becoming the power behind two thrones.

The Dayang-Dayang and her husband lived in the colonial governor's mansion, the first Moros ever to do so. It was the grandest residence in Jolo, and Adil, on his way to the palace kitchen where the cooks always treated him to tidbits of royal food, would peek into the reception hall and see the sultana's servants crawl toward her to kiss her feet.

One day, a squadron of American warships, like great grey leviathans, appeared in their sparkling bay of brightly colored sailboats—a battleship with destroyer escorts and two submarines. Presently, four naval officers in crisp white uniforms arrived at Kuder's house to take coffee with him on the veranda. Eavesdropping, Adil learned that the officers were from the submarines and, curious beyond containment, he paddled his boat out to inspect them. As he circled the first submarine, both taller and longer than he had imagined, a sailor on deck called out to him, "Come here boy, what do you want?" Adil steered his dugout to the sub's side, its hull slick with green moss. He told the sailor that he had come from the house where the submarine's captain was visiting, and the sailor invited him aboard and led him below to an underworld of pipes, tubes, gauges, and valves, all, to his surprise, brightly lit by electric bulbs. Then he showed him the galley, fed him some crackers, and sent him happily on his way. When he arrived home, the Americans were still there. Kuder asked him where he had gone, and he told them of his adventure. The officers laughed, and Kuder smiled and hugged the boy to his side.

One day in the schoolyard at Sulu High School, an older boy punched Adil hard in the mouth without provocation, cutting his lip and knocking him to the ground. Adil stood up, spit blood, then pulled his dagger and chased the boy who, when cornered, produced his knife. They circled and feinted, toes gripping the packed dirt until a crowd gathered and a teacher stepped between them. Kuder heard about the incident and demanded the knife.

A few weeks later, a box arrived at the house. Kuder told Adil it was for him. He opened it and found two pairs of boxing gloves. Kuder tied the gloves on him, then put the other pair on his own hands. He knelt and said, "Now hit me." Adil swung at him, and he deflected the blow. "Again. Come on, box!" They practiced for hours until the boy could punch, parry, and counterpunch. "Remember," Kuder told him, "the first target you aim for is his nose because if you connect, it will bleed, and he'll run away. From now on, use your fists when you fight. Don't use that knife." When his vigorous lesson in American sportsmanship was over, Adil sat happily exhausted, his gloved hands dangling with fatigue, and thought to himself, "Yes. He loves me!"

Adil in Boy Scout uniform at Sulu High School

Before he knew it, six months had passed, and it was time to return home for the December school holidays. His companions on the interisland ferry were Salipada Pendatun and his wife Matabay, who recently arrived from Manila, where he was a law student at the University of the Philippines, and she attended the Philippine Normal School, the most prestigious teacher's college in the

Philippines. A few years later, still in her twenties, Matabay Pendatun, one of the only Moros to have studied in the United States,
would be called "the most influential woman in Cotabato—not
only among Moros, but also Christians."[4] She and her husband had
stopped off in Jolo to pay their respects to Edward Kuder before
continuing home to Cotabato. Kuder introduced Adil to the still-
young Pendatun, 14 years his senior and making a national name
for himself as a spokesman for the Moros. Having been invited by
Pendatun and Matabay to share their cabin on the ferry, Adil traveled home in style.

His family was happy to have the runaway back home, if only
for a few weeks. When it was time for him to return to Jolo, his father
sent him back to Edward Kuder with a shiny red Japanese-built bicycle and a brand new air rifle. His uncle, Datu Manguda Ibad, a man
of enormous power and prestige in Cotabato, met him at the wharf
as he was about to board the steamer. His subordinate datus walked
in single file behind him, as was customary. His uncle slipped the
American wristwatch off his arm and onto Adil's, where it dangled,
saying *"pangagi ka,"* study hard. The next datu in line handed him a
Parker fountain pen, the next placed a few pesos in his palm. Every
elder gave him something. The American, Edward Kuder, would
know without a doubt that this boy came from a family of means.

* * *

By 1926, Edward Kuder, age 28, had been in the Philippines for
four years and was growing bored with his assignment as a colonial
teacher in a typical town on the principal island of Luzon, one that
included Christian churches, modern conveniences, and familiar
lifestyles. "The average American," he wrote in 1944, looking back
on his early days in the colony, "would feel more at home in the

ordinary Philippine town than anywhere else among native peoples from Suez to San Francisco, and between Russia and Australia." Kuder, who had left home and travelled halfway around the world seeking adventure, did not want to feel at home. He wanted to live in an extraordinary Philippine place.[5] His chance came later that year when he was appointed colonial superintendent of schools for Cotabato Province, a vast, unfamiliar territory on the huge and lightly populated island of Mindanao. He bought a Winchester pump-action shotgun and a Colt .45 revolver and boarded a steamer for the long journey south. Over the next five years in the province, he did find adventure, along with the blizzard of paperwork required of a midlevel colonial official anywhere in the Philippines. He also found Salipada Pendatun.

More precisely, 16-year-old Salipada Pendatun found him. In Cotabato, Kuder first began taking in male high school students to live in his house (in those years, almost no Moro girls attended high school). For a province the size of Massachusetts, there was just one high school, in the capital, Cotabato town, where Kuder was stationed. Kuder travelled frequently throughout the province, and when he found a promising young student whose family could not support him to attend high school in the capital, he would offer to help.

Pendatun presented himself at Kuder's door one day in 1927 and asked to be taken in. Already at that age he had a commanding presence, and within a week he was issuing orders to the other boys in the house. Like Adil, he had run away from home and at first tried to conceal his background, telling Kuder only that his father was dead.

Kuder did not learn the boy's full identity until he woke one morning a few weeks after Pendatun's arrival, to find an enormous, fearsome-looking Moro, hand on the hilt of his kris, bending over his bed curiously observing him. The man told the startled Kuder, now fully awake, that he had come to see Salipada. Kuder then made inquiries and learned that Pendatun was the son of the Sultan of Barongis. His father, who had recently died, had told his son to seek an American high school education, but his current guardian had forbidden him to leave the territory of his father, so he ran away from home.

Edward Kuder with the young Salipada Pendatun, 1927

A dual portrait taken not long after Pendatun's arrival, hints at their complex relationship. Kuder, seated in a white tropical suit, black tie, and brogans, seems the personification of American colonial rule. A closer inspection, however, reveals contradictions; the full lips are sensuous rather than stern, the hooded eyes belie the inquisitive eyebrows. It is not an entirely coherent face that gazes obliquely past us from 1927. Pendatun stands next to Kuder. He is barefoot and dressed in the simple white cotton garb of a Philippine schoolboy. But this seemingly straightforward depiction also reveals nuance on closer examination. Pendatun stands separate and distinct from Kuder, as his own man, and, unlike Kuder, who is gazing softly into the middle distance, he stares intently at the camera. His schoolboy garb is augmented first by a *tubao* tied high on his head in the style of the Moro nobility and, second, by an ornate *kris* tucked, like an umbrella, under his arm. It is a portrait of a colonial teacher and his pupil. It is just as much a portrait of two allies coming together from different worlds.

In late 1929, Kuder and Pendatun, still, a legal minor, partnered on an unusual land venture. Under the colonial regime, Christian settlers from northern islands were beginning to move in small numbers into the Cotabato Valley, and arable land in that vast territory was beginning to acquire monetary value. Colonial surveyors had begun in the mid-1920s to map parcels and establish existing landholdings. They started near the coast in more populated settlements and working their way eventually to the wilder and roadless interior.

By late 1929, the surveyors had reached the remote upriver district of Buluan, the territory of Pendatun's deceased father, the Sultan of Barongis. On the massive and lightly populated island of Mindanao, sultans and chieftains controlled people, not property.

Before the house of every local chieftain stood a great bronze gong suspended from a hardwood frame. All who could hear the beating of the gong counted themselves as within the chieftain's domain. For the Sultan of Barongis and his ancestors, the land where he ruled had significance only in respect to the number of laborers available to clear forests, drain marshlands, and plant crops.

But with the arrival of the surveyors in 1929, the land in the sultan's domain took on an entirely new significance. Individuals were now required to legally claim the land that they had lived on, farmed, or ruled for generations. If the colonial Bureau of Lands did not recognize their claim, the land would be designated as public domain—essentially owned by the colonial government—and anyone in the Philippines would be able to apply for title to it.

Pendatun and Kuder responded to the surveyors by filing an application to register a vast tract of land, over 3000 hectares (about 7500 acres), in the name of Pendatun and his siblings. Was it Kuder who heard about the surveyors and suggested the venture to Pendatun or, more likely, was it the precocious Pendatun who grasped the implications of the survey and, knowing that neither he nor his minor siblings had legal standing, offered Kuder a stake in the land in exchange for his assistance?

Although the originator of the land partnership is unclear, the court documents show that Kuder made himself the legal guardian of Pendatun, his younger brother Abu-Bakar, and his sisters Tinomimbang and Bagutao, at least for the land registration. Pendatun needed an adult to make the application but also to pay the application fees. Kuder did so, and then kept paying because the Bureau of Lands challenged their claim in court. Kuder hired a lawyer and, in 1931, won the case, but the Bureau of Lands appealed to the Supreme Court of the Philippines.

The court fight dragged on until Salipada Pendatun was no longer a minor. In 1932, he became the first of Kuder's students to attend university in Manila and one of the very first Moros to do so. Pendatun wanted to study military science and become a constabulary officer but Kuder, who was paying for Pendatun's college education, convinced him to study law at the University of the Philippines instead. The young man did so, while also enrolling in the ROTC program for four years. College required more money, and "the boy was to ask for plenty," according to a 1939 profile of Kuder and Pendatun in the Philippines Free Press. "All the way through college, he asked for money for tuition, money for books, money for clothes, money for fun. Sometimes he asked for more than he needed." Kuder gave freely, never refusing a request and never asking for the return of any of the money.[6]

In late 1931, shortly before Pendatun left for college, Kuder made a visit home to his family in Pennsylvania, the first since he had arrived in the Philippines almost ten years earlier. In his hometown, the effects of the global depression were evident, with shuttered banks, foreclosed farms, and widespread layoffs. Christmas was less bright with more than half his siblings unemployed.

He booked passage back to the Philippines on the SS President Monroe. Writing to his parents about the voyage, Kuder told them that the ship departed Shanghai on January 28th, 1932, just hours before the first Japanese attack on that city. At midnight, aircraft launched from a Japanese carrier had rained incendiary bombs on Chapei, the Chinese quarter of the city, engulfing the district in flames and killing thousands. The air raid, which occurred more than five years before Luftwaffe planes appeared over Guernica, was the first-ever aerial terror bombing of a civilian population.

The attack appalled American and European observers and, as

Kuder reported in his letter, sent shock-waves through the Philippine colony. In Manila, he wrote, it was nearly the only topic of conversation among Americans. At the dock in Manila, he handed his overcoat to the ship's freight clerk, gave him a dollar, and asked him to mail it to his family house when the President Monroe reached New York, sending the coat back halfway around the world so that one of his brothers would have it to wear the following winter.

* * *

Soon after Mohammad Adil first told me about Edward Kuder, I set out to learn more about him. I immediately found his five-part 1945 Saturday Evening Post series. Written with Pete Martin in the rat-a-tat style of the day, it was exciting and informative but left me wanting to know much more about Edward Kuder the man. At the Bentley Historical Library at the University of Michigan at Ann Arbor I found the very valuable papers of Joseph Ralston Hayden, his friend and superior in the colonial civil service in the Philippines. There I found a variety of materials by and about Edward Kuder, including the 1943 wartime classified report on Mindanao that Kuder had assembled with Hayden for MacArthur's staff and the OSS (Office of Strategic Services).

From there, however, I hit a wall. I could find no personal letters or journals of Edward Kuder. Nearly all of his papers, work journals, and personal diaries had been lost or destroyed during the war. As a long shot, I began to spend time on Ancestry.Com, focusing on Pennsylvania, where Mohammad Adil had told me his parents had last lived. Census data eventually led me to a house in a small town in southeastern Pennsylvania. I sent the house a letter, saying that I was looking for any personal correspondence from or about Edward Kuder. In a few weeks, I received an email reply from Kuder's nephew, Ted Kuder, who still lived in the family home. Ted, who barely remembered his uncle from his visit to the house in 1945, wrote that he "might possess some meager results." His uncle had had a trunk shipped to the house later that year, and it had been in the attic ever since.

A forgotten trunk in the attic is every biographer's dream, and I replied to Ted, barely containing my excitement, telling him I could be there in a few days to go through it. But he replied that he would just send the material to me, and in a few more weeks I received a Federal Express package accompanied by an email from Ted apologizing that "the pickings" were so poor and that he had not seen much of importance in his uncle's letters.

A quick look through what he had sent confirmed that it was, in fact, a treasure trove, and I told him as much in my reply. There were 52 letters in all, dated from 1932 to 1969. Almost all were written by Edward Kuder, most but not all to his parents and siblings, and most before 1942. They revealed his hopes, fears, political opinions, money problems, and, by suggestion, the objects of his love. They also vividly described extraordinary events, such as the Moro frontal attack with krises and spears in 1935. Thanks to the care and generosity of Ted Kuder and his siblings and cousins, Edward Kuder, though still in some ways a mysterious figure, had come finally and fully to life.

* * *

In an April 1932 letter to his parents from his new posting in Lanao Province, Kuder told them that he had recently borrowed "a considerable sum of money" from a fellow American in the colony for his "venture" with Pendatun.[7] Defending a Supreme Court case required expensive attorneys. Kuder wrote that his motive was financial and that he expected a very significant payoff for his substantial investment when the case was won. But it was likely not purely profit-seeking that motivated him to take on a powerful agency of his own colonial government in a prominent court battle.

Kuder was already gaining a reputation as an advocate for the Moros, particularly in his insistence that they receive equal opportunities and equal treatment under the law. The colonial government had recently touted Mindanao as the "land of unfulfilled promise" and increased its assistance to Christian homesteaders from the northern islands, including providing free passage for some of them. But little or nothing was being done to assist Moros in obtaining legal title to their land. If Filipino notables in the North could hold title to vast agricultural estates established during the Spanish period, why not the Moro notables of Mindanao and Sulu, who possessed written genealogies reaching back over 400 years? Why not his own foster son? Like other datus, Salipada Pendatun was being disadvantaged under American colonial policy simply because the Moros had never been conquered by the Spaniards.

The Supreme Court decision was released in March of 1934 and it went against them for the very reason Kuder had feared. The majority opinion stated that a genealogy establishing five generations of rulers on the land in question was inadequate as evidence of ownership because "political authority…does not establish…private possession."[8] The land was declared to be public domain, and Kuder's investment was lost.

A year earlier, the U.S. depression had hit him personally when salaries for all civil service employees in the colony were reduced by 15 percent. He was now deeply in debt with no near-term prospect of getting clear of it. He helped Salipada and his three siblings file homestead titles for 144 hectares each, a tiny portion of the land they had originally claimed. In a 1934 letter to Joseph Hayden, then the colonial vice-governor general, Kuder railed against the "Bureau of Lands skullduggery" that placed advertisements for homesteaders in Manila newspapers but made no homesteader application forms available in its Cotabato office for Pendatun's Moro followers.[9]

Later that year, he was transferred again, this time into exile in faraway Sulu Province. He had picked a fight with the most powerful colonial institution of all—the Philippine Constabulary—and would not back down. The target of Kuder's ire was an American constabulary lieutenant stationed in Lanao who had been soliciting bribes from Maranaos. The constabulary closed ranks, and Kuder lost the fight when the Lanao Governor, John Heffington, recommended his removal. Sulu, however, was a fortunate banishment. It was where Mohammad Adil found him, and it became the place in the Philippines that he loved most of all.

Salipada Pendatun passed the Philippine Bar examination in 1938 and was almost immediately appointed to the Cotabato Provincial Board thanks to the influence of his foster father. In 1941 he joined the USAFFE as a first lieutenant and, in January 1942, he was assigned to the regimental command post at Digos to act as a liaison to the Bolo Battalion led by his brother-in-law Datu Udtug Matalam.

The two men could not have been more different. Datu Udtug spoke no English and could neither read nor write in any language. He preferred going barefoot, including in the Cotabato Governor's office that he would eventually inhabit for almost two decades. Pendatun and Datu Udtug nevertheless became comrades in arms and the closest of political allies, sharing the loyalty and dedication of Mohammad Adil.

On the right flank of the Digos line, Datu Udtug led nightly forays into the mountain jungle against the Japanese until he was struck down by malaria. Pendatun took leave to accompany him home to Pikit, in the upper Cotabato valley. They were still at Pikit when they heard news of the sudden American surrender. Pendatun, the American-trained lawyer, was inclined to obey orders and surrender with the rest of the USAFFE officers and men, but Datu Udtug forbade it, telling him they would continue the fight on their own.

And so they did, gathering fighters and collecting guns from USAFFE soldiers who had deserted from their surrendering regiments to walk away from the lost war. Soon they had gathered 200 men, and in August 1942, they attacked the Japanese garrison in Pikit, seizing the town from the Japanese and holding it. That initial success brought them more fighters. In September, they attacked the town of Kabacan and secured control of the only drivable road between the Cotabato interior and the Japanese-held port of Davao on the east coast. Their operation grew again but, as in Lanao, suffered from a chronic shortage of ammunition.

Pendatun's successes brought him to the attention of Don Manuel Fortich, a wealthy rancher and former governor of Bukidnon Province. Bukidnon, just north of Cotabato, in the island's geographic center, was rich in resources, including ammunition—it had been the headquarters of USAFFE in Mindanao, and still had stores of munitions not found by the Japanese—but lacked an effective guerrilla movement. Fortich invited Pendatun to expand his guerrilla movement into Bukidnon, offering the hidden ammunition stores as an enticement.

Pendatun leapt at the chance, leaving Udtug to oversee operations in Cotabato and marching half his force north up the rainforest slopes, following the course of the Pulangi River, to the high plains of Bukidnon. Those plains were the nursery for the Pulangi, The Rio Grande de Mindanao, which meandered through its pastures, fed by countless mountain streams before falling into the vast watershed of the Cotabato basin and flowing to the sea. With a new supply of ammunition and a still-growing force numbering more than 2000 men, Pendatun quickly drove the Japanese from their Bukidnon garrisons. One after another, Kiyawe, Maramag, Valencia, and Mailag fell to his fighters.

On the plains of Bukidnon, Pendatun was harrying the Japanese in the same way as the Maranaos of the Lanao Plateau, but his was a far more organized resistance. By the end of 1942, the 30-year-old Pendatun led a highly-disciplined armed force that was larger than Fertig's, and he had certainly won more victories against the Japanese than had Fertig. Pendatun's movement was both quasi-military and multi-ethnic. Some of his officers were unsurrendered Americans, including Major Frank McGee, a West Point graduate. Among his staff officers were a former Philippine senator, a former governor of Cotabato, and the former chief of the Philippine Air Service. All of them were older than this young man, who possessed an ability to inspire confidence far beyond his age.

He was also a leader admired by civilians—Moros, Filipinos, and Americans. After he freed her family from Japanese house arrest in Malaybalay in 1943, American teenager Dorothy Dore regarded Pendatun as a romantic hero, and he looked the part when he rode his Arabian horse captured from the Japanese while inspecting his troops. His soldiers respected him for his courage on the front lines, and civilians appreciated his administrative skills. In the territory he controlled, he set up a civilian government and, like Fertig, provided basic services.[10]

In January 1943, at Casisang, Pendatun's men staged the first-ever raid against a Japanese POW camp. The POWs were Filipinos. The American prisoners, including the officers serving under the murdered General Fort, had recently been transferred out—the enlisted men and junior officers to Davao and the senior officers on to Japan. The Japanese guards fled to nearby Malaybalay, the provincial capital, taking the prisoners who had not escaped with them. Pendatun then laid siege to Malaybalay. Miguel Fortich, though elderly and in poor health, insisted on accompanying him for the initial attack. Don Miguel rode to the front on his horse and cheered on the attackers while Japanese bullets whined past him. He returned home in high spirits and went to bed, where his son found him the next morning, dead in his sleep with a smile on his face.

When Wendell Fertig first contacted Pendatun by radio in January 1943, telling him of his organization, Pendatun offered Fertig a position on his staff. The eldest foster-son of Edward Kuder admired Americans to such an extent that he strove to be the best among them. In Mindanao at the beginning of 1943, he had evidently succeeded.

Pendatun's guerrillas had driven the enemy from large swathes of central Mindanao and had recaptured Del Monte airfield, from where MacArthur had escaped the Philippines. He had acquired more stores of gasoline and ammunition than any other guerrilla commander, and he had American officers reporting to him. Unlike Fertig, who had assumed that rank on his own in an attempt to impress Filipino guerrilla commanders, Pendatun's men had elected him to the rank of Brigadier General. And for good measure, Pendatun and his wife Matabay, who were childless, had adopted an orphaned American girl, Bessie Mae, now eight years old, blonde, and speaking perfect Magindanaon.[11] Why, he wondered, shouldn't he, rather than Fertig, be the guerrilla chief of Mindanao?

While the middle-aged Luis Morgan was an annoying thorn in Wendell Fertig's side, this young Moro rival, Pendatun, was both an affront and a profound threat to his leadership of the Mindanao guerrillas. In January 1943 Fertig sent an emissary, Edward Haggerty, an American Jesuit priest, to Pendatun's headquarters in Bukidnon to seek his submission. Haggerty made the arduous journey east on foot, crossing a mile-high pass through some of the tallest mountains in the Philippines. He then struggled down the steep eastern slope through a gloomy and stifling rainforest until he reached the great central plain of Bukidnon and found his way, after days of hard travel, to Malaybalay, the site of Pendatun's headquarters.

Paternalism came naturally to Father Haggerty. In occupied Mindanao he risked his freedom and his life traveling almost constantly to minister to a widely scattered flock of Filipino settler faithful, most of whom he viewed as superstitious and ignorant and loved them all the more for it. The Moros, however, he distrusted, reportedly regarding them as "treacherous semi-savages."[12] He was thus fully prepared to be unimpressed with Salipada Pendatun. Instead, he found "an energetic and intelligent young man with fierce purpose and intense ambition" and came to quickly understand "why Christian officers and men were willing to follow his lead."[13] Pendatun took to Haggerty as well, reportedly telling him, "After Mr. Kuder's, I value your friendship most of any American's."[14] On parting, Pendatun provided Haggerty with vague reassurances that he would travel to the coast to visit Fertig soon, which Haggerty took to mean that he intended to submit to Fertig's authority. Haggerty reported as much to Fertig on his return, but Pendatun had no intention to submit, and he never made the trip.

* * *

Back in the upper Cotabato Valley, Pendatun's brother-in-law, Datu Udtug, had also been busy. On a trip later in 1943 to minister to his Cotabato flock, Haggerty visited the guerrilla leader at his headquarters in the middle of Liguasan Marsh. He found that Datu Udtug had so harassed the local Japanese garrisons that they had gone to extraordinary lengths to avoid his ambushes, even "to the extent of sending his soldiers medicine and cigarettes." East of the marsh, in M'Lang, "cultured" Christian evacuees from Davao lived under Datu Udtug's protection in a town the Japanese had never visited—one with plentiful food, "a library, an orchestra, and a club-house." Based on his tour, Haggerty reported that Datu Udtug was "doubtless the most influential and efficient of all guerrilla leaders in Cotabato."[15]

* * *

After moving to Fertig's headquarters in early February 1943 and learning of his foster-son's extraordinary achievements, Edward Kuder was proud but perturbed. General MacArthur had just anointed Wendell Fertig as military chief of the Mindanao guer-rillas, and there could be only one guerrilla chief. Kuder, based on Haggerty's report, wrote mistakenly in his first letter to his younger foster son that Pendatun had already submitted. As weeks went by without Pendatun reporting, Adil recalled that Kuder wrote to Pen-datun again, urging him to submit immediately to Fertig so that his guerrilla force would be recognized by General MacArthur. Kuder's published words on the matter also make it clear that he never con-sidered supporting his foster-son's claim to at least equal standing as a guerrilla leader in Mindanao. To Kuder's mind, the need to main-tain American authority trumped his foster son's impressive victories in the field.

By the spring of 1943, Pendatun was apparently becoming a problem even for MacArthur's senior staff. Mindanao played an outsized role in MacArthur's plan to retake the Philippines, and a united Mindanao guerrilla movement under his control was key to that plan. Chick Parsons was not only MacArthur's eyes and ears in the Philippines but also his enforcer. In May of 1943, when Pendatun had still not been brought into the fold, Parsons, decided to pay him a personal visit, following the same route that Father Haggerty had taken over the mountains to Bukidnon. Edward Kuder would likely have accompanied him had he been well enough for the arduous journey.

Like MacArthur and Kuder, Parsons was an American who had been formed in the Philippines, though in his case, at a much earlier age. Born into a problem-ridden Tennessee family, he had been sent to the Philippines by his mother at the age of five to live with an uncle, a colonial public health official in Manila who could provide him a more stable life. He returned to Tennessee as a teenager and finished high school there, but traveled back to the Philippines at age 19, working his way across the Pacific on a freighter and arriving nearly penniless in Manila.

Parsons found employment quickly and travelled throughout the islands for his work, learning at least one Philippine language on the way. He settled first in Mindanao and, as a buyer for an American logging company, spent years sailing in and out of the bays and inlets of the great island's west coast. At the age of 28, he married Katrushka, the 16-year-old daughter of a prominent Czech-American businessman in Zamboanga and his California-born wife. The couple soon moved to Manila, where Parsons managed various trading enterprises, and they gradually became fixtures in Manila's social scene, socializing with, among others, Douglas and Jean MacArthur. Like MacArthur and Kuder, Parsons defied convention and socialized with Filipinos, counting them among his closest friends.

Chick Parsons was a notable colonial success story. Twenty years after his arrival, the Tennessee boy from the troubled family was ready to retire at the age of 39 and spend his time playing polo. The war put an end to those plans. In early 1942, Parsons found himself trapped with his family in a Manila under Japanese occupation. When American civilians in Manila were herded into detention camps, Parsons posed as Panama's consul general to the Philippines (an honorary title he possessed because of his trading ties) and evaded the roundup. Speaking only fluent Spanish in public, which he had learned as a schoolboy in Manila, he maintained the fiction for months while carrying on his real work as a naval intelligence officer.

The audacious ruse worked so well that the family was repatriated to the US in late August 1942 as part of a diplomatic exchange. They sailed on a Japanese hospital ship to Formosa and then on a succession of European liners on a roundabout wartime route to Shanghai, Singapore, Mozambique, and Rio de Janeiro. In Brazil, he finally revealed his real identity and boarded an American ship with his family for New York. Within days he had reported to the War Department in Washington D.C. for debriefing. Four months later, he was in Australia with MacArthur, preparing to return by submarine to the occupied Philippines he had so recently escaped.[16]

From left to right, Robert Bowler, Salipada Pendatun, and Chick Parsons, Bukidnon, 1943

A photographer captured the meeting between Parsons and Pendatun. Parsons, tan and robust, flashes his characteristic winning smile. It was the smile that had won him his wife, his financial success, and his freedom from Japanese internment. It did not quite win over Salipada Pendatun. Pendatun stands between the two older, taller Americans (the second is Lt. Colonel Robert Bowler, one of Fertig's commanders) in crisp khakis, riding boots, and forage cap. His gaunt face, framed by a coal-black beard, is unsmiling. While his companions stand at ease, he strikes a general's pose with hands-on-hips, his eyes, as in his schoolboy portrait, staring intently into the future.

Parsons, the enforcer, knew he had no power to compel Pendatun to submit to Wendell Fertig, MacArthur's chosen guerrilla leader. Pendatun's guerrilla force rivaled Fertig's in strength. He could only attempt to persuade Pendatun of the benefits to be had from accepting American leadership. Parsons was sure that the young Moro general would be impressed by the arms and supplies arriving with increasing frequency in Fertig's territory via American submarines.

But Parson's arguments about superior armaments were not as persuasive as he had imagined. As part of a tour of his operation, Pendatun brought Parsons to the site of a standoff between the Japanese garrison in Malaybalay—whose soldiers had fortified themselves in a concrete-walled school—and his guerrillas. Conventional weapons and Molotov cocktails had not dislodged them (In writing about this and other stalled guerrilla attacks on Japanese positions, Edward Kuder could not avoid expressing a certain pride at the superior construction of American schoolhouses built under his administration).

Parsons seized on the impasse as a teaching opportunity, pointing out the advantage of American mortars and bazookas in such a situation. But Pendatun had prepared a secret weapon—a water buffalo with 100-pound aerial bombs salvaged from the Del Monte airfield strapped to each side. With the fuses lit and a sheaf of straw tied to the animal's tail and set on fire, the unfortunate beast was driven toward the school building. The bombs exploded just as it reached the concrete wall. The water buffalo disappeared in the explosion, but so did the front of the school building. Pendatun's guerrillas immediately rushed the schoolhouse and Japanese soldiers attempting to escape through the rear were cut down by Moro fighters with krises.

The next morning, Pendatun greeted Parsons by informing him, "I will serve under General MacArthur." On his uniform collar he had replaced his general's stars with the gold oak leaves of a major. Recalling that day, Parsons believed that it was his powers of persuasion that convinced Pendatun to submit to Fertig. But Carlos Quirino, in his biography of his friend, Chick Parsons, relates a more plausible story. It was Pendatun's own subordinates, in particular his chief of staff Edwin Andrews, who convinced him to submit to American control.

Andrews, a Filipino pilot in the Philippine Army Air Corps, had an American father but was no great friend of America. Before learning to fly, he had graduated from the Philippine Constabulary Academy in 1927. He was then sent for intelligence training to an FBI school in the U.S., where he endured months of racist insults, which he never forgot nor forgave. But he made a practical appeal to Pendatun, arguing that unless they were recognized by MacArthur, none of them would receive their military back pay after the war. Resigned now to the reality that MacArthur would never recognize him without his submission to Fertig, Pendatun reluctantly agreed for the sake of his men.[17]

Fertig wasted no time asserting his authority. He ordered Pendatun to leave Bukidnon, the province he had seized from the Japanese, and return to Cotabato. Fertig's final insult was delivered a few months later in October 1943 when he ordered Pendatun's former subordinate, the American West Pointer, Frank McGee, to replace him as commanding officer of the Cotabato guerrillas, forcing Pendatun to step down to command a local regiment. Fertig's justification for replacing Pendatun—that Filipino guerrillas had told him that they wished to serve only under American officers—was objectively false. Pendatun not only had Filipino officers and men serving happily under him, he had American officers as well, including, of course, Frank McGee. The purpose of replacing Filipino or Moro commanders with American ones seem to have been, once again, the maintenance of the colonial racial hierarchy, even at the cost of military effectiveness.[18]

The remarkable accomplishments of Salipada Pendatun, a young guerrilla leader so talented and charismatic that he impressed even those, such as Edward Haggerty and Chick Parsons, predisposed to dislike him, were never properly recognized by Fertig, MacArthur, or, for that matter, his American foster father. In the first grim year of the war, while American fugitives in Mindanao were stunned, scattered, and disheartened, the Moros, on multiple fronts, fought the occupiers with astonishing results. However, their deeds were lost in the postwar stories of American wartime resistance told by Wendell Fertig and others. The first and most effective guerrilla chief on Mindanao was Salipada Pendatun, who had reason to expect that his American foster father would help him obtain the American recognition and support that he deserved. But Edward Kuder, the man who could never refuse him, was, in this instance, unwilling to provide Pendatun what he most desired—an equal opportunity to excel at war.

5
"DIG UP YOUR GUNS"

With his main rival for guerrilla leadership neutralized, Wendell Fertig turned his attention to expanding his zone of operations south to Cotabato. The upper Cotabato Valley, to which Pendatun had returned, was now under his command, but the entire Cotabato delta, a Japanese stronghold, was his weak flank. It was the land of the Sinsuats, who had cast their lot wholeheartedly with the Japanese. Fertig asked Edward Kuder if he knew anyone willing to challenge the Sinsuats in their home territory. Kuder said he did, and he also knew the perfect courier to enter that hostile territory to make contact.

And so, in August 1943, Mohammad Adil was sent on his first mission. He was to return to his home province and only as a messenger, but his excitement was boundless; he might not yet be fighting, but he was at least *in* the war. His return to Cotabato would be more dangerous than his original trek to find Kuder in Lanao. If the Japanese captured him with his dispatches they would torture him before killing him, so his orders were to avoid their patrols at all costs.

He followed his guide on a circuitous route through the jungled ravines that spilled from the Lanao plateau. They spent days struggling up or slipping down muddy slopes and slashing their way through densely tangled undergrowth amidst clouds of mosquitoes. Finally, weak and pale from relentless attacks by biting insects and jungle leeches, they emerged from the gloom and squinted into the brilliant green vista of the broad Cotabato Valley. Adil exulted gazing once again upon the "wide green land" evoked by Magindanaon bards. After so many days spent in dark, forested, ravines, every shade of sunlit green was now laid out before him—the gilded green of coconut fronds, the somber blue-green of banana leaves, the brilliant jade green of young rice plants—all arrayed under a bright blue sky. His heart immediately lightened to see his homeland.

They hid until nightfall, then made their way to the town of Malabang on the coast. There they contacted friends, and Adil found a fisherman to take him south by boat to the mouth of the Pulangi. The fisherman dropped him north of the river in the coastal marshlands of Sulun, and he walked home the long way round to evade Japanese checkpoints, finding small boats to ferry him across the creeks and rivers.

His family was overjoyed to see him but shocked at his condition. They had sent off a healthy, robust boy two months earlier. The boy who came back was gaunt, his eyes glazed with fever. The leech bites had become infected, and some had grown into ghastly tropical ulcers as jungle bacteria consumed the flesh of his ankles. His father sent for the healer—an expert in mixing remedies from herbs, barks, and roots—who saw to his treatment. Within two days, the old woman's medicine had quieted the infections, allowing him to regain his strength and complete his mission.

But before he did, his father held a *kanduli*, a ritual feast, to give thanks for his safe return. At the ceremony, he sat surrounded by relatives. Across from him, on the floor of his father's house, five *panditas*, elders who performed the most important rituals, sat shoulder to shoulder. At a signal from the senior *pandita* they began a rhythmic chant, their bodies swaying in unison side to side; *Laa ilaaha illa Allah, Laa ilaaha illa Allah.* Their chanting was slow and soft to start before gradually building, the tempo faster and more punctuated. The *panditas'* voices rose and fell, the meter of the chant sometimes changing abruptly, but always the sound was deep, soothing, entrancing.

The sacred words of the litany—"Only God is worthy of worship" —filled the room, swirling to the rafters with the smoke from the incense. The boy let the voices and the pungent smoke wash over him until the chanting gradually tapered to a whisper and ended. Then he joined the others as they began to eat with pleasure the food set out before them on *talams*—beautifully engraved round brass trays. Every morsel of food was now sanctified by the chanting of the litany over the *talams*, so the act of eating was itself a prayer. Adil washed his right hand with the water offered by a serving girl and reached for the food on the *talam* nearest him. Chinese porcelain plates crowded the tray. They held young yellowfin tuna roasted on a greenwood spit, precious red mountain rice, grown in forest gardens in the coastal highlands, and from his father's taro patch, tender taro shoots stewed in coconut milk. He saw half a dozen other delicacies as well, all his favorite foods. It was good to be home.

Before dawn the next morning, he set out from his father's house on the six hour hike to Dulawan, the traditional upriver capital. He followed old trails, avoiding the river and its Japanese patrol boats. In Dulawan he found the house of his father's close friend, Gumbay Piang. It was not easy to miss. Above the lintel was a large sign in English reading: "Captain G. Piang, Prisoner-of-War."

Gumbay Piang had been Salipada Pendatun's counterpart in the USAFFE defense force at Digos. College educated like Pendatun, he was commissioned as a Captain and served as a liaison between the Digos commander and the Bolo Battalion led by his half-brother Pindililang, the man who presented the severed Japanese head to Colonel John McGee. When the order to surrender arrived, Gumbay, who was a trusted aide to General Joseph Vachon, the American commander of Cotabato forces, surrendered with him, apparently the only Moro to do so (his half-brother and his men had already slipped away).

Gumbay Piang, the fifth son of Datu Piang by his sixth wife, Polindao, had another half-brother, Ugalingan, who was the elected representative for Cotabato in the Commonwealth Congress. Seeking Ugalingan's support, the Japanese released his half-brother, whose health had suffered badly in the prison camp, on parole to him. Gumbay Piang had become, he told Adil, a *prisionero caballero*, an unguarded gentleman prisoner sitting out the war in his hometown. Japanese officers visited him at regular intervals asking him to use his influence to pacify the population. He invariably refused, pointing to his sign and reminding them of his status as a prisoner of war.

* * *

Gumbay Piang's father, Datu Piang, was for more than 40 years the most powerful man in Mindanao. Despite its aristocratic structure, Moro society had always made room for self-made men. None of them was more successful or less ashamed of his commoner status than was Datu Piang. Born around 1850 in Dulawan, he was the son of a Magindanaon mother and a Chinese trader from Amoy.

Long-distance traders from south China had been settling in Cotabato for centuries, a number of them marrying local women and converting to Islam. Piang's father, Tuya Tan, died when his son was 11 years old, still owing a significant debt to Datu Utu, the upriver Sultan of Buayan and the most powerful ruler of his time. The debt was due to loans that the sultan had forced on him to pay various fines and ceremonial expenses. Piang, his mother, and his older siblings inherited the debt and worked to pay it off. But when it became unmanageable, Piang, at 15, surrendered himself to Datu Utu as an *ulipun*, a debt slave. He now belonged to the sultan until his family's debt was cleared.

The boy was industrious and ingenious, and within a few years, he had paid off his family's debt and regained his freedom. He had sufficiently impressed Datu Utu in a few more years that he was made one of the sultan's trusted ministers. Then, slowly and cannily, he began to repay differently the man who had impoverished his family and forced him into slavery.

Datu Utu, a ruler most remembered for his cruelty and caprice, was known to reduce followers who displeased him to *mga itik a tau*—human ducks—by crushing their knees and depositing them to live in the mud beneath his house. Utu was also under extraordinary pressure from the Spaniards, who had finally succeeded in occupying Cotabato, though not in controlling it after centuries of trying. Like the Japanese occupiers 70 years later, the Spaniards had begun to garrison key points on the Pulangi River, gradually boxing Datu Utu in.

Working quietly, Piang struck alliances with Utu's key vassals, took control of strategic parts of his territory, and made a separate peace with the Spaniards until, the story goes, one morning Datu Utu woke to find that his followers had all deserted him during the night and gone over to his former slave, Piang. In 1890, Datu Piang allowed his former master to retire downriver under Spanish protection. He then set out to make himself wealthier and more powerful than Utu had ever been. He moved his seat of power to be close to the new Spanish fort on the river at Reina Regente. The fort protected him from the few Moro enemies who had not yet submitted to him, and at the same time, he enriched himself by selling food to the garrison. He increased his influence with the Chinese trading community downriver in Cotabato town, and he controlled the upriver areas that provided the products—tobacco, coffee, beeswax, resins, and hardwood they desired. Within a few years, he dominated every part of the flourishing trading network on the great river, taking his percentage at every stop along the way.

Datu Piang with visiting American officers, 1899.
*Under his feet are two lantakas, **traditional bronze cannons.***

The Spaniards withdrew from Cotabato in early 1899 as their rule in the Philippines ended after more than 300 years. Datu Piang immediately sacked Cotabato town, protecting the Chinese community but killing the leading Christian Filipinos who had worked for the Spanish occupiers and driving hundreds more to the hills. When the American occupying forces arrived at the end of the year, Piang chose the path of least resistance. He cooperated with the latest occupiers of his homeland and required his vassal datus to do the same. He then sent his sons to the new American schools and quickly learned how to benefit from the new colonial regime.

Piang continued to control all trade on the river while also expanding into the American-introduced enterprises of lumber and commercial coconut production. He built roads and schools for the Americans using the free labor of his followers, then pocketed the construction fees and high rents for himself. In a 1926 letter, Joseph Hayden, fresh from a visit to the "King of Mindanao," reported on his current wealth:

> The old fox has accumulated much wealth during the three or four decades of his power: 42,000 coconut trees (they are good for $1 per tree each per year) thousands of carabao, thousands of hectares of rice land, horses, cattle, buildings, boats, and what not—to say nothing of the tithe paid him by his loyal subjects. He is also reputed to have a huge hoard of gold coins.[1]

Piang ruled as an overlord with little American interference, still collecting tribute from his subjects, still casting the occasional recalcitrant to the crocodiles. So powerful had he become in the eyes of ordinary Magindanaons that they said he was able to kill a man merely by pointing at him with his index finger and uttering the magical word "*enemigo.*"

Datu Piang with the young Gumbay Piang, 1933

As every visiting American wanted a picture of, or preferably with, the "King of Mindanao," Datu Piang was probably the most photographed Moro of his time. In early photographs his heavily pocked but nonetheless handsome face projects the calmness and self-assurance associated with absolute authority. In later photos, his now-bespectacled face has the bemused look of a man who has achieved all his dreams.

He would have been bemused as well by the English title "King of Mindanao" because he had always rejected nearly all the titles and trappings of the Moro nobility. He declined even to call himself "Datu," preferring instead, following the practice used by Moro commoners, to name himself after his eldest child. He was Amai Mingka (short for Ama ni Mingka) father of Mingka, his first daughter. As befitted a Moro ruler, however, he had ten simultaneous wives and fathered 33 children.

* * *

Adil found his father's friend sitting on his porch under the sign and handed him the letters he was carrying—one from Edward Kuder and one from Wendell Fertig. But there was more to deliver. As Gumbay Piang read the letters, Adil reached deeper into his knapsack for the physical proof that the Americans were indeed fighting their way back to the Philippines. He pulled out a carton of Philip Morris cigarettes, a gift to Piang from Fertig. From Kuder there were recent copies of Time and Life magazines and two remaining chocolate bars (the other two Adil had given to his sisters). And there were matchbooks, pocket mirrors, and leaflets, all of them featuring the same image of Douglas MacArthur, standing and saluting, with stiffened spine and determined gaze, above the bold-lettered caption, "I shall return."

Captain G. Piang, Prisoner-of-War, was overjoyed. He kissed the carton of cigarettes, "I told you! I told you the Americans are coming!" he exclaimed to his followers who had gathered. "It's time to dig up your guns!" For Gumbay Piang, the timing was right. The Japanese officers who visited him had begun to change their tone because his brother, Ugalingan, was not cooperating with them in the way they had hoped. Gumbay expected to be arrested in a matter of days and returned to the POW camp, where he would likely die.

The letters from Kuder and Fertig requested that Gumbay travel to Fertig's headquarters in Lanao and formally join the guerrilla movement. He was ready to break his parole and go, but first, he had to prepare a hideout in the hills of Talayan for his fighters and see to the safety of his family and followers. Adil and Gumbay agreed to meet in a week on the coast in Lusayin on the Lanao border, where they would rendezvous with their guide for the trek to guerrilla headquarters.

* * *

Cunning and clever as he was, Datu Piang never inspired a single Moro—his sons included—to fight a guerrilla war at great odds against a powerful foreign invader. That distinction belonged to Datu Ali, Piang's aristocratic and charismatic rival in the early days of the Moro Wars. And Gumbay Piang knew his story well. Datu Ali was the high-born nephew of Datu Utu, the powerful upriver sultan who had been deposed by Datu Piang. Unlike Piang, he decided to fight the American invaders, and from 1903 to 1905, he led an armed uprising in the vast upriver territory formerly controlled by his uncle.

At first, Datu Ali fought traditionally, building the largest wooden fort ever seen in Cotabato—mounted with 85 bronze cannons— and challenging the Americans to come and fight him. They did and brought with them enough firepower to demolish his fort and disperse his followers. Datu Ali escaped with about 50 warriors and led the Americans on a chase across the wild marshlands of the upper Cotabato valley, eluding capture for almost two years. Out of necessity, he had become the first Moro guerrilla leader.

The American commander, General Leonard Wood, who twenty years earlier had taken part in the military offensive against Geronimo, the Chiracauha Apache warrior who led the last major Indian uprising against the U.S. government, was experienced with "hostiles." However, he was still unprepared for Datu Ali's next move.

In May 1904, Ali and his fighters launched a surprise attack on a small company of about 40 American infantrymen. The soldiers, led by a Moro guide, were following a trail along the edge of the upriver Liguasan Marsh near the tiny hamlet of Simpetan. They had pushed through mile after mile of white-tufted talahib, wild sugar cane that stood higher than the tallest American and interlaced overhead. The dank air of the tunnel-like passage was oppressive, the cane on either side of the trail so thick it was difficult to see beyond it. It was from behind that wall of matted grass, at a spot on the trail where a carabao wallow blocked their way, slowing the column, that Datu Ali's men fired their first furious volley, the well-aimed rounds dropping the company's lead soldiers.

The trail quickly became a trap as the troops in the rear pressed forward and were shot in turn, the firing coming now from three directions. Those who tried to escape the trail, crashing through the tangled stalks on either side in a desperate effort to outflank the unseen enemy, were cut down by sharp krises scything through the tall grass. As more and more men fell, discipline broke, and the company, its guide long gone, made a disordered retreat down the marshland trail leaving more than half its men behind in the black mud. Nineteen infantrymen had paid the price of empire with their lives, struck down by an unfamiliar foe on the far side of the world.

Two young soldiers, lying wounded in the wild cane, were spared. Datu Ali tended to their wounds and eventually set them free in exchange for showing his men how to use the Krag repeating rifles taken from their dead comrades. One of the young men was Private Colin Mackenzie, a 19-year-old English immigrant from the West Midlands who had joined the U.S. army looking for opportunity and adventure.

Despite his close brush with death in Mindanao, Mackenzie

spent the rest of his long life there. After being discharged from the army, he became one of the first American teachers in Cotabato. He married a fellow teacher, Eufemia Navarro, from the island of Cebu, and they raised two children. A colleague of Edward Kuder when he was stationed in Cotabato, Mackenzie was principal of the Upi Agricultural School in the years that Mohammad Adil attended. He affectionately called the boy Peanut because of his small size and spoke to him in Magindanaon, the language he learned during his months as a prisoner of Datu Ali.

General Wood, after leading an expedition to retrieve the remains of the slain soldiers, declared that Datu Ali would be pursued until captured or killed. Soon he sent several companies of American soldiers and PhilippineScouts out on a single mission—to avenge the 'Simpetan Massacre'.[2] Despite the military resources that Wood threw at the task, it still took 18 months and the treachery of a former Moro guerrilla for the Americans to corner Datu Ali. Multiple accounts were published of Datu Ali's last stand, some of them quite fanciful. Only one was based on the firsthand recollections of Moros, and it was written by Gumbay Piang.

Early one morning in October 1905, in a hidden valley on the eastern slopes of the Cotabato Basin, Datu Ali was awakened in his refuge by a runner who informed him that American troops had found him and were only about a mile distant. Most of his warriors were attending a market more than a mile away. The runner proposed that he would go and get them but Ali, realizing "the futility of making his poorly armed men resist the Americans in open combat," did not send for them.[3] Datu Ali's only companions in the house were his wives and his youngest son. Father and son, still dressed in their sleeping *malongs*, sat at adjoining windows with rifles ready and softly recited together the Ayatul Kursi, the Verse of the Throne, *"Allahu la ilaha illa...."*

Captain Frank McCoy, through an interpreter, demanded Ali's surrender, and he interrupted his recitation to refuse. McCoy then ordered his men to open fire, and they poured volley after volley of Krag bullets into the frail house. Bright morning sunlight followed the bullets into the dimly-lit dwelling, streaming through hundreds of newly torn holes in the woven-palm walls and illuminating the carnage within. Datu Ali fell first with a bullet in his chest as he fired at his attackers. His son hit again and again, continued firing until the supply of bullets in front of him was exhausted. As he turned to reach for more ammunition behind him, an American round struck him in the back of the head, scattering his brains across the floor.

The women in the house crawled beneath the storm of bullets and those who could, escaped through the rear, led by Bagungan, the youngest of the women. She was wearing Ali's amulets, which he had forgotten to put on that morning and which she had slipped on her wrist for safekeeping. It was to them that she attributed her deliverance. After one ferocious volley, she raised herself slightly from the floor to find that a child she was trying to protect with her body had been shot dead.

Ali's first and favorite wife, Mingka, was shot several times while trying to escape. This was the same Mingka—Datu Piang's eldest child—from whom he took his popular name—Amai Mingka—the Father of Mingka. Piang had arranged her marriage to Datu Ali years earlier. It was a good political match, bestowing his first daughter on his highborn ally, and assuring that his grand-children would be members of the traditional nobility. When told that his men had critically wounded Datu Piang's firstborn daughter,

Captain McCoy had her brought immediately to the army hospital in Cotabato town and treated by army surgeons. She survived her wounds and lived another 11 years.

Datu Ali was a skilled guerrilla leader, and in order to surprise and defeat him, an informer was required. That role was played by Datu Inuk, a former lieutenant of Ali, now allied with Datu Piang, who offered to guide the Americans to Ali's hideout. The expedition, composed of 77 hand-picked men, was arranged with the greatest secrecy to avoid word of it getting to Ali's many spies. The boat carrying the expedition sailed to Davao, and Inuk guided them over the Digos pass (where 37 years later the Bolo Battalions would make their stand) to approach Ali's valley hideout from an unexpected direction, which allowed them to get so close before being detected.

On the question of why Inuk betrayed his former chieftain and how Bagungan, the niece of Datu Piang, came to be in the hideout with Datu Ali, the Moro accounts vary. The one Gumbay Piang relates is that Bagungan, a young woman of exceptional beauty, intelligence, and determination, was Ali's youngest wife and Datu Inuk was utterly infatuated with her. In the hopes of obtaining the woman he desired most, Datu Inuk used the Americans to defeat his rival Ali. He did so with Datu Piang's knowledge, and possibly at his bidding. Neither man imagined that the Americans would open fire on women and children, a severe violation of *maratabat*. They had much left to learn. Just a few years later, at Bud Dajo, Major General Leonard Wood made clear to the Moros that he would not hesitate to massacre women and children to achieve his objectives.

Bagungan, fortunate to have survived the deadly consequences of Inuk's betrayal, nevertheless married him shortly after Ali's death. She went on to outlive her second husband, Inuk, and marry a third—a younger man of lower status—whom she chose against tradition and

the express wishes of her uncle, Datu Piang. When the post of munic-
ipal district president (a colonial office equivalent to mayor) became
vacant in 1918, she was appointed to fill it after receiving an overwhelming vote of confidence from the male electors of the district.
Bai Bagungan, as she was universally known—a Moro, a survivor,
and a breaker of traditions—thus became the first female mayor in
the Philippines. She was an active official and a strong proponent of
public education, especially for girls.

* * *

A few days later, Adil began his journey back to Lanao by paddling
a dugout canoe through the tangle of creeks, sloughs, and estuaries
that laced the lower delta, heading for Cotabato town to find a small
sailboat that would take him to Lusayin. The town was defined by
the water that flowed around it in three small rivers and one great
one, the Pulangi. Adil was paddling his dugout on one of the smaller
rivers, the Matampay, near the public market when he met a larger
dugout paddled by three men heading in the opposite direction.

His father's servant, Kadungan, was steering in the stern. His
father sat stonefaced in the bow, and Adil's stepmother sat crying
behind him. Across her lap she held a small still figure wrapped
in white cloth, and Adil realized with a shock that it was the body
of his six-year-old sister Norma, who three days ago was gleefully
nibbling the chocolate bar he had given her. When she had fallen
suddenly ill with a high fever, the old woman healer could not help
the child, so they had brought her to the hospital in town. But at the
hospital, there was no medicine for her, only a bed and the tender
care of a doctor and nurse while she died of meningitis.

They were taking her home to bury her. Adil's father knew
where his son was going and told him he had to turn back. When

Adil balked, his father reminded him that of all the ominous signs one could encounter when starting a long and dangerous journey, meeting a dead relative on the way was the worst, and ignoring such an ill omen would be utter foolishness. He must postpone his trip. Eventually, they convinced him, and he turned his boat around and followed them home.

Magindanaon dugout canoe on the Pulangi River, 1933

Gumbay Piang travelled to Lanao without Adil and returned before the end of the month, recommissioned by Fertig as a captain in MacArthur's U.S. Forces in the Philippines (USFIP). Fertig gave him an infantry regiment to command—the 119th—and a territory in which to operate—the entire lower Cotabato Valley. He had little else to give him. Gumbay would have to man and arm his regiment on his own. Fertig had already told him as much in the letter Adil had delivered to him: "You will note that it is necessary for every applicant for induction…to be armed. We do not furnish the arms; the men furnish their own." Despite the modern weapons coming off American submarines and Chick Parson's promises to Pendatun, the Moros of Cotabato were, once again, expected to fight the Japanese as part of an American army without having been issued American arms.[4]

Adil was there to meet him on his return and asked for news of his foster father. Piang told him that Kuder's health had deteriorated rapidly while he was in Lanao, so much so that he had been evacuated by submarine to Australia. Kuder had learned of the evacuation order only a few hours before boarding, and Piang had been unable to say goodbye or relay any messages for him.

Adil was relieved that Kuder had escaped Mindanao, but also feared for his foster father's health and worried he would never see him again. There was no point in returning to Lanao. Kuder had wanted him to join the force of Pendatun, now in the upper Cotabato Valley, so that is where he would go. But his father had other plans for him. And this time, he listened to his father. Gumbay Piang was severely in need of weapons and men for his guerrilla regiment. Hadji Adil had the largest cache of firearms in the delta and close ties to seasoned fighters. He told his son that he would have more opportunities for advancement under Captain Piang than in Pendatun's much larger and older force. It was time for his son to fight, he knew, but he wanted him fighting on home territory surrounded by kinsmen who would protect him.

On the first day of September 1943, 19-year-old Mohammad Adil became one of the youngest officers in General Douglas MacArthur's guerrilla army, commissioned as a third lieutenant in the 119th regiment.[5] He brought nearly 50 guns with him from his father's cache and an eager group of fighters, some young, some less so. Most were his kinsmen. Two—Rudolfo Carillo and Anecito Valdez—were Christians as well as childhood friends. Rudolfo's parents, immigrants from the island of Iloilo, had contracted leprosy when he was young, and he could no longer stay with them. After asking his father's approval, Adil invited his classmate to live with his family, and Rudolfo became Hadji Adil's foster son.

His father had also insisted that his distant kinsman Hadji Hashim Ali, a man already in his fifties, accompany Adil to the hills.

As his name signaled, Hadji Hashim, a cousin of Adil's mother, had made the pilgrimage to Mecca. He had left on the same ill-fated journey as Adil's father, traveling as a bodyguard for another pilgrim. Hadji Hashim, a quiet man with a soft smile and the cold eyes of a cobra, was a specialist at killing, having been both an executioner and an assassin. He could behead a condemned man with a single stroke from his *kampilan*, a long single-edged sword. He had done so multiple times in the service of Datu Sinsuat Balabaran, who still occasionally sentenced offending followers to death, despite the formal imposition of an American colonial legal system. Hadji Hashim was renowned as a man fully ready for any fight. In battle he bristled with weapons—shotgun, pistol, panabas, kris, dagger, awl, and brass knuckles. Whatever he needed to get the job done, he said, he kept near at hand.

Adil, seated far left, is still the smiling schoolboy on the eve of being commissioned as a guerrilla officer in 1943. In this studio photo he poses with the older fighters who will accompany him to the hills, including, seated next to him, the well-armed Hadji Hashim Ali and his wife.

The story of how Hadji Hashim became a retainer of Hadji Adil begins with a minor infraction. Pimbarat, the teenaged nephew of Hadji Hashim, was riding his carabao home one day and took a shortcut across the corner of his neighbor's rice field. The sons of Ama ni Sulik, both young men, were working in the field and angrily accused Pimbarat of ruining their plow work. He responded that they were overreacting. They were going to plow the field once again anyway before planting rice. More words were exchanged and led to blows. The brothers pulled the boy off his carabao and beat him to the ground and then, as a final cruelty, stripped the clothes from his body as he lay prone in the black dirt. It was a grievous and inflammatory insult. The boy limped home, covering himself with his hands, and told his father he wished they had killed him instead, so great was his shame.

Pimbarat's father appealed to Datu Sinsuat, demanding justice for his son. The datu heard the case, but as Ama ni Sulik, the defendant's father, was one of Sinsuat's most loyal enforcers, the datu imposed only a small fine on his sons. Pimbarat's father then gathered the family elders, who agreed that such a severe violation to family *maratabat* had not been satisfied by the fine, and retaliation was required. They also agreed that Ama ni Sulik, the most powerful member of the offending family, should be the target of their vengeance. Young Pimbarat would carry out the reprisal to relieve his shame. The goal was to injure Ama ni Sulik but not to kill him, to avoid a lethal feud.

Hadji Hashim prepared the weapon, a two-foot-long hardwood club concealed in a woven hemp bag. He then brought Pimbarat to the weekly market in Pagalamatan, which Ama ni Sulik was known to frequent, handed his nephew the bag, and pointed out his target. Pimbarat made several rounds of the market stalls, twice passing Ama ni Sulik, who was carrying a .38 revolver, but he couldn't summon the courage to attack him with his club.

When Hadji Hashim saw this, he beckoned the boy and took the bag from him. He then walked directly to a fishmonger's stall where Ama ni Sulik was asking the price of a string of mudfish. When the seller told him "20 centavos," Hadji Hashim stepped up behind him, grabbed one end of the string, and said, "I'll buy these fish for 25 centavos." Ama ni Sulik turned and began to argue, but when he saw Hashim and caught the gleam in his eye, he reached for his .38. In one smooth motion, Hadji Hashim pulled the hardwood club from its bag and swung it backhanded against Ama ni Sulik's skull. He swung again, this time forward, and Ama ni Sulik dropped his revolver and crumpled to the ground. At the hospital, the doctor had to pry the man's cigar from between his clenched teeth, but he was still alive. Hadji Hashim the killer, also knew how *not* to strike a killing blow.

Hadji Hashim's daylight attack in a crowded market attracted notice and was soon the talk of the lower delta. Datu Sinsuat was furious at him for defying his ruling and exacting revenge against a loyal retainer. The family of Ama ni Sulik filed charges against him, and the Philippine Constabulary sought him out to arrest him. Hadji Hashim asked for assistance from his distant cousin Hadji Adil Tambis, who was known to have influence with the constabulary. Hadji Adil, the bail bondsman, first invited him to stay on his land, where he could avoid the constabulary, then arranged a bond to keep him out of jail while awaiting trial. The charges were eventually dropped for lack of witnesses willing to testify, and, from that time on, Hadji Hashim never left Hadji Adil's service except to protect his benefactor's son.

On paper, the 119th infantry regiment was just one of about

20 local guerrilla forces in Mindanao and Sulu under the command of Wendell Fertig and recognized by Douglas MacArthur. But the 119th would be the only one of those local forces required to fight the Japanese *and* their Moro allies. Several Moro datus, such as Gumbay Piang's brother Ugalingan, had remained neutral during the occupation or signed separate peace agreements with the Japanese, but only the Sinsuat clan, along with their close allies, the Ampatuans, had actively sided with the Japanese. It was certain that when the guerrillas of the 119th attacked the Japanese, the Sinsuats would retaliate with fury. Mohammad Adil had volunteered to fight the Japanese invaders. But he was also going to war against his clan enemies who were, at the same time, his neighbors and distant kinsmen. It would be, in the custom of the Moros, a conflict both bloody and intimate.

* * *

Adil had already witnessed the wrath of the Sinsuats more than once, most recently at the oath-taking induction for the Bolo Battalion in late December of 1941. The young men stood in line in the riverside square in Tamontaka to place their hands on the Holy Qur'an and swear the Moro Oath of Service in a language poorly understood by most of them. It was Gumbay Piang, his father's good friend, who had asked him to swear in the volunteers and keep the enlistment records.

Gumbay Piang had arrived at the oath-taking by a launch with Brigadier General Joseph P. Vachon, the USAFFE commander for Cotabato and the counterpart of Brigadier General Guy Fort in Lanao. The two of them had conceived the idea of the Bolo Battalions. As Gumbay Piang stepped onto the shore, he was immediately challenged by Odin Sinsuat, the son of Sinsuat Balabaran and his chosen heir as the ruling chieftain of the traditional territory of the Sinsuat clan, covering much of the lower delta.

Odin thrust his finger at Piang and shouted, "Come no further. This is not the territory of the Piangs!" Gumbay's bodyguards immediately raised their weapons. The men of Odin leveled theirs in response. General Vachon paled. Adil watched as his father, blood-related to both men, stepped between the two mortal enemies, speaking soothing words to each of them, working to avert a gunfight. Gumbay Piang agreed he would not stay long, easing the tension for the time being, but it was clear to all present that the coming war would aggravate old enmities, not erase them.

Nor was it Adil's first encounter with an enraged Odin Sinsuat. A few months before the Japanese invasion, he had been home on school vacation when his father asked him to guide the district land officer and his assistant on a trip to survey lands in Dalican. He met them at the Pagalamatan ferry landing with a long dugout canoe and two boatmen, and they paddled with the tide up the wide Tamontaka River. Upstream, they left the main channel to follow a network of tributaries south—narrower rivers fringed with nipa palms and carpeted in the quieter stretches with water-beaded lotus leaves— bejeweled green backdrops for the pink-tinged magnificence of lotus flowers by the hundreds. Bamboo thickets and coconut palms and a lone basking crocodile slipped past, as well as shaded hamlets close by the shore and, beyond them, sun-soaked rice paddies.

A final passage up a narrow stream overhung with spreading narra trees brought them to his uncle's house in Dalican, where they stayed while the inspectors conducted their land survey. On their last day, Odin Sinsuat invited the officials to a wedding feast to celebrate his marriage to Limbang, a beautiful village girl more than ten years his junior. Dalican was part of Datu Odin's territory, and, as his father had before him, he laid claim to any beautiful maiden in his domain that caught his eye, whether she consented to the union or not. Not yet thirty, Odin already had wives in several local villages. The village square was decorated with red, green, and gold embroidered hangings, and the sound of a *kulintang* rang out. Datu Odin wore a long-sleeved khaki shirt and turban, and his unsmiling bride, in gold sash and veil, sat beneath a decorated umbrella. The *pandita* pronounced the marriage ritual, and the village feasted.

At dawn the next day, as they were preparing to leave, a dugout with five men passed his uncle's house, heading upstream. Two men were poling the boat, two stood with Enfield rifles slung on their shoulders, and one man knelt in the middle of the boat, his hands bound behind his back. Adil immediately recognized him as Abu Dimatinkal, a teenager his age. His uncle wondered aloud, "Why did the men of Odin arrest that young boy?" A short while later, they heard the unmistakable sharp snap of four quick pistol shots from upstream and saw people running along the bank from the village. His uncle asked them, "What happened?"

"Odin just shot Abu." Adil and his uncle walked warily to the village. As they approached the wedding celebration site, Adil saw Abu, no longer young and hopeful, slumped awkwardly on the ground, head on destroyed chest, arms still pinioned behind him and tied to the house post. Dark blood had pooled and thickened beneath him, and flies were gathering. The villagers, he saw, were afraid to remove the body. He had died slowly, they whispered, despite four point-blank shots. And when he had begged for water, Adil's cousin was the only one brave enough to bring it to him.

Odin was nowhere in sight. The villagers told Adil that when Odin had tried to consummate the marriage the night before, he discovered that his bride was no longer a virgin. Furious that someone had gotten to his prize before him, he demanded of Limbang, "Who was here ahead of me?" She told him, "Abu Dimatinkal," and

Odin sent for the boy, had him tied to the post, and shot him there in the square in front of the assembled villagers.

The slain boy was from an upriver clan, the Baguingedin, his family having moved downriver a few years earlier to live with in-laws. A number of fighters in Datu Udtug Matalam's upriver guerrilla band were the boy's kinsmen, and in June of 1942, just after the American surrender, he approved a raid far downriver to kill Odin Sinsuat. [6]

The raiders, 30 men in three boats, paddled more than 60 miles down the great river that the Japanese did not yet control. They followed the Pulangi as it narrowed and twisted, creating the tightest bend of its long course at Masakit, the Tight Place. At Pagalungan, the Mirrored Place, the river opened into a broad marshland, and its flow slackened as they slipped across its glassy surface. When the river reached Tumbao, the Raised Place that forced it to divide, the raiders chose the south fork, the Tamontaka, to continue west toward the sea. At Malages (Strong), the river first met the powerful tidal currents of the sea. Finally, a few miles from the sea, they saw their destination on the south bank. A small, fast-flowing river, the Dimapatuy (Cannot Be Turned Back), fell from the rugged coastal range known as the Cotabato Cordillera and emptied into the Tamontaka River with such hydraulic force that its flow could not be reversed even by the strongest tide. They had reached the heart of Sinsuat territory and the main village of Odin Sinsuat.

Having timed their arrival for the predawn hours, they moved in a single file up the trail that led to Odin Sinsuat's great house and waited in a stand of coconut palms for him to appear. When he did so shortly after dawn, they attacked, first firing from behind the trees then moving forward into the open for the kill. Odin dodged the first bullets, took cover, and called for help. Armed men came running, and one of them, Gumanti, a man of more than fifty years, carried by its wooden handle a Browning Automatic Rifle (BAR), a fearsome weapon that no Moro had ever owned and most had never seen. Gumanti, a former Philippine Scout with the U.S. Army had deserted with the gun when the Americans surrendered and brought it to Odin Sinsuat who, he calculated, was now the most powerful Moro on the winning side. Gumanti immediately went prone, set the BAR's bipod, and began directing bursts of automatic fire at the raiders.

Unable to match the BAR's fierce firepower, the raiders fell back into the trees. Having halted their advance, Gumanti stood and began a walking fire with the gun at his hip, *chung-chung-chung-chung, chung-chung-chung-chung*, as the men of Odin fell in behind him. In unrelenting gusts, .30 caliber bullets ripped through the coconut bark and into the bodies of the raiders, killing one man and wounding two others. The leader of the raiding party, Ali Dimatinkal, ordered his men to withdraw. His nephew would not be avenged today. When Gumanti stopped to reload, the raiders fell back rapidly to the boats, dragging the wounded with them but leaving their slain comrade behind. It would be a bitter journey back upriver. The opening shots of the guerrilla war in Cotabato had been fired, and they were exchanged between Moros.

* * *

Though not what he had hoped for, Third Lieutenant Mohammad Adil's first assignment was a prominent one. In late October, he and his men were ordered to escort the new guerrilla commander of the entire Cotabato sector (Fertig's 106th Division) on his inspection tour through the territory of the 119th Regiment. Lt. Colonel Frank McGee was formerly one of Salipada Pendatun's guerrilla officers and now his superior. The territory of the 119th Regiment covered all of the lower Cotabato Valley as well as the northern cordillera. Adil's mission was to meet Colonel McGee and his men on the narrow coast south of the delta and escort them to the territory of Pendatun's 118th Regiment in the upper Cotabato Valley.

McGee was a graduate of the West Point Class of 1915. Known as "The Class the Stars Fell On," it produced Dwight Eisenhower, Omar Bradley, and a record 57 other generals. No star fell on their classmate Frank McGee, only a German artillery shell at the battle of Chateau-Thierry, one of the first American offensive actions of the First World War. Three years out of West Point and serving in France with the American Expeditionary Force under General Blackjack Pershing, McGee, by then a captain, suffered a grievous wound when, during a counterattack by combined American and French forces, a steel fragment from an exploding artillery shell sliced through his scalp and punctured his skull. The battlefield injury left him with a silver plate in his head, permanently slurred speech, agonizing headaches, the Distinguished Service Cross, a promotion to Major, and disability retirement from the army.

Involuntarily separated from the life he loved but still young and seeking adventure, Frank McGee made his way to Mindanao and spent the next 20 years managing a plantation in Cotabato. As with Chick Parsons, he thrived in Mindanao and came to love it and its people, only returning to the U.S. mainland periodically to have the plate in his head adjusted. When the Japanese invaded, he volunteered for active duty at the age of 52. When the surrender order arrived, he decided to take his chances in the mountains of Bukidnon. There he gathered a group of other USAFFE holdouts and they struggled with shortages of food and medicine until Salipada Pendatun arrived in the province and they joined his guerrilla force.[7]

Adil led his platoon to the Cotabato coast, where he met

Colonel McGee, who had about thirty men with him. At the meeting point on the beach, Adil saw a huge man walking toward him— old, in the teenager's estimation, but overflowing with energy. Adil saluted, introduced himself, and related his orders. McGee smiled at him, then shook his hand in a welcoming vice grip and threw his other arm around him in a bear hug. Adil noticed with satisfaction that, despite his rank, McGee was as ragged as the rest of them. He had hacked the sleeves off his uniform shirt with a knife, and the loose cotton threads hung down in a fringe.

They set out across the thickly forested hills on the three-day trek that would take them to the headquarters of the newly-formed 119th Regiment in Bagan at the head of the Talayan Valley. As they made camp the first night, Colonel McGee pulled an army-issue jungle hammock from his pack and tied it between two trees. It was the first hammock Adil or any of his men had ever seen. McGee was a large man, enormous by Philippine standards, and when he climbed into the hammock to test it, it immediately broke, sending him tumbling headfirst to the ground. Adil's men clapped their hands over their mouths to keep from laughing out loud. McGee jumped up, laughing himself, and asked in a loud voice, "How many broke? How many broke?," referring to the hammock strings. To the men that sounded like "Ama ni Broke," or, in English, "Father of Broke." Still stifling laughter, some of them walked off to cut cogon grass to make a traditional mattress for him, repeating to each other in low voices, "Ama ni Broke, Ama ni Broke." The name stuck, and McGee was known among the fighters of the 119th as Ama ni Broke for the rest of the war.

In Bagan, McGee planned to spend a few days consulting with Gumbay Piang and then, still guided by Adil, proceed upriver to Sapakan, where the territory of Pendatun's 118th Regiment started.

Adil had his own plan for Colonel McGee and his men, who had arrived on the Cotabato coast with brand new guns and abundant ammunition. McGee's bodyguards carried Thompson submachine guns, and most of his men had M1 carbines slung over their shoulders. The 119th had less than one gun per man, most of them First World War relics, and was pitifully short of ammunition.

The young third lieutenant was curious to see what those guns could do against Japanese weapons. He had decided to take a slight detour on the way to Sapakan and guide McGee and his men past the Japanese garrison at Salebo, with the hope of getting them involved in some action. In his enthusiasm, however, he shared his plan a little too widely. The night before they were to leave for Sapakan, he was called to Captain Piang's office.

"Lt. Adil, is it true that you were planning to guide Colonel McGee and his men past the Japanese detachment at Salebo?

"Yes, sir."

"And why would you do that?"

"Well, they have guns, beautiful guns, and so much ammunition! I just wanted to test their firepower against the Japanese."

"Those were not your orders!" If something happened to Colonel McGee because of you, I'd have to answer for it. I'm relieving you of your assignment."

A new guide was assigned to Colonel McGee, who completed his tour without incident. Piang ordered Adil to return to his outpost and wait for instructions. He had failed his first assignment. He wondered if there would be another.

In late December, another order did come from Captain Piang, and it was the one he had been waiting for. He and his men were ordered to attack the Japanese garrison at Dulawan, the capital of the Piangs. The attack was to be carried out on New Year's Eve when the Japanese soldiers celebrated their most important holiday of the year.

He gathered his best men and immediately scouted the location. The garrison sat on the point of land formed where the Dansalan River emptied into the wide Pulangi. The land upriver from the garrison was swampy and impassable for most of the year, so the only approach was by water. Adil's plan was to take a boat across the Dansalan River, about a hundred yards wide at that point, attack the garrison from close range, and escape the same way.

He presented his plan to the five guerrillas who would accompany him, all of them older and more experienced than him. To a man they shook their heads no. "They have machine guns and searchlights. They will slaughter us on our way back across the river."

Adil was frustrated. "I want to be close! I want to see my target!" He turned to Hadji Hashim, but even the professional killer disliked the plan. Faced with unanimous disapproval, Adil acquiesced. They would fire on the garrison from across the river.

Shortly after midnight on the first day of 1944, the six men stood obscured in the tree line at the river's edge listening to the sounds of drunken celebration from the opposite bank. About 30 Japanese soldiers were raucously celebrating New Year's Eve in the main building of the garrison. Adil, the best marksman of the group, chose a dim figure in the distant lamp-lit building with a white cloth tied around his head. On his signal, they fired, and he saw his man drop. It was over in seconds. Each of them had only enough ammunition to fire two rounds.

As Adil retreated with his men through the dark, his heart racing, he wondered if he had killed his first enemy. He had expected elation but sensed only dissatisfaction. The attack had felt feeble and ineffectual—a mosquito bite on a carabao's rump. He wanted to defeat the invaders, not irritate them. The attack on the garrison was not, however, without effect. The Japanese commander in Cotabato had taken notice. The beast had felt the sting and was about to stir.

* * *

Over 14 years, I made four more trips to the Philippines to visit Moham-mad Adil, staying at his home and enjoying his hospitality while serving as an audience of one for a superb raconteur. His stories were charged with physical courage, violence, loyalty, and love, and it sometimes seemed as if I were listening to a twentieth-century oral epic. But as our relation-ship grew closer, the stories broadened and deepened and revealed him in unheroic, even unflattering, circumstances. There were stories of comic blunders and tragic missteps, disappointments, and regrets. Thanks to his self-discernment and forthrightness, the narrative of his life took on a fully three-dimensional form.[8]

In the same way, I gradually came to know the multi-sided indi-vidual behind the reputation. By 1986, he was widely known as a fear-some man who personified the fighting spirit of the Moros—a man about whom songs were sung and legends were told. He was described in terms used for forces of nature: dangerous, unstoppable, uncontrollable. He was said to inspire fierce loyalty in his soldiers, who told him they would gladly jump into the mouth of a crocodile if he gave them the order. He was also known as a "man without mercy" because, as a constabulary officer, he could not be bribed and would arrest even his kinsmen. And he was reputed to be both fearless and, when provoked, deadly.

He was, without a doubt, the man described by that reputation. But as I spent more time with him at his home, I gradually gained a fuller perspective on his life. He was also a man who quoted Kipling, Tenny-son, and William James and considered himself an environmentalist. He wrote beautifully composed letters in a graceful hand, preferred classi-cal music, and appreciated beauty in all forms, especially in women. He had a robust, unselfconscious sense of humor and enjoyed making people laugh. Married to his first wife for 47 years until her death, he raised three daughters to be courageous and uncompromising and four sons to be thoughtful and wise. Later, he doted on his grandchildren, raised orchids, and had a warm and playful relationship with his second wife, whom he addressed with great tenderness as "friend."

6
WAR IN THE CORDILLERA

As far as he could see down the Talayan Valley, a long fertile hollow nudged into the Cotabato Cordillera from the delta floodplain; the landscape was smeared with twisting columns of blue-gray smoke, one above each burning hamlet. The smoke pillars, 30 or more of them, drifted and merged as they reached above the surrounding hills, where Adil lay watching, and formed a thick acrid pall. The Japanese and the Sinsuats were burning every house in the valley.

The riverside path through the valley's center was crowded with the newly dispossessed, walking away from their doomed houses, their crops, and their hopes. As they walked, carrying what they could and leading their children by the hand, they passed Japanese soldiers setting fire to thatched roofs and using their bayonets to prod those too slow to evacuate their homes. They kept walking out of the valley, unsure of where to go.

Before the combined force of 300 Japanese infantry and their Sinsuat allies marched through the Talayan Valley, torching houses as they went, they had attacked the main guerrilla camp at Bagan at dawn, surprising and scattering Gumbay Piang's fighters. It was the first week of February 1944, just over a month since Adil's New Year's Eve attack on the Dulawan garrison. As Japan's war effort in the Pacific had begun to falter in the autumn of 1943, the Japanese military drew in its line of defense in the Pacific, heightening the strategic importance of Mindanao. With the stakes having increased, the Japanese commander of Cotabato had no choice but to respond to the new guerrilla threat with immediate and crushing force. To bolster his forces, he had the men of Datu Sinsuat Balabaran, organized into a local unit of the Bureau of Constabulary (BC), a national police force formed by the occupation government and modeled on the Philippine Constabulary.

Adil had no idea what had become of Captain Piang and the bulk of the guerrilla force. He had been with his men at his mountain outpost in Sigawa, higher in the hills and more than a mile from Piang's headquarters. With him was Captain Macario Guballa, Piang's executive officer. Captain Guballa, a graduate of the Philippine Military Academy, had taken a liking to the young man and was teaching him the everyday duties of a junior officer—preparing rosters, writing orders, and other administrative work. Pleased with his pupil's aptitude, Guballa had told him, "You have a great future in the military, lieutenant."

Hearing the shooting coming from the main guerrilla camp, Guballa told him to withdraw his men to an even higher position. There, as the sun lit the valley floor, they could see the headquarters of the 119th, now occupied by the Japanese and their allies, and watch as the burning of houses in the lower valley began. Captain Guballa knew what would come next as rank and file guerrillas hiding in the jungle saw their camp overrun, their leaders killed or captured, and the homes of their relatives destroyed. He directed Adil to establish checkpoints on the major forest trails leading from the western hills down to the valley and confiscate guns from any guerrilla attempting to desert or surrender to the Japanese. By nightfall, the valley below them still illuminated by burning houses, he and his men had collected nearly 50 guns.

The flames had extinguished themselves by morning, leaving only sooted outlines where more than 400 houses had stood in the now silent valley. After salvaging the guns, the next priority was food. Because most of their stores had been left behind when they evacuated their camp at Sigawa, which was now also occupied by the Japanese, Captain Guballa ordered Adil back down to the valley to look for rice. The only houses in the Talayan valley that had not been burned to the ground were at its mouth, where the valley opened into the marshes of Butiran, The Place of Water Lilies. The Japanese had spared those few structures because Butiran was known to be infested with crocodiles. In their desperation, hundreds of civilians had nevertheless fled to Butiran for refuge after their homes were destroyed. Adil decided to try there first.

Cotabato, a land of dark rivers and vast marshlands, was famous for its crocodiles. With an average length of fifteen feet and a bite four times more powerful than a Bengal tiger, the crocodiles of Cotabato were killing machines, and the Moros of Cotabato paid them the attention they deserved. They called them *buaya*—a word that, when voiced evoked the gaping and snapping shut of massive jaws. They enclosed their riverside bathing areas and carabao wallows with sturdy bamboo fences to fend off the underwater predators. And to express their terror of sudden violent death from the dark water, they told each other stories of the *balangitaw*, a preternaturally strong crocodile, astonishingly ferocious and rapacious.

But the people of Cotabato also felt an affinity for the crocodiles that prowled their rivers and marshes. Some crocodiles—those with yellow bands around their necks—were believed to be the spirits of dead ancestors and were called *pagali*, kin. Offerings were still left on riverbanks at night to petition them for favors. Spirit crocodiles were also known to be occasional instruments of divine wrath, or *busungan*, punishing individuals who had defied the will of God and the natural order of the world. The most famous case of crocodile-delivered divine retribution in Cotabato was that of Datu Balabaran—the father of Datu Sinsuat and the founder of the Sinsuat clan. In the first years of the twentieth century, Balabaran was on his way to proclaim himself Sultan of Magindanao, a title for which he lacked the requisite noble blood, when a huge crocodile dragged him from his decorated boat on the Tamontaka River and devoured him. Only his severed forearm was recovered, which was brought to his land and buried.

The Magindanaons, the Moros of Cotabato, were not crocodile hunters by tradition. They did not consider the meat of crocodiles edible, and their skins had no commercial value prior to the American period. Only crocodiles identified as man-eaters were actively hunted. But in the early 1930s, a new market developed in Europe and the U.S. for crocodile skins, which prompted the creation of a local crocodile-hunting industry.

It was, in fact, the birth of luxury-brand handbags that changed the nature of the relationship between the people and crocodiles of the Cotabato basin. At the start of the 1930s, long-established European leather-goods companies such as Hermes, Louis Vuitton, Prada, and Gucci, began to expand beyond luggage into creating luxury shoulder bags for women made primarily from crocodile leather. After a wartime hiatus, crocodile handbags became even more popular in the U.S. in the 1950s, led by the market success of the iconic Kelly Bag by Hermes.

Ugalingan Piang, Gumbay's half-brother, was the first to finance upriver Magindanaon hunters, who soon became highly efficient at killing crocodiles, hunting at night from small boats with torches and harpoons. The hunters had noticeably reduced the upriver crocodile population by the time the crocodile skin buyers disappeared with the Japanese occupation. Hunting resumed after the war, and by 1952, Piang was exporting 500 salted raw crocodile skins per month to a tannery in New Jersey.[1] By the end of that decade, the Cotabato crocodile population had collapsed, and hunting had ceased.

Nowhere in Cotabato were the crocodiles larger, more aggressive, or more numerous than in Butiran. So closely associated was Butiran with its crocodiles that it had inspired a famous oath; "May the crocodiles of Butiran devour me if I am not telling the truth." The refugees fleeing to the Butiran swamp in February 1944 were wagering their lives that, in the two years of Japanese occupation, the crocodiles of Butiran had not yet recovered from the depredations of the crocodile hunters.

Among those refugees was Adil's uncle, Abdul Tambis, his father's younger brother. Abdul told him that he had been in the marshes for more than a week with his wife and children, crowded into a tiny dugout canoe. None of the evacuees, he said, had any rice to spare, but he knew of a location on the edge of the swamp where he had seen some recently harvested rice. They agreed that Abdul would guide him there the next morning.

They set off to the southwest before dawn. At this edge of the Cotabato basin, the foothills of the cordillera tumbled straight down to the Butiran swamp, separated from the flooded land only by a narrow verge of grassland. It was through that grassland that Adil and his men and his uncle Abdul walked. They had not gone far before they saw a large Japanese patrol heading toward them from the south with scores of civilians fleeing before them. The Japanese had cleared out a smaller valley to the south of Talayan and were driving its inhabitants into the marshes.

Adil told his men to unfasten one end of their rifle slings and drag their weapons in the tall grass behind them so the Japanese would take them for civilians. As the Japanese neared, he motioned his men down, and now they were creeping through the grass to avoid detection but were also unable to see the enemy because of the civilians all around them. After crawling some distance, they stopped near a group of Magindanaon carabao herders armed with spears to ward off crocodiles, who would attack calves when given the opportunity. Adil stood and asked them in Magindanaon, "Where are the Japanese?" As the words left his mouth, he realized Japanese soldiers were just off to his right within hearing distance. He froze in place, happy to be shielded by a grazing carabao. The herder, clearly petrified, stayed silent.

Adil crouched back down and looked around. Not 40 yards to his right, a Bureau of Constabulary soldier—a Sinsuat man—stood on a large mound of harvested but unthreshed rice while five Japanese soldiers lounged in a nearby open-walled shed. Adil felt his anger swell; the enemy had found the rice first. He pulled his rifle toward him and signaled his men to prepare an ambush. But his uncle began to plead with him in a frantic whisper: "Nephew, please, if you shoot, we'll all die right here, and the civilians too. The Japanese are all around. They'll kill us all before we reach the hills." Adil grimly swallowed his anger and motioned his men back down. But he was still hungry and determined. They lay in the grass for hours, waiting for the Japanese squad to move on, leaving the rice to them, but the soldiers stayed right where they were. Eventually, Adil and his men crawled and then crouched away west toward the nearby foothills, empty-handed and unsatisfied.

When they had reached the cover of the forested hills, Adil chose the trail that led to the house of Guiwan. He knew Guiwan would have rice and would likely know where more could be found. Guiwan was a Tiruray, and the Tiruray's were forest people who had inhabited the jungled highlands for as long as the Magindanaons had occupied the lowlands. A longtime trading partner of his father, Guiwan had aided him in the past. He lived in a small hamlet in a clearing at the confluence of two highland streams not far from Adil's outpost in Sigawa.

The hamlet consisted of eight thatched houses raised high on hardwood stilts and fields of corn and upland rice. The lives of Guiwan and his close kinsmen had been transformed by what had taken place in the nearby Upi Valley in the previous decades, including the establishment of the American agricultural school. His eldest son, Matias, had attended the school with Adil. They were now settled and were using plows and carabaos to plant their fields. But Guiwan still wore his long hair, uncut since his first birthday, wound around his head and tucked into a colorful cotton turban.

* * *

Ten years earlier, Mohammad Adil had traveled with his father from his delta home to the coastal highlands to enroll in the Upi Agricultural School and begin his intermediate education. They bounced on the back of an empty logging truck heading up the Cotabato-Upi Road, which twisted through the blue-gray hills of the Cotabato Cordillera, leaping fast streams and hugging steep ravines. Over the narrow crushed-coral road gouged into thickly-forested slopes, emigrants were moving into the high Upi Valley, and lumber was moving out. The school had been opened by Irving Edwards, who had been a captain in the Philippine Constabulary. Its current principal was another former military man, Colin Mackenzie, who had been spared by Datu Ali.

The school, the road, the settlers, the logging, the appearance of the Upi Valley itself, a green and gold checkerboard of corn and sugarcane fields with crops arrayed in Iowa-straight rows—everything within their view as Mohammad and his father hopped off the logging truck at the end of the road—was set in motion by one man, Irving Edwards. Edwards performed many roles in the colonial government after he left the Philippine Constabulary. He became a teacher and taught Hadji Adil Tambis. He served as Superintendent of Schools for Cotabato, the same post Edward Kuder would eventually hold. He later became chief justice of the provincial court and, for a while, the provincial governor. Still, he was best known as the man who transformed a pristine forested valley in the northern Cotabato Cordillera into a populous agricultural settlement. In 1915, Edwards built the Cotabato-Upi road, opened the Upi Agricultural School, and began advertising for Filipino homesteaders from overpopulated parts of the Philippines to settle in the Upi Valley. At the same time he began commercial logging operations in the valley and invited various church groups to establish missions there.

All of these efforts were directed at a single, specific objective. Edwards had fallen in love with and married a young woman of a local family, the Tenorios. The Tenorios were Tirurays, the native people of the Cotabato Cordillera, but, living close to the delta lowlands, they had been converted to Christianity by Spanish Jesuit missionaries two generations earlier (Tenorio was the family name given them in 1862 when the first family members were baptized). Edwards became fascinated with the Tirurays, about 30,000 in all, who continued to live traditionally in the highland rainforests. He took it as his personal mission to "civilize" and Christianize them. His efforts in the Upi Valley were directed at them—to convince them to come out of the forest, settle down, take up plow agriculture, and, in general, model their lives on the new Christian settlers in the valley.[2]

The Tiruray were forest people and had been for countless generations. They lived by growing mountain rice, yams, corn, and bananas in temporary gardens, and by hunting, fishing, and gathering wild plants and fruits (more than 80 varieties in all). They were nomads who lived in dwellings so quickly constructed of such simple materials that an early chronicler compared them to "the nests of doves." They wore their hair long, dressed in loincloths, and carried blowguns and bows with poison arrows. Both men and women filed and blackened their teeth for beauty, painted their lips and eyes, and wore earrings. Women also wore necklaces and bracelets and anklets, and rings on every finger and they tied tiny tinkling bells at their wrists and around their waists. They worshipped local spirits, consulted shamans, and made charms of grasses, stones, and shells to repel illness, encourage kindness, or "capture the beauty of the moon and stars." They regarded their forest as a sacred place and lived according to their beliefs, treating it with reverence and acting as its caretakers. [3]

*A young Magindanaon man wearing a tubao and carrying a panabas
stands on Irving Edward's road to Upi, 1933*

The Upi Valley that the father and son beheld in 1935 was
not a sacred place. It was surely not a traditional place and the Upi
Agrigultural School perfectly reflected its rapid social and environ-
mental change. By 1935, Magindanaon farmers, including some of
Adil's relatives, were, for the first time in their history, ignoring the
age-old separation of valley people from hill people and venturing
into the uplands from the delta as traditional bonds loosened under
American rule and Irving Edwards' road brought highland and lowland closer together. At the same time, increasing numbers of traditional Tiruray from the northernmost portion of the Cordillera
were abandoning their beloved but dwindling forest and, as Irving
Edwards had hoped, coming into the Upi Valley to settle down. In
the meantime, Filipino emigrants from outside Mindanao continued

to flow into the valley. The 100 or so students in the all-boys agricultural boarding school were roughly evenly divided among Magindanaon Moros, Filipino settlers, and Tirurays. With its volatile mix of students and its location on a wild frontier, Upi Agricultural School was almost certainly the most unusual American boys' boarding school of its day.

As at any boy's boarding school, competition and fighting were prominent features of school life, but Irving Edwards had created a unique environment by bringing together for the very first time boys from three ethnic communities that, for hundreds of years, had only known each other through raiding, exploitation, and warfare. To gauge the explosive potential of that unique environment, try to imagine a boys' boarding school in 1915 located in the hill country of Texas and populated in equal parts by the descendants of Comanche warriors, Anglo settlers, and Mexican farmers—all armed with sharp blades. At Upi Agricultural School, mutual antagonisms didn't just develop among classmates; they had been seeded in the cradle.

Nine years old and still short for his age, Mohammad Adil was the smallest boy at the school when he started. All the boys worked at the school farm every day to pay for their room and board, and the older boys would sometimes carry him piggyback as they walked from the fields. Some of the boys in the intermediate school, especially the Tirurays, were 10 years older than him because they had been late starting school. All the boys had knives in their belts and carried some form of machete for farm work.

Mohammad Adil's strongest memories of his years at Upi Agricultural School were of the drudging work and the fights. The most memorable of those fights was a pitched battle that started over a stolen light bulb. One of the Filipino boys, a bully by the name of Leonardo Solisa, had stolen the precious lightbulb from the room of the Tiruray students. The Tirurays were looked down upon by the other boys, who considered them uncivilized, and they were the usual victims of such stunts. But on this evening they had had enough. The Tirurays asked the Moro students to join forces with them to stop Solisa once and for all, and the Moros, also tired of Solisa's bullying, agreed to help. Although this was primarily a fight among high schoolers, Mohammad, now 11 and still small for his age, rushed to join them because he was anxious to punish Solisa for tormenting the Tirurays, whom he "pitied."

The Tirurays and Moros marched out of their dormitory yelling for Solisa, who had rallied the Filipino boys around him, but not all of them; some had refused to join in because they too were tired of his bullying. Seeing that they were now badly outnumbered, the Filipino boys ran to the nearby house of Mr. Devera, the acting principal, while Mr. McKenzie was away from the school. But Devera had not yet returned home from the school building. The Tiruray and Moro boys surrounded them at the house's front door and grabbed Solisa by the arms. Other boys punched him, and someone yelled to throw him in the well. They began to drag him to the well, but the Filipino boys were pulling him from the other side, and Solisa himself was big and strong and eventually escaped their grip. He and his companions ran back to their dormitory and tied their door shut with a rope. Inside, they picked up their machetes to defend themselves, shouting, "Come and get us!"

In response, the Tiruray and Moro boys ran for their blades and began hacking at the door, trying to get at them. Mohammad ran to his dormitory to find his *panabas*, but when he saw a bamboo spear that a Tiruray boy had made for him, he grabbed it instead. He was one of the only boys in the melee small enough to move easily under the Filipino dormitory, and he did so. Looking up through the bamboo floor slats he saw, by the light of the stolen bulb, Solisa, machete in his hand, directing the other boys to reinforce the door. Solisa's bare feet were impossibly tempting, and Mohammad thrust straight up with his spear. Just as Solisa howled in pain and fell to the floor, a sudden shotgun blast shattered the night and froze every boy in place except Solisa, still rolling and moaning on the bamboo floor. Mr. Devera, recently arrived, had fired his gun in the air to restore order.

As Devera began to make sense of the havoc he had witnessed, he sent young Mohammad Adil ahead to his house. By the time he met him there, he was livid and ready to punish. Devera made the boy lie flat on the kitchen table in his short pants and whipped him hard with a rattan cane across his bare thighs until the cane broke. And with every stroke, he spat the words, "You criminal, you criminal! You Moro, you criminal!" words that stung him just as sharply as the rattan.

Adil was too ashamed to tell his father, but soon enough, his older cousins who were also attending the school spread the word about what Mr. Devera had done and said to him. When his father learned of the incident, he sent two formidable young men with krises in their belts to speak with the acting principal. Within days Devera had left the school and moved away from the Upi Valley forever. Back in the dark hills ten years later, short on food and ammunition and on the run from the Japanese, Adil still felt happier and freer than he ever had while at his old boarding school.

* * *

The war and the Japanese occupation had placed tremendous new stresses on the Tiruray, both the traditional nomads who had retreated deeper into the forest and those who had settled in permanent communities and taken up plow agriculture. Despite their physical isolation, the forest-dwelling Tiruray had, for hundreds of years, been tied into a global trade system in much the same way as the lowland crocodile hunters of Cotabato because their upland rainforests provided wild products valued by faraway purchasers. For nearly a hundred years, the Tiruray had brought tree saps—gutta-percha and almaciga—to a small number of trusted lowland traders waiting at the edge of the forest. Gutta-percha was a natural plastic used for insulation, most importantly in the first transatlantic telegraph cable. Almaciga, the hard resin of the almaciga tree, was used to make a maritime varnish highly valued by European shipbuilders. For centuries, buyers far off in Europe had also valued the beeswax, rattan, and rare hardwoods that the Tiruray brought to the edge of the forest to trade. In return, they received the cloth and iron implements, and salt they needed but could not produce themselves.[4]

With their trade networks disrupted, the Tirurays faced new privations, and with new armed groups penetrating their forests, they encountered new dangers. For the most part, they disappeared in response to the threat of armed violence, but occasionally, they responded differently. In his debriefing in Australia, Edward Kuder reported more than one successful ambush of small Japanese patrols by Tirurays armed with bows and arrows. Of the thousands of Japanese soldiers who died in the jungles of the Philippines, a few, to their surprise, were killed by poison arrows shot from the bows of long-haired forest nomads.

The sedentary Tirurays of the highlands faced different difficulties. Because they could no longer easily disappear into the forest, they were in constant danger of having their crops stolen or their labor exploited by both the Japanese and the guerrillas. Guiwan, who was well-respected and well-connected in the highlands, needed protection from the new marauders as much as any settled Tiruray. Nothing happened anywhere in the cordillera without him knowing about it. He provided valuable information to the young guerrilla officer who, like his father, was a lowlander who could be trusted. In exchange, the presence of Adil's men kept bandits at bay and had not yet drawn the attention of the Japanese.

Adil liked spending time in Guiwan's hamlet because of what he could learn there and because of Guiwan's beautiful daughter Yamani. With her long hair tied up in a colorful scarf, she would cook *kamote* (sweet potatoes) for him and his men. Bright beaded necklaces hung to her waist, and brass bangles encircled her forearms from wrist to elbow. She wore a high-waisted blouse and a *malong* of simple but vibrantly colored cotton, and she always had a sweet smile for him. His men told him, "you really should marry that girl."

Guiwan greeted Adil warmly. He had a small amount of rice to spare, and Adil assigned two men to carry it back to Captain Guballa. Guiwan told him that he might find more rice at Muti, another small Tiruray hamlet further into the hills. He also warned him that Japanese patrols had been combing the highlands searching for guerrillas who had escaped from Gumbay Piang's camp.

Adil was not surprised to hear this. At a Magindanaon settlement they had passed on the way to Guiwan's hamlet, two of the villagers led them to the badly mangled body of a guerrilla lying face down midway up a nearby ridge. Two large monitor lizards were picking and pulling the flesh from the corpse where the Japanese bullets had pierced the skin, retreating resentfully only when Adil approached and turned the body over. It was the first guerrilla casualty he had ever seen and the bloated face that stared blankly back at him, he realized with a shock, belonged to his second cousin, Baguio, who was nearly his same age. Baguio had escaped the Japanese attack on Gumbay Piang's headquarters only to die on this lonely hillside.[5]

His cousin had fired his shotgun at his pursuers from the base of the ridge, then tried to escape by running up and over it but only made it halfway. The Japanese had cut him to pieces with gunfire. Seeing his cousin's corpse brought home to him what others, including his uncle, had tried to teach him. It was essential for guerrillas, who were always outgunned, to have a viable means of escape. He had been foolish to ignore it, but he had been lucky to be surrounded by more experienced fighters. They buried his cousin there, and as they walked back through the settlement, he angrily berated the inhabitants for leaving a fellow Muslim unburied.

They stayed the night at Guiwan's hamlet and set off the next morning in the dark to arrive in Muti with the first light. Muti was a Tiruray hamlet of four houses sitting on four graduated knolls that formed a large half-circle. The knolls enclosed a cleared valley of about 10 acres planted in foot-high tobacco. The hamlet was silent and empty. There was no rice to be found and not a soul in sight.

Adil decided to wait for the inhabitants to return with their rice or, better yet, for the Japanese patrol that had killed his cousin to pass by. He had his six best men with him, and he deployed them across the four knolls, with Hadji Hashim and himself taking the highest knoll, the one with the best view of the trail from the bottom of the valley. He told his men to dig in and camouflage themselves. He and Hadji Hashim settled into a drying shed, hiding beneath dried sheaves of broad brown tobacco leaves.

Shortly after seven in the morning, six Japanese soldiers came into sight, walking from the bottom of the valley. They entered the tobacco field with their eyes to the ground, apparently tracking footprints across it. When they were all in the open, now moving toward the knolls less than a hundred yards away, Adil sighted his Springfield on the lead man and fired. This time, he knew immediately that he had killed him. His men, following his lead, opened fire as Adil tracked and shot a second Japanese soldier and watched him slump to the ground.

They continued firing until all six members of the Japanese patrol lay motionless among the tobacco plants. Adil was about to leave his hiding place under the tobacco leaves when an entire Japanese infantry platoon—more than twenty soldiers—suddenly appeared at the bottom of the valley, advancing up the trail through the field at a run. The soldiers they had ambushed had been advance scouts for a larger force that was now shouting and pouring gunfire at their positions on the knolls.

It was Adil's first experience under enemy fire, and it was more terrifying than he had imagined. The drying shack was disintegrating under a furious hail of high-powered rounds as shredded tobacco leaves, bamboo, and palm thatch rained down on them. But after a few moments, a feeling other than terror also seized him—a wild exhilaration like nothing he had felt before, a sense of indestructibility. He threw off the tobacco sheaves, stood tall, and shouted for his men to advance against the Japanese.

Hadji Hashim, who had once been possessed by the same feeling, immediately pulled him back down. Turning Adil to face him, he shouted over the gunfire, "No, no, that is *takabbur*! That is arrogance! Do not tempt fate!" Hearing Hadji Hashim's insistent voice, Adil found his head again, shaking off the feeling of invulnerability and remembering his men. He passed the order to fall back just as the Japanese platoon's light mortars found their range, and percussion grenades began falling on the four knolls. The guerrillas withdrew one by one under covering fire, using the terrain to their benefit, each man racing down the back slope of his knoll to the forest and a Tiruray trail that led them deeper into the highlands.

Adil set a rearguard to watch for the Japanese to follow, but they did not advance into the forest beyond the knolls, likely out of fear of walking into another ambush. When he was sure that the Japanese patrol was not in pursuit, Adil halted his men, and they rested for most of the day on a ridge with a good view of the trail. Later in the afternoon, they ventured back to Muti to retrieve the knapsacks they had left behind in the undergrowth when they withdrew. The Japanese had returned to the Talayan Valley, and the hamlet was again empty. They recovered all the packs but one, which had been found by their pursuers and contained some of Adil's possessions, including photographs. The Japanese and their Sinsuat collaborators later displayed the photographs widely, claiming that they had killed him. His father and stepmother were devastated, believing him dead, and held a solemn funeral feast for him. When the truth became known, it launched his reputation as a young man with powerful protective magic. It also made him a wanted man.

Moving out from Muti for the second time that day, Adil, who was walking at the head of the column, saw an apparition on the trail ahead. He raised his rifle at the peculiar sight. It was a man, but with his head thrust far to one side, almost sitting on his shoulder. His elbows were pressed tightly to his sides, and he walked with a jerking, halting gait that reminded Adil of a Frankenstein movie he had seen in high school.

As they approached the man, the air reeked of putrefying flesh. He had a gaping bayonet wound in his neck oozing blood, and his trunk had been wrapped with copper wire, binding his arms to his body. The skin around the wire had swollen, and burst and maggots were crawling in the wounds. The others stood back from this zombie-like creature and told Adil to shoot him to end his misery quickly, but he couldn't do it. Instead, he cut the wire and pulled it carefully away from the man. Then he found a stalk of wild elephant ear taro, which the Tirurays used as a disinfectant, and squeezed the juice from it. He rubbed the juice on the man's arms and dressed the wound in his neck, and gradually the odor of death dissipated.

By the next day, the swelling in the man's arms had subsided, and he was able to speak. He told Adil his name was Leopoldo Aguirre. Along with two other guerrillas, he had been captured a few days earlier by the same Japanese patrol they had ambushed at Muti. The men were bound and forced to guide the Japanese through the hills, and when they were no longer of use, the soldiers had bayonetted them and left them to die at the side of the trail. Aguirre alone had survived, and he had been walking for hours to find help. He told Adil that he wanted to join his unit when he recovered, but he never fully mended, dying of his wounds seven months later.[6]

Because the main guerrilla camp and Adil's outpost were occupied by the Japanese, they slept that night in a refuge camp higher in the hills, which could only be reached by wading up a creek for more than 100 yards. Early the following day, they heard the splash of footsteps in the water coming toward them from downstream. Adil sought the cover of a nearby mango tree overhanging the creek and took aim at the lead figure as he came into sight. He lowered his rifle when he recognized Gumbay Piang, who was carrying the M1 carbine presented to him by Colonel Fertig, the first one given to any Moro.

Gumbay had avoided capture by the Japanese but was exhausted and barely able to walk. His command was scattered, and he had only two companions, one of them wounded in the leg and the other an old man armed only with a rusty shotgun. Adil ran through the creek to meet him, shouting to his men that Captain Piang had arrived. He helped carry Gumbay, wheezing and gasping for air from a severe asthma attack to a nearby hut. Between gulps of air, he cried and cursed. "How shameful that the clansmen of Amai Mingka should surrender to their enemies!"

Adil asked his commander about the reports of surrenders. Piang replied bitterly that it was true. His chief of security, Mamasu, was caught completely unaware by the attack and, leaving his guns behind, escaped in his underwear. A few days later, likely expecting to be blamed by Piang for their headquarters being overrun, he surrendered to the Japanese in Dulawan. Since the attack on his headquarters less than a week ago, his most prominent half-brothers had all signed or renewed cooperation agreements with the Japanese. And Gumbay's beloved younger brother—the brave and capable Pindililang, who had paralyzed the invasion force at Digos with his Bolo Battalion—was dead; betrayed by a fellow Moro, lured into an ambush, and killed by the Japanese. As with Datu Ali, only treachery had allowed the invaders to catch and kill him.[7]

Gumbay was now the only Piang still openly fighting the Japanese, and, with his men scattered and communication lines disrupted he did not know how much longer he could hold out. That he should be the last Piang brother fighting was an unexpected outcome, for he had not trained to be a warrior or a leader of men. His brothers, following their father's lead, had learned to be political leaders, warriors, or traders. Gumbay was the only one of Datu Piang's sons to choose a different path. At the University of the Philippines, where his father had sent him, he studied anthropology and education. Like his two American mentors, Joseph Hayden and Edward Kuder, he was a scholar by inclination. He had an abiding curiosity about the cultural history of his people, the Magindanaons of the Cotabato

Basin, and an ability to write beautiful English prose. We know the full story of Datu Ali's uprising against the Americans only because of Gumbay Piang.

He was also a natural educator who, like Edward Kuder, was convinced of the absolute value of Western education. In 1934, he wrote an open letter to the recalcitrant Magindanaon parents who still refused to send their children to the American schools. In it, he reminded them how much cultural change had already occurred in the previous 30 years.

> When I was a little boy, I was told that I would not be able to atone for the sin I committed by eating rice which was milled by a machine. Yet, the very persons who told me that idea are the owners of rice mills today in our communities.
>
> When I was a little boy, I was made to throw away the first pair of shoes I had because it was against our customs and traditions to wear shoes—there is practically not a single hadji at this time who does not own a pair of shoes.
>
> I learned from my mother that it was wrong for panditas and hadjis to sell anything... Now...our best merchants and peddlers are panditas and hadjis.[8]

Like his good friend Hadji Adil Tambis, Gumbay Piang believed in following the American path to the future because he had experienced the practical benefits of that path. But he was no less a Moro for it. He indeed followed the Americans into a Japanese prison camp—he may have been the only Moro to do so—but his decision likely hinged as much on *maratabat* as on the orders of his American superiors. Gumbay Piang was a close aide and friend to the American Brigadier General Vachon, and Vachon, though he hated the idea, was required by his orders to surrender. Gumbay Piang was required by *maratabat* to uphold personal loyalty. Surrender without defeat was a violation of *maratabat*, but just as great a violation was the abandonment of a commander and comrade.

His decision to surrender with the American troops, as well as his decision to join the American-led guerrilla resistance rather than collaborate with the Japanese, may very well have ruined his fragile health and cost him his life. He became a congressman for Cotabato Province after the war but was only 39 years old when he died of respiratory illness a few years later in 1949. His promise as a writer and educator died with him, as did the political prominence of the entire Piang clan.

But there in the refuge camp in early 1944, Gumbay Piang and his 119th guerrilla regiment, thanks in large part to young 3rd Lt. Adil, were badly battered but not broken. Adil had found rice for the guerrillas but had provided an even more important service by ambushing their pursuers. He had raised the morale of what was left of the regiment and sent the Japanese invaders a message that no matter how aggressive they became, they would always be prey in the homeland of the Moros. Now Mohammad Adil was nursing his commander back to health and more loyal kinsmen were arriving at the refuge each day bringing food and weapons. Gradually the regiment regrouped—smaller, but more disciplined and better armed.

Though Gumbay Piang and his men knew little of it, the allied forces fighting the Japanese in the greater Pacific War were also finding their situation improving after their initial disasters. In the Central Pacific in February 1944, the U.S. Navy launched Operation Hailstone, a massive air and sea assault against the stronghold of Truk, one of the strategic islands that Japan relied on to surround, and now defend, the Philippines. The Americans destroyed 40 ships and 250 aircraft and effectively removed Truk as a threat.

In late February, in the Southwest Pacific, Douglas MacArthur surprised his staff by announcing that he would accompany an advanced assault group on a "reconnaissance in force" to the island of Los Negros, one of the Admiralty Islands, an archipelago lying 200 miles northeast of New Guinea. It was a risky decision. MacArthur hadn't joined an assault force since his days on the Western Front in the First World War. But on February 27th, he observed the landing from a cruiser and then followed his troops ashore. He had wanted to be there personally for the landing because Los Negros held special significance for him. Its magnificent protected harbor would be his forward base for the reinvasion of the Philippines via Mindanao.

A few weeks later, Edward Kuder was making his way across the Pacific, in his case, toward the U.S. mainland. He had survived a submarine trip and emergency surgery in Australia. Now he was island-hopping by plane to San Francisco, where he would undergo a second and a third surgery to repair critical damage from the tropical disease that kept trying to kill him.

* * *

At his home in Tamontaka, Mohammad Adil would tell me his stories across a low table in his cool, dark sitting room, or under the imposing mango tree in his front yard, or at his dining room table, where his wife served extraordinary meals, often with ingredients from his gardens. Sometimes we would walk through his land beside a narrow river where fishermen threw nets from slender dugouts, across rice fields, and along garden patches of taro and okra.

Gradually, he began to show me papers from the back room where he would occasionally go to rummage; sometimes just one or two greyed sheets at a time, at other times, thick stacks. As I read them, I realized with amazement that I was looking at the historical record of the Moro anti-Japanese resistance in Cotabato. Over 50 years, through innumerable military postings that required changes of residence, and despite the challenges of a tropical climate and the ravages of a war on the Moros in the 1970s brought on by the dictator Marcos, he had preserved original documents, some of them created in his guerrilla camp in the hills above Talayan.

A few came from the earliest days of the war. There was an order from Brigadier General Vachon on January 21st, 1942, announcing the appointments of Pindililang Piang and Udtug Matalam, the leaders of the two Bolo Battalions at Digos, as First Lieutenants in the USAFFE. I also read a February 25, 1942 telegram message from Gumbay Piang to Douglas MacArthur on the occasion of Washington's Birthday.

> *The old friendship of our families remain [sic] unshaken..*
> *The...Moros enlisted as Bolomen and I greet their great com-*
> *manding general and join their brave comrades of Bataan in*
> *celebrating the birthday of the father of the American nation.*
> *MacArthur replied:*
> *For Datu Gumbay Piang: I and my comrades in arms*
> *in Bataan and other parts of the Philippines are deeply*
> *inspired by the words of loyalty in your...birthday message.*
> *Your devotion and patriotism will have its full reward in the*
> *liberty and freedom which will be yours when we success-*
> *fully expel the invaders from these shores. Ultimate victory is*
> *certain.*

From the last days of the war, Adil also showed me a casualty roster for Gumbay Piang's 119th regiment listing the 43 guerrillas who lost their lives fighting the Japanese invaders under his leadership. They included his younger brother Pindililang and his nephew, Guialudin Piang. Gumbay Piang, who initiated the memo, could not have known that in a few short years he as well would become an indirect casualty of the war.

7
ESCAPE

When his illness flared again in September of 1943, Edward Kuder lost even more weight, and by mid-month he was so weak he could no longer walk the 200 yards from home to office. On September 29th, the day before Gumbay Piang returned to Cotabato from Fertig's headquarters carrying his new commission, Edward Kuder was told that he would be leaving immediately on a submarine to Australia. If he stayed, the medical officer had informed Fertig, he would quickly die. He had time only to gather a few papers before boarding a launch that evening to take him to the submarine waiting at the dark mouth of Panguil Bay. His friends, Moros, Filipinos, and Americans, had followed the launch in small boats to see him off and when he said goodbye to them, he was more "emotionally stirred" than ever before in his life, but also, he later recalled, "so sick and exhausted that I was afraid to fully express my feelings for fear that I would completely collapse."[1]

He climbed with difficulty up the rope ladder that hung over the side of the dark hull, then made his way through a hatchway and down into the submarine. Inside, he sat wide-eyed with exhaustion and watched two sailors paint three small Japanese flags on the riveted inner hull. Eventually, he was led to his bunk in a forward compartment, and he did not leave it again, even at mealtimes, for the entire journey to Australia.

He was being carried nearly 3000 miles south, through the Makassar Strait and along the edge of the Indian Ocean to Perth by the U.S.S. Bowfin, which was on its very first patrol of the Pacific War and its only mission to support the Mindanao guerrillas. Earlier in the month the Bowfin, skippered by Lt. Commander Joseph Willingham, had delivered its cargo, which included a shipment of newly-developed M2 automatic carbines, to Fertig's headquarters before heading out to hunt in the Japanese shipping lanes of the South China Sea. A few days before returning to Mindanao to take on its passengers, it had made its first kills—sinking or mortally damaging a Japanese freighter, a troop transport, and a tanker, and earning the first three flags on its inner hull.

Kuder's eight fellow evacuees included Samuel Grashio, an American fighter pilot who had survived the Bataan Death March and escaped from a Japanese prison camp in Davao to join the Mindanao guerrillas. Three crew members of the PT boat that had brought MacArthur from Corregidor to Mindanao were also on board. They had ignored the May 1942 order to surrender and fought with the guerrillas instead. The only Filipino passenger was Captain Luis Morgan, whom Fertig was exiling to Australia to remove him as a threat to his leadership, ignoring MacArthur's express orders to the contrary. MacArthur had sent a radio message to Fertig on September 28th specifically denying his request to send Morgan to Australia by submarine. Fertig, claiming not to have received the message in time, sent him anyway, noting in his diary for September 29th, 1943 that, "It was too late for the easiest solution of Morgan was to send him out...." Reflecting on seeing off the submarine that held both Morgan and Kuder, Fertig added, "there in that thin steel shell are some of my biggest problems, some friends, and my letters to my loved ones."[2]

Early the following morning, the Bowfin got its fourth kill by using its four-inch deck gun to sink a Japanese troop barge carrying more than 100 soldiers. The submarine then continued south, leaving the surviving Japanese soldiers struggling in the water miles from any shore.[3] It was another ordinary encounter in a Pacific war overflowing with casual brutality.

Ten days later, the Bowfin docked at Perth in Western Australia. Edward Kuder, now unable to walk at all, was carried ashore on a stretcher and taken straight to a local hospital, where doctors observed him for a week before diagnosing an abscessed liver. When they operated, Kuder recounted, "they removed seventy-two ounces of pus from my body," telling him that "it was a record of some kind." When he had recovered enough to travel, they flew him 1,700 miles east across the desolate Nullarbor Plain to Melbourne on the Tasman Sea. His plane refueled before continuing another 850 miles up the eastern coast to Brisbane, where MacArthur had his headquarters. In addition to 3000 miles of sea, he had now put a continent between himself and the Japanese-occupied Philippines.[4]

The details of Kuder's stay in Brisbane are unclear, including when he arrived and when he left for the U.S. mainland. The military had imposed a communication blackout on evacuees from the Philippines to avoid alerting the Japanese to any further evacuations. Kuder was not allowed to write his family or friends in the U.S. to let them know that he was alive and safe. Almost two years earlier, in late January of 1942, his mother had contacted the Red Cross seeking information about him. Four months later, presuming him dead, she had sought to collect on his government life insurance only to learn that it had lapsed. Kuder had borrowed on each of his two policies in the mid-1930s, presumably to pay back the money he had borrowed for the Philippine Supreme Court case. He had never repaid the loans. His insurance expired in 1937.[5] Because of strict military censorship at MacArthur's headquarters; he was also not allowed to take any written materials with him when he left Brisbane, not even his journal.

What is certain about Kuder's time in Brisbane is that most of it was spent being debriefed by Joseph Hayden, whom MacArthur had brought over from the Office of Strategic Services (O.S.S) to act as his advisor on Philippine affairs. Hayden was MacArthur's point of contact with the guerrillas in Mindanao. Every radio message from Fertig's headquarters came across his desk, and he drafted replies signed by MacArthur. Hayden also organized the evacuations by submarine. It is likely that he personally approved the evacuation of Kuder to save the life of his former colleague in the colonial service, but also because of the uniquely valuable information he possessed.

Hayden, a professor of Political Science at the University of Michigan, was both a scholar of the Philippine colony and a high-level colonial administrator before joining the wartime O.S.S. From 1933 to 1935, he had served as Vice Governor and Secretary of Public Instruction of the Philippines, and as such, was Kuder's immediate superior. He was also one of the few American colonial officials other than Kuder with significant knowledge of Mindanao and Sulu and its politics. He had traveled throughout the region and, through Kuder, he had met and corresponded with Salipada Pendatun and Gumbay Piang. In what was a rare occurrence of maximum military efficiency in wartime, there was simply no one better qualified to debrief Edward Kuder on conditions in occupied Mindanao than his friend and former supervisor Joseph Hayden.

Mindanao was key to MacArthur's strategy to retake the Philippines. It was the southernmost island, it had the largest and strongest guerrilla force, and it possessed the only large airfield outside of the capital region. High-quality intelligence about current conditions in Mindanao was essential, and Edward Kuder was the man to provide it. Chick Parsons, who was in Brisbane at the same time as Kuder, knew more about military matters in Mindanao, but Kuder was the person with extensive knowledge of the political and economic landscape, the attitudes of the Moros, and the propaganda efforts of the Japanese.

Hayden and Kuder produced an extraordinarily detailed report primarily focused on the province of Lanao before and during the war but also covering events and issues throughout Mindanao. Hayden wrote the report but Kuder, still recuperating, edited the entire document and wrote most of the appendices and recommendations himself. Relying only on his memory and the few papers he could gather before boarding the submarine, Kuder not only related his own experiences but provided information on the political sympathies and activities of almost every former official or prominent person in the Moro provinces of Mindanao. With the cold calculus of an intelligence asset, he identified collaborators, resisters, and untrustworthy neutrals among his colleagues, former students and employees, acquaintances and friends.[6]

MacArthur and his staff were particularly concerned with how the people of Mindanao, and the country as a whole, would respond to the American invasion. Would they fight? Remain neutral? Aid the enemy? In one of his appendices (written in the third person),

Kuder addressed that question directly, and he used a personal anecdote to do so. A section of the report titled "Filipino gratitude to individual American benefactors" begins:

> In June of 1938, a small Moro boy in Cotabato
> province got 15 pesos from his father for his 'expenses'
> in connection with the closing exercises of his sev-
> enth-grade class. Instead of attending the closing
> exercises, he bought a 3rd class ticket on an inter-island
> steamer and a few days later presented himself to Mr.
> Kuder, then stationed in Sulu.

Kuder had chosen Mohammad Adil—whom he had taken into his household and sponsored through high school—as his exemplar of "Filipino gratitude." Their first meeting, more than five years earlier, had left an indelible impression on him, but he chose another story to illustrate his point:

> At an entertainment in the High School auditorium
> some time [after that first meeting], a sudden uproar in
> the back caused Mr. Kuder to leave his front-row seat to
> investigate. He found a stranger with a badly mussed-up
> once nice sharkskin suit and a bruised face, with a furious
> Mocamad, forcibly restrained by onlookers, still flailing
> away in his efforts to get loose and finish the job. The
> stranger turned out to be a petty government employee
> who had commented to a companion on the amusing
> appearance of Mr. Kuder's partly unthatched head seen
> from the rear.

Adil, sitting directly behind the man, and angered beyond words at his quip, had stood up and punched him, and the ruckus began. The boxing lessons had paid off.[7]

Kuder's story was, of course, intended as an analogy. Just as the 13-year-old Mohammad Adil had defended his benefactor out of "loyalty and gratitude," so many thousands of other Filipinos who were benefited directly or indirectly by American colonizers had been willing to fight for the U.S. and to shelter American soldiers and civilians after the ignominious U.S. defeat and surrender. It was a sincere analogy and an inapt one. The great majority of American colonialists had no informal social relations with Filipinos. The journalist Florence Horn observed the extent of that social separation during her extended trip to the Philippines in 1940:

> Americans insulate themselves as thoroughly as
> possible against the life of the country they are in. ...
> Their knowledge of Filipinos is limited to their houseboy
> and chauffeur...and...[they] berate the miserable natives
> bitterly and endlessly."[8]

The colonialists' interactions with Filipinos were entirely formal and impersonal and rarely if ever included helping individual Filipinos in any significant way. Kuder and MacArthur were rare exceptions in that regard. Most Filipinos and Moros resisted the Japanese not out of "loyalty and gratitude" to Americans but because the Japanese were such brutal occupiers and they believed MacArthur when he said that he would return. Most Filipinos who assisted Americans in hiding did so in exchange for desperately needed resources.

Kuder's analogy was somewhat inapt even with respect to his foster son. Although, in general, Mohammad Adil felt significant "loyalty and gratitude" toward Edward Kuder, those sentiments probably did not motivate his actions in this instance. He regarded Kuder as his foster father, and any insult to Kuder violated his honor. It was *maratabat* that sparked Adil's anger and motivated his newly-trained fists to fly. In the end, it didn't matter why Filipinos and Moros supported the American return, only that they did. But the story that Kuder told himself and others, including MacArthur—with Adil in a starring role—was likely comforting to those whose overseas colony had been seized from them by an upstart Asian empire.

By March of 1944, Edward Kuder was heading to the United States mainland, where he had not set foot for 12 years. He traveled, as did his fellow evacuee Samuel Grashio, by air from Brisbane to San Francisco. Staying south to avoid the still-vast Japanese-held zone that stretched from New Guinea to China and from Burma to Guam, the plane hopped across the South Pacific from one island way-station to another: New Caledonia, Fiji, tiny Kanton and Christmas Islands, Oahu in Hawaii, and then the final leg to the U.S. mainland and through the Golden Gate to land at last at Crissy Field at the edge of San Francisco Bay on the Presidio military base. Kuder's flight may have been a medical evacuation because he appears to have been taken straight to the U.S. Marine Hospital, a federal public health service hospital for civilians tucked away in a quiet corner of the bustling Presidio. He underwent two more surgeries in the next few months and convalesced looking out over the relatively quiet northwest quarter of the war-busy city.

From the upper floors of the hillside hospital, an urban panorama would have greeted him when not obscured by fog rolling in from the southwest. Straight ahead, Golden Gate Park, an unbroken band of green more than three miles long, stretched east to west from the city's central heights to its ocean shore. In the long valley between the hospital and the park, three-story Edwardians crowded the streets of the Richmond District. Away to his left, on Lone Mountain, rose the campanile of the San Francisco College for Women and the nearby spires of St. Ignatius church. And far off to his right, the pastel mansions of Seacliff looked west to China Beach and the Pacific Ocean, whose steel-blue swells had also travelled from Mindanao.

Kuder's principal concern, after his health, was the state of his finances. He had been in debt and scraping by before the war. Now he was destitute. The only salary he had drawn in more than three years was nine months of half-pay in ersatz money that he had printed himself using wooden plates and paper delivered by submarine. On his return to the U.S., Kuder had learned of a congressional bill authorizing the federal government to pay and hold the full salaries of all its employees detained by the enemy. He wrote to the Auditor General of the Philippine Commonwealth in Washington D.C. and requested his back pay, noting that, although he had not been detained, his situation was comparable.

When the Auditor General replied asking for more detail, Kuder responded that, although the colonial administration in Lanao had been disbanded by the Japanese, he had remained in the province and "rendered service in helping hold a large part of the Lanao population loyal to our cause…and raising armed resistance, where feasible, among the Lanao people against the enemy." Even with the financial stakes as high as they were, he could not resist adding a qualifier.

> The uprising in Lanao was a real and spontaneous fight
> for freedom and their homeland against the invader by the
> Filipino people — Christians and Mohammedans both. It
> would have happened if I had never been there. But I *did* do
> what I could to help start it and keep it going.[9]

By mid-July 1944 he had been discharged from the hospital and was traveling east to collect his compensation, having borrowed

$200 from his brother Ted to make the trip. The Philippine Com-
monwealth had granted him $2,625 in back pay and the check was
waiting at his family home in Pennsylvania. He was too late to see
his parents alive. His father had died in 1935, after Kuder's last visit
home. His mother lived until the previous February, less than a
month before he arrived in the U.S. Because of strict military censorship, she likely died never knowing that her son was alive and safe
and had escaped the Philippines.

* * *

Edward Kuder's family roots ran deep in American soil. The Kuders
had been in Pennsylvania for five generations, and his mother, born
in Alabama, could trace her descent from a Virginian Revolutionary
War officer. His parents, however, had spent a good deal of their
adult lives in a foreign land. His father, Calvin Kuder, was ordained
a Lutheran minister in May of 1891, married Mattie Ferguson that
summer in Salem, Virginia, and two weeks later set sail with her for
India. They were part of an American foreign missionary movement
building momentum since the mid-nineteenth century and now in
full surge. Their destination was an American Evangelical Lutheran
mission in Madras, first established in 1851, where Calvin Kuder
had been commissioned as the new principal of the elementary and
middle school.

By 1896, Mattie Kuder had borne three children at the mission,
the youngest of whom, Mary, died there at six months. Soon after,
Mattie, "on account of weakness," left Madras with her two surviving children, arriving at her parents' home in Salem in the spring of
1896. A few weeks after her arrival, she gave birth to Edward, her
fourth child and the first one not born in India. A little more than
a year later, when she returned to the mission and her husband, she

carried her baby son aboard the ship bound for Madras but left her two other sons, four and five years old, behind in Salem to be cared for by her parents. It was time for the boys to begin their education, but she may also have been trying to shield them from the fate of their younger sister Mary.[10]

Edward Kuder's earliest memories were of India. His strongest, he told Adil, was of a Hindu street magician, who raised his cupped hands above an empty basket and brought forth a miniature mango tree with real fruit, grown in an instant from thin air. He had limited time to make memories because by the end of 1898, when he was not yet three, his father had fallen ill, and the family, which now included Edward's baby brother, sailed home to the U.S.

For the next nine years, the family lived together in Pennsylvania, where Calvin served as pastor at various congregations and Edward acquired four more younger siblings. Mattie now had eight children to care for. Then, on the first day of 1908, his father sailed alone from New York to resume his work at the mission, staying away for five years until he returned in 1913 to collect his wife and three youngest children and bring them back to Madras with him. Edward, age 16, and his two younger brothers lived with their grandparents in Salem until his parents finally returned permanently to Pennsylvania at the end of 1916.

By that time, Edward Kuder had graduated from Salem's Roanoke College, his father's alma mater, and begun teaching high school in West Palm Beach, Florida. When the U.S. entered the First World War, he joined the army as a private in September 1917, serving stateside, and leaving the army at war's end as a second lieutenant of artillery. After his discharge in January 1919, he moved to Flint, Michigan, where he worked in the offices of the Buick plant before talking to a government recruiter, taking the civil service exam, and signing on to teach in the Philippines.

He was, it could hardly be denied, following in his father's footsteps, and his return to Asia had not been a sudden decision. In his college yearbook, his classmates had nicknamed him "Shanghai" and predicted that he would "win fame as a teacher in the Orient." Like his father, he had graduated from Roanoke and taken an assignment as a school principal on the other side of the world. And like his father, he was also a scholar by inclination, fascinated by language and culture.

In a 1914 book presenting the history of the Madras mission, Calvin Kuder, the primary author of this co-authored work, provides a detailed description of the way of life of the two and a half million Telugu-speakers of southern India—"the...population for whose Christianization we feel responsible." The elder Kuder does not disguise his admiration for the "musical" Telugu language (he had just finished translating the Lutheran Church Book into Telugu). But neither does he hide his disdain for Telugu religion, a local expression of Hinduism consisting, to his mind, of "the most absurd superstitions, the grossest sensuality, the subtlest dishonesty, and the most inhumane religious practices." The individuals whom he lived among, taught, and supervised for more than 15 years—very few of whom ever converted to Christianity—were, in his estimation, "spiritually benighted and morally degraded."[11] Edward Kuder wrote of his admiration for his father, remembering him in a letter to his mother shortly after his death in 1935 as "a good soldier, rigidly honest, the kindest father to all of us, and a true son of God." But the gap between father and son was epochal. Calvin Kuder was a man of the previous century and its activist Protestant expansionism. He was a "good soldier" in the American missionary movement to evangelize the world, and he readily sacrificed himself, as well as his wife and children, to that cause. [12]

Edward, a teacher like his father, also sought to spread the gospel of American civilization to Asia, but he felt no compulsion to preach Christianity and no responsibility to save souls. He viewed the world through the lens of a new century. Like his father, he had an unwavering conviction in his superiority as a white man and an American. But he had also been influenced by a new American science—in effect, a new secular creed—that opposed American evangelism. Cultural anthropology, exemplified in the widely-read works of Franz Boas, Ruth Benedict, and Margaret Mead, taught that each culture had its own moral imperatives and that it was wrong to denigrate the beliefs and values of a culture different from one's own.

In his official memos and letters about the Moros, Edward Kuder employed the language and precepts of cultural anthropology. He declared the Moros to be "interesting, likable, and vital people." He corrected those who called them uncultured, noting that the better term was "differently cultured"; and he sought to hire American and Filipino teachers who could "disassociate themselves from their own...cultural bias sufficiently to acquire a correct...view of the local culture."[13] He may have followed his father to Asia, but, once there, he strode adamantly in the opposite direction—rejecting Christian proselytizing just as vigorously as Calvin Kuder had pursued it.

Edward Kuder did not devote himself to saving Moro souls. Instead, he committed to improving the well-being of Moros, all the while convinced of the rightness of America's overall imperialist project in the Philippines. Though soft-spoken, he wielded a sharp pen, and his memoranda bristled with complaints and criticisms. It was a "mistaken idea" that Moros should be tracked into vocational schools and a "deplorable pander to expediency" to shorten their high school curriculum. Moros were being denied training and employment opportunities and equal access to land ownership because of the "thick passiveness" or "skullduggery" of colonial bureaucrats.

He knew he was racing the clock. America's colonial rule in the Philippines was scheduled to end before the halfway mark of the twentieth century. It was to be replaced by a single Philippine nation—one that, for the first time in their shared history in the archipelago, would bind Moros and Filipinos together under a single government. Moros had been somewhat protected under U.S. rule, but in the Philippine Republic there would be no buffer from the demographic and cultural domination of Filipinos. Kuder had been preparing the Moros to be a national minority, using education to inculcate them with "compatible" values. But he was also working to remove impediments and carve out opportunities for them—including his foster sons—before the arrival of the new nation.

* * *

Edward Kuder spent the rest of the war on the east coast, most of it in Washington D.C., the global capital of the allied war effort. There he stayed with his Salem cousin, Claudine Ferguson, in her fourth-floor apartment in Mt. Pleasant, which had a view of the neighboring National Zoo. By the time he arrived in August 1944, the district's mood had brightened with news of crucial victories on both American fronts. In Europe, all four allied invasion armies had broken out of the Normandy beachhead and advanced rapidly toward the River Seine and Paris. In the Pacific, U.S. Marines had captured Saipan and the rest of the Mariana Islands, putting American heavy bombers, for the first time, within easy striking distance of the Japanese mainland.

In the last weeks of that muggy, war-weary summer, district residents could, for the first time in almost three years, sense a palpable shift in allied fortunes, and the more optimistic among them even began to imagine life after victory. In the meantime, as Claudine wrote to her Aunt Mattie, they continued "working overtime, struggling onto crowded buses and streetcars, standing in long lines to get a bite at lunch time, and going to cheap out-of-door concerts in the evening." D.C. was, she said, "a jostling, hurrying, mixed-up mess."[14]

Amid that mess, Edward Kuder decided it was time to write. On his own, he wrote a short article, The Moros in the Philippines, for the *Far Eastern Quarterly* and an engaging story of his early days in Mindanao for *The Collegian*, Roanoke College's alumni magazine. But there was a bigger story to tell and a much larger audience waiting. In the autumn of 1944, someone in the War Department (Joseph Hayden of MacArthur's staff?) informed Edward Kuder that it was time for him to tell his story of occupied Mindanao to the nation.

Kuder was one of the very first American civilians to be evacuated from the Philippines. Only a handful of high-value Americans had left on submarines before him. But less than a month after Kuder left the Philippines, MacArthur altered his evacuation policy. In an October 4th, 1943 message to Fertig, he (or more likely Joseph Hayden writing under his signature) authorized the evacuation by submarine of 100 American civilians, specifically mentioning Edward Kuder as a model for a civilian who met the criteria for evacuation by submarine:

YOU ARE AUTHORIZED ARRANGE EVACUA-
TION ON RETURN TRIP VESSEL OF ONE HUN-
DRED AMERICANS... INCLUDING THEREIN ALL

AMERICAN WOMEN AND CHILDREN ALSO MALE
CIVILIANS WHOSE SERVICES NOT NEEDED YOUR
AREA AND CAN BE ACCUMULATED WITHOUT
UNDUE RISK PD INSTANCES SUCH AS KUDER ARE
IN ORDER PD

In a message sent on October 10th he added:

"NOW THAT THE MEANS ARE POTENTIALLY AT
HAND CMA I DESIRE THAT EVERY EFFORT BE
MADE TO EFFECT SUCH EVACUATION AS SPEED-
ILY AND SAFELY AS POSSIBLE." [15]

The means now at hand were two cargo submarines that had
just been assigned to the Philippines, the Narwhal and the Nauti-
lus—underwater behemoths that could carry 50 tons of supplies and
30 extra passengers as opposed to the Bowfin, which could com-
fortably accommodate only 5 to 10 tons of cargo and six passengers. These "supersubs" made it possible for Fertig to organize the
first large-scale civilian evacuations beginning in November 1943.[16]
The pace of those evacuations quickened considerably in December
when the Japanese high command in the Philippines announced
that its "amnesty" for unsurrendered Americans was ending on January 25th, 1944 and that any Americans captured in the islands, either
soldiers or civilians, would be "executed without trial."[17]

The killing squads didn't wait for the deadline. On the morning
of Sunday, December 19th, at a hillside hamlet on the island of Panay,
a Japanese patrol captured 13 American civilians. They were primarily Baptist missionaries: four married couples, two single women,
and three young children. The soldiers held them for two days while
they searched for more Americans, then told them they were to be
executed the next day. The captives were allowed to meet together for
a final prayer the following morning, and then, beginning precisely

at 3:00 P.M., they were beheaded one by one in a palm-thatched hut, which was then burned to the ground.

Also in the hamlet was a young Filipino couple, Federico and Catalina Condino, and their three-year-old daughter Bienvenida. Federico and Catalina were household servants brought to the upland hideout by their employers, Claude Fertig (the brother of Wendell Fertig) and his wife Laverne. They did all of the domestic work for the Fertigs; Federico cooked every meal, and Catalina was an accomplished seamstress. The Fertigs escaped the hamlet that Sunday morning a few minutes before the Japanese soldiers arrived. Federico and Catalina lagged, slowed by their little girl. The three of them were captured just outside the hamlet by Japanese soldiers and their fate was even more terrible than that of the American missionaries. Witnesses saw the soldiers hang Federico by his heels from a bamboo beam before torturing him and saw them beat Catalina, possibly to death. They then bayonetted the three-year-old Bienvenida and set the hut the family was in on fire. The Japanese wanted to know from the couple where their American employers were hiding, but neither one knew where Claude and Laverne Fertig had gone so could not reveal their whereabouts. The Fertigs and their American companions eventually made it safely to a waiting American submarine.[18]

When the Panay killings came to light, American evacuations intensified, as did the requirement for absolute secrecy of those already evacuated to Australia so as not to alert the Japanese to the submarine missions. The evacuees, most of whom had been hiding in upland jungles for more than two years, presented novel problems for the submarine crews. They came aboard carrying infants and leading small children. Some were quite sick or elderly, and all were barefoot and ragged. They brought their head and body lice, boils, tropical ulcers, and cockroaches hidden in their meager belongings. The boats' cooks fed their passengers steaks and sandwiches, apple pie, and coffee with cream–all the American foods they had gone without and dreamt about for the past two years. Back on shore, the Filipino and Moro civilians who had assisted and protected them faced yet another year of deprivation and danger. [19]

By the autumn of 1944, all American civilians in hiding who could be found and wanted to be rescued had been. In all, 472 individuals were evacuated by submarine from the Philippines, most of them from Mindanao. With the rescue missions completed and MacArthur's concerns allayed, it was now time for the evacuees to tell their stories, and Edward Kuder was one of the very first to relate his. [20]

He had been contacted by the *Saturday Evening Post,* the venerable illustrated magazine with a weekly circulation of 3 million, offering to tell his story. The Post provided him a co-writer, Pete Martin, for his first-person narrative and allocated five weeks of space to tell the extensive story, titled *The Philippines Never Surrendered.* The first installment appeared on February 10, 1945, and included an artfully lit portrait of Kuder on its first page. His classmates' unlikely prediction in his college yearbook that he would "win fame as a teacher in the Orient" had, quite improbably, come true.

For 21 years as an American colonial official, Edward Kuder had been inundated with memos, letters, and documents. Now he lacked even a single piece of paper to supplement his memory of his time in the Philippines. Nevertheless, he provided a vibrant and richly detailed account of his wartime experiences in occupied Mindanao. He told of the Japanese invasion, the American surrender, and the Maranao resistance. He gave the first public account of the Battle of Tamparan, the murder of General Fort, and the birth and expansion of the American-led guerrilla movement. He portrayed the Moros (colorfully if inaccurately described as the "Irishmen of the Pacific") as fearless fighters, clever tacticians, and loyal friends throughout it all. That positive portrayal—starkly different from the derogatory depictions of the Moros in subsequent published memoirs by Wendell Fertig, Edward Haggerty, and others—was undermined somewhat by the illustrations that accompanied the series. In his story, the handsome, fine-featured Moros described by Kuder appear jarringly in the hand-drawn illustrations as squat, brutish creatures with simian faces. The unnamed illustrator had years of experience depicting America's Asian enemies—the Japanese—as subhumans, and habit won out when drawing America's Moro allies.

In the Saturday Evening Post story, Edward Kuder presents himself as a witness to extraordinary events rather than a heroic protagonist. Had Kuder been otherwise inclined, we may have seen a very different depiction. Pete Martin did his best to dramatize the story of a brave Westerner, alone among Muslim tribesmen, leading them in an audacious revolt against a seemingly invincible Asian military empire. Someone else telling his own story for an audience of 3 million—a man more in the mold of Wendell Fertig or, for that matter, MacArthur—might have embraced a role as the T.E. Lawrence of Lanao, leading fierce Muslim warriors in a land far removed from Arabia.

But despite Pete Martin's best efforts, the Edward Kuder who emerges from those illustrated pages is a mostly modest man who had found more adventure than he bargained for when he volunteered for an assignment in Mindanao as a still-young man twenty years earlier. Modesty aside, Kuder's accomplishments in wartime Lanao did, in fact, closely resemble the main contributions of the real-life T.E.Lawrence (mythologized by the journalist Lowell Thomas as Lawrence of Arabia) to the Arab Revolt of 1916. Both acted alone as strategists and liaisons to Muslim resistance forces by helping to plan attacks and persuading resistance leaders to cooperate with Western allies. In sharp contrast to Lawrence, however, Edward Kuder insisted on making the Muslim insurgents the primary heroes of his story.[21]

* * *

Ten months earlier, in April 1944, as Edward Kuder was recovering from his first surgery at the U.S. Marine Hospital in San Francisco, one Muslim insurgent led his guerrilla fighters down a familiar jungle trail in the Cotabato highlands. All of them were barefoot—those who owned shoes had walked them to shreds months earlier—and all were singing God Bless America at the top of their lungs. When in friendly territory, 3rd Lt. Mohammad Adil often required his men to join him in boisterous song while marching. He had taught them the words to God Bless America and other American patriotic songs. Many of his older fighters spoke no English but had learned the words phonetically and bellowed out their nonsense syllables ("GAHDU BULESA MELIKA...") along with the rest.

The trail opened onto a ford of the Talayan River, and Adil saw a man in fatigues holding a rifle over his head crossing the river from the far bank, thirty yards away. Assuming he was a fellow guerrilla, Adil, still singing and with his rifle now at high port, stepped into the water. As he took his second step, the man, waist-high in the river, dropped his rifle to his shoulder and fired at him. Adil felt the bullet snap past him and instinctively fired back. His round did not miss, and he saw the stranger's body fold into the river.

The opposite shore immediately erupted in gunfire, a deafening crash of rifles over the deep bup-bup-bup-bup of a Japanese "woodpecker" machine gun. As water and dirt exploded at his feet, he scrambled with his men up the bank for the cover of the trees. Halfway there, he realized he had lost his ancient steel helmet at the riverside, so ran back to retrieve it. Skidding to a stop at the water's edge, he could see Japanese soldiers firing at him from the cover of the trees on the opposite bank, their machine gun tucked behind a coconut palm. He grabbed his helmet, dancing as bullets pocked the ground around him, and sprinted back up the bank to his men in the tree line, now returning fire.

Soon their ammunition ran low, and Adil motioned his men back into the forest, moving soundlessly this time. On the trail, his men searched his body for bullet wounds, not believing he hadn't been hit. Within days, the Japanese were boasting that they had killed him, and the Sinsuats celebrated the news of his death, but this time he sent word to his parents that he was unhurt and asked them to hold a *kanduli* to give thanks for his deliverance. The story of the young warrior invulnerable to Japanese bullets made its way, travelling by water, from village to village upriver and down, then north and south along the coast. It buoyed the spirits of those with no way of escape, now facing their third year under Japanese occupation.

* * *

The Bentley Historical Library—a low-slung modern brick building, tucked behind crisply-trimmed hedges in a quiet corner of the University of Michigan Ann Arbor campus—is a world away from the Lanao Plateau and the Cotabato Cordillera. Still, this archive of Michigan state history is the unlikely repository of some of the most valuable documents on Mindanao in the American colonial period because it holds the papers of Joseph Ralston Hayden. Like other anthropologists, I've conducted most of my research amidst the mud, dust, pollution, crowding, and ever-present noise that are everyday features of the modern world as experienced by most of its inhabitants. That research environment is what I signed up for, and it is an exciting place to be. But it is no surprise, then, that every time I walk into a research library—invariably a quiet, clean, and sedate place filled with treasures—it is with a sense of self-indulgence as well as anticipation. It was how I felt entering the Bentley Library looking for clues to the colonial world of Edward Kuder, and I wasn't disappointed. Within minutes I had laid out before me an assortment of letters, clippings, and reports covering 30 years of American rule in Mindanao and Sulu. There were letters from Edward Kuder and letters about Edward Kuder. There were travel journals and confidential memos and reports of attacks by crocodiles and by Moro "outlaws."

But when I saw the name "Mokamad" appear toward the end of a long classified report, my heart jumped because I knew I had found the treasure I was seeking. On the page was Edward Kuder's story of how he first met Mohammad (Mokamad) Adil. The report was a draft edited with his own hand, and the story was virtually identical, down to the smallest details ("Mokamad...got 15 pesos from his father..."), to the story that Mohammad Adil had told me on the first day I met him. And there, one page later was Kuder's version of Adil's story about punching the young man in the school auditorium who had made an insulting comment about his foster father's bald head. It was, again, identical in almost every detail to the story that Adil had told me.

Adil had never seen this report and was not even aware of its existence until I showed it to him more than 50 years after it was written and he read with joy the passage about him. Edward Kuder, who didn't possess a copy of the report, had never told him about it. The only known copy had been sitting quietly in the Bentley Library. It was a historical document that validated Mohammad Adil's recollections, but it did far more than that. It provided a surprising mirror image of the relationship. The "small Moro boy" had clearly made an impression on Edward Kuder as indelible as the one Kuder had made on the boy, for there he was, five years and 5000 miles away in Brisbane, Australia in 1943, writing about their first meeting in Jolo town in 1938 with a fineness of detail only made possible by a lasting memory. Their cross-cultural and cross-generational relationship had been even more emotionally reciprocal than I had imagined. Mohammad Adil's story of his American foster father had now become dynamically two-sided.

8
BULLETPROOF

By the late spring of 1944, the 119th Regiment, diminished now but hardened, had recovered from the Japanese attack meant to annihilate it. Captain Gumbay Piang was ready to reward the guerrilla officers who had stood by him through the assault, particularly Mohammad Adil, who had found rice to feed the remnants of the regiment, had nursed his commander back to health, and, most importantly, had taken the fight to the Japanese. He decided to make the young lieutenant the commanding officer of the newly formed G Company.

But the other Moro officers, most of them in their thirties and forties, angrily protested the move. "He's still a boy!" they objected. "We used to tickle his balls when he was a baby!" Piang finally succumbed to the pressure, assigning the much older third Lieutenant Ruffino Billedo as CO of G Company, although it was understood that Adil would be the de facto commanding officer, with Billedo acting, as Captain Guballa had done previously, as his mentor.

Mohammad Adil was, indisputably, still a youngster. He insisted on keeping his pet fighting rooster in camp with him, antagonizing the other officers so much that they reported him to Captain Piang, complaining that the headstrong teenager was giving away their position to the enemy because the crowing of his tame rooster was distinct from that of a wild one. The pet rooster eventually was sent home to his father's house.

Adil was a restless young man and disliked staying in camp, preferring to roam the Cotabato Cordillera with his men, covering scores of miles in a few days. The Tiruray aided and sheltered him, and he assisted them. Traditional Tiruray communities continued to suffer terribly from the occupation, with their forest gardens disrupted and their trade networks destroyed. Some were subsisting on famine foods such as *krut*, a wild root that was poisonous if not carefully prepared. Adil gave them rice when he could and salt, which they could no longer obtain in trade. Once, returning from a four-day trek across the hills to Lebak on the coast to collect supplies brought by a U.S. submarine, he met a Tiruray family whose small child had a gaping gash in his arm from an accident. Adil used a packet of powdered sulfanilamide that had just come off the submarine to dress the boy's wound. Twenty years later, the boy, now a young man, sought him out to thank him for saving his life.

Whenever the young lieutenant was in camp and heard the deep metallic throb of the *agung*, a large bronze gong usually played as part of a *kulintang* ensemble, pulsating through the forest night, he would shiver with pleasure and tell his men, "let's go!" They would then walk through the darkness to find the source—a wedding or other celebration—and he would play the *agung* till morning. It pleased him even more that the low tones of the *agung* ringing and echoing across the black hills were known to chill the hearts of Japanese soldiers lying awake in their valley garrisons.[1]

The impatient young officer, who had encountered the enemy more often than anyone else in the regiment, had lost only one man wounded, and even that wounding was not a result of direct enemy fire. Surviving the ambush at the river, where a mixed platoon of Japanese soldiers and Bureau of Constabulary men had lain in wait for them, had further burnished his reputation among the guerrillas. The ambush, he had to admit, had been nearly perfectly set. But for a single ambusher caught out of position, he and his men would have been surprised and slaughtered in midstream.

When the firing had erupted from the opposite bank, terrifically intense and unbelievably loud, one of his men, Dadoy, had run. Insane with fear, he lost the trail and crashed his way through thorn bushes, and knife-sharp saw grass. It was only the next afternoon that they had found him, crouched and still shivering with fear under a broad banyan tree. He was wild-eyed and badly bloodied, and he threatened to shoot anyone who approached until one of Adil's men crept up from behind and disarmed him, and they brought him, shaking and muttering, to a nearby village.

There they found a curer, a white-haired woman with crossed eyes, to help him. She lit incense and chanted herself into a trance to contact the demon that possessed him and negotiate the return of his soul. By the end of the exorcism Dadoy's mind was almost back to normal but his body was badly torn by his mad rush through the forest. As the curer prepared poultices for his wounds, Adil asked him, "Why did you run? You would have been safe if you had stayed with me." Dadoy quickly recovered from his physical injuries but he never fought again. The rest of Adil's men took the lesson to heart. Safety lay in staying close to their bulletproof commander, even when his bravery approached recklessness.

* * *

Fifteen years would pass before Mohammad Adil discovered the culprit behind his ambush, which had taken place in guerrilla-held territory and so had likely been initiated by someone known to him. In 1959, Adil, now a captain, was appointed company commander of the 68th Philippine Constabulary Company in Cotabato Province. To welcome him to his post, the datus of Cotabato held a grand *kanduli* to honor Captain Adil, who was, after all, the first Magindanaon datu ever to command a Philippine Constabulary company in Cotabato.

Hundreds of people gathered for the celebration under colorful pavilions flying green, red, and gold banners, and two *kulintang* ensembles played for the arriving guests. After the prayers were chanted and the feasting had ended, the speeches commenced. When it was his turn to speak, Datu Mama sa Gindulungan Midtimbang of Talayan, offered a surprising story about his distant kinsman, Captain Adil. Holding his cigar, he told the gathered datus that many stories had been shared that day about how Captain Adil was a great man, but "perhaps no one else here has witnessed that greatness firsthand as I have." Adil looked at him inquiringly, and Datu Midtimbang turned to address him. "Did you not know, Kapitan, that I was the one responsible for your ambush in 1944 at the Talayan River?"

Datu Midtimbang recounted how he had not complained when the guerrillas requisitioned rice from him every week. The harvests had been plentiful that year. But the arrogant young guerrilla officer who collected it always demanded that the rice be polished. Every week the villagers worked for hours pounding rice by hand for Adil and his men because there was no diesel-powered rice mill near their village as there was in Tumbao, where Adil's father had his mill.

The villagers were tired, and the constant hollow pounding echoed through the hills, attracting Japanese patrols and endangering the whole village. Finally, he said, he could tolerate no more. He told the Sinsuats, who informed the Japanese, and an ambush was prepared.

"Kapitan, do you remember the man crouching behind the Japanese machine gunner? That was me! I went along to identify you and to see that machine gun in action. And the Japanese gunner was surprised that he couldn't hit you, especially when you were retrieving your helmet. The bullets were tearing up the ground all around you. I was a witness. To this day, I still can't understand how he missed you."

Adil smiled slowly before answering. "*Babuy ka* (You pig!), Mama sa Gindulugan. If I *had* known back then that it was you, I would have cut you to pieces." The assembled datus roared with laughter. To cut the tension, Mama sa Gindulugan's father, Datu Midtimbang Palti, a very old man, stood and declared that he would gift Captain Adil with one thousand hectares. Adil's face softened as he said, "Thank you *apo* (grandfather), but I don't think you know how much land that truly is. Anyway, I did not come here today to acquire land. Maybe another time." Soon after, the festivities ended, and Captain Adil returned to his quarters with an old mystery unexpectedly solved.

* * *

Third Lieutenant Adil was learning more about the challenges of leading irregular fighters. The Japanese were still patrolling in the Talayan valley, assisted by Bureau Contabulary collaborators who guided them and translated. The most prominent of them was a Moro named Salik Malugayak, who was given special privileges and wore the Bureau of Constabulary armband. Adil wanted to stop his activities, so he sent Hadji Hashim Ali and a young guerrilla named Sanday Undung, down to the valley to arrest him, telling them to bring him back to the hills so they could interrogate him and use him as a laborer in their camp. The two guerrillas seized Salik and started back but when they arrived in camp he was no longer with them. Adil asked them what had happened. Sanday spoke up: "I pleaded with Bapa Hadji but he wouldn't listen! He just took his kris and killed Salik." Adil turned to Hadji Hashim; "Why did you do that?"

"Well, I felt he might escape, and my finger was itching, and it has been a long time since I bled my weapon. So I just sliced his neck and left his body there by the side of the trail." Adil made to reply but thought better of it. Hadji Hashim the former assassin, had only done what was in his nature. But Adil never sent him to arrest anyone again.

Adil's growing reputation in the regiment had become difficult to ignore. Mentang Semama, Captain Piang's executive officer, had made known his dislike for the young upstart. Still, in September 1944, he offered him a challenging assignment to wipe out the nearby Japanese detachment in Salebu. As an incentive, he provided Adil with ten M2 automatic carbines. The new rifles, first delivered nearly a year earlier to Fertig's guerrilla headquarters by the submarine that carried Edward Kuder to Australia, had finally made their way to the Moro guerrillas of Cotabato.

Adil took up Mentang's challenge and began to plan the attack. The Salebu detachment was located on an embankment beside a small river and garrisoned by a squad of Japanese soldiers. He wanted a closer look, so Adil had one of his men paddle him past the detachment in a dugout. The beardless young man borrowed a silk *malong* and headscarf to disguise himself as a woman, keeping his rifle tucked beneath the *malong* as they passed the detachment. He saw that it was heavily fenced with two gates, the main entrance and a small doorway leading down to the river used for fetching water. The surrounding riverbank had also been fenced with barbed wire.

The cook for the detachment was a local man, short and grizzled, by the name of Tungkaling—the Magindanaon term for a small bell put on a pet or a small child to keep track of them. Adil found him in his hamlet one evening and learned that Tungkaling kept careful track of his Japanese bosses and was willing to share what he knew. The cook told him that there were ten Japanese troopers currently in the detachment but that some were sick with malaria. The soldiers had both a light and a heavy machine gun to defend themselves. Early every morning, they assembled on the drill ground just outside the main gate to perform calisthenics clad only in their breechclouts and guarded only by a single sentry, leaving Tungkaling, the sick soldiers, and their weapons inside.

Adil told Tunkaling that in two days' time, he needed him to close the main gate and bolt it when the soldiers started their calisthenics, then rush to open the small gate by the river. If Tunkaling accomplished that, he said, most of his men would attack the soldiers outside, while Adil and a few others would cut the barbed wire, enter through the back, and dispatch the soldiers still inside. Tungkaling, who despised his employers, readily agreed to do what Adil asked. Mentang Semama approved Adil's plan and issued him ten M2 carbines, each with a single 15-round magazine, to carry out the mission.

Neither Adil nor any of his men had ever fired an M2, so he brought them to a nearby clearing to test-fire the weapons. The M2s looked nearly identical to the M1s they had been carrying but had been modified for automatic fire. Ten men took prone positions facing the targets that had been set out and, on Adil's command began firing. Each man fired off one or two rounds and then BRR-RRRRRRRRRRRRRRRRRRRP, the ten magazines were immediately emptied. The men jumped up from their firing positions, staring at their carbines in disbelief.

"*Da den!*" Empty!

"*Da den su pangelu!*" No more bullets!

"*Ngin i sinapang a niya?*" What sort of gun *is* this?

Adil returned to Mentang for more ammunition for the M2s but received a tirade instead. "You've wasted ammunition, Lieutenant! "You haven't killed a single Japanese with these guns yet here you are asking for more ammunition?" Now angry himself, Adil countered, "Goddamnit, how do you expect me to attack the enemy when my men don't know how to use their weapons?" They shouted back and forth for a few more minutes until Adil threw his carbine at Mentang's feet and yelled to his men, "bring those guns." They stacked the rest of the M2s in front of him. Then Adil saluted, turned on his heel and walked away with his men, and kept walking until he had reached his satellite camp in the hills. He had disobeyed orders and knew he could be seriously punished, but it was now a matter of *maratabat*. No unit in the regiment had killed more enemy soldiers than his, and he could tolerate no more disrespect.

Mentang and Adil came close to having their own war, but the elders spoke to Mentang, advising him that Adil was no ordinary boy and should not be treated as one. Mentang reluctantly listened, eased off, and a feud was averted. No one else in the regiment used the M2s to attack the Salebu detachment, and a few months later, the outpost was abandoned when the squad stationed there was pulled back to join the main body of Japanese troops at Dulawan. [2]

Life in the upland forests eventually took its toll on the guerrillas. On one occasion, Adil and his cousin were so weakened by malaria they could barely walk. Despite the submarine deliveries, no quinine had yet found its way to the guerrillas of Cotabato. Adil sent a message to his father to come with a boat to meet them at the seacoast in Tabuan. With their companions supporting them, the stricken men half-slid down the steep western slope of the Cotabato Cordillera to the narrow beach at Tabuan where they waited. His father arrived with a companion in a small sailboat, and the four men sailed north in the afternoon through rough seas and adverse winds and made it only as far as Ledteng, where they beached the boat.

They had no food and would have spent a hungry night, but for the Tirurays of that place, who brought them *sabah*, boiled bananas, which they ate with gratitude. By morning, the sea had calmed, and they set out again, and in a few hours, they had rounded Bulusan Point and entered the wide brown mouth of the Tamontaka River. The tide was with them, and by one in the afternoon, they were approaching the ferry crossing at Tamontaka, guarded by a Japanese detachment on its southern bank.

Adil and his cousin were both wanted men, so his father had them lie on the bottom of the boat, then covered them with *salang*i, mats woven of nipa palms. Stifling in the heat under the *salangi*, Adil looked at his cousin, Gulam, who was shivering so hard with malarial chills that the rifle in his hand was shaking. As they drew near the detachment, Adil looked out under the *salang*i and saw the Japanese soldiers signaling his father to bring the boat in to be searched. He thought he could hit two or three of the soldiers from where he lay. In his current condition, Gulam could shoot no one. That left plenty of soldiers to use the heavy machine gun on the military barge tied to the ferry dock to shatter their fragile boat and the bodies of its passengers.

He asked his father, "What now?" and he replied, "Allah will protect us. Let's recite the Ayatul Kursi and utter the names of the Seven Sleepers of Ephesus." The four men, two above, two below, immediately began to recite in Arabic the protective Verse of the Throne from the Holy Qur'an, which they had all memorized as children:

Allahu la ilaha illa Huwa, Al-Haiyul-Qaiyum La
ta'khudhuhu sinatun wa la nawm, lahu ma fis-samawati
wa ma fil-'ard Man dhal-ladhi yashfa'u 'indahu illa
bi-idhnihi Ya'lamu ma baina aidihim wa ma khalfahum,
wa la yuhituna bi shai'im-min 'ilmihi illa bima sha'a Wasi'a
kursiyuhus-samawati wal ard, wa la ya'uduhu hifdhuhuma
Wa Huwal 'Aliyul-Adheem.

None of them understood the meaning of the sacred words they spoke in unison, but all knew stories of how the verse had delivered from evil those who recited it.

When they had finished the Verse of the Throne, Adil and his father began to whisper the secret names of the Seven Sleepers of Ephesus over and over—the names they had both learned as children from their uncle and great-uncle, the Sufi master Saik a Datu Barat. Reciting the names of the Seven Sleepers was said to make one invisible while moving through enemy territory. Saik a Datu had told them that the effect was not literal invisibility. "Your enemies can see you but they no longer care who you are. They lose awareness for a while. But when you are safely away, they'll wake up and exclaim, 'Ah, an enemy has passed this way!'" [3]

His father held the tiller steady, and the boat continued straight upriver with the tide. Soon they were abreast of the detachment, and the soldiers had stopped signaling. Adil, still whispering the secret names as fast as he could, winced in anticipation of their gunfire, but none came. They sailed past the ferry crossing, and in less than an hour, they had arrived in Pagalamatan, where his family, overjoyed to see him home, nursed him tenderly back to health.

* * *

Mohammad Adil owed his very existence to his great-uncle, or so his grandmother had told him when she recounted the story of his birth. He had not wanted to enter the world, and for more than a day he resisted the birth pangs that convulsed his mother and ignored her exhausted pleas. Finally, the midwives sent for Saik a Datu, who walked out of the Talayan hills and paddled downstream to reach her. When he arrived, he touched her tormented body where it was most swollen, spoke a few potent words, and her firstborn son immediately slipped out, giving the loudest newborn cry anyone could remember.

Saik a Datu Barat was a healer, a teacher, and a Sufi warrior. Wherever he went, a crowd gathered to hear his words and witness his powers. As a boy, Mohammad Adil tried to be in that crowd as often as possible to listen to his great uncle teach that the world created by God was an entirely sacred place and its desecration was the most grievous human sin. And Saik a Datu Barat not only taught about the sanctified world, he lived according to his principles.

He never wore factory-made clothing or shoes of any kind, which, he said, would separate his feet from God's earth. His clothes were of cotton grown, spun, woven, and sewn by the members of his clan—the Tampakanens. He refused to eat rice milled by a machine or any food or drink that came from a store. His coffee was locally grown and his sugar was made by his children. He would not travel in a motorboat or in any form of transportation powered by machines. In these practices, he was not so different from traditionalists such as his brother Pangilamen, but Saik a Datu Barat went further. He even refused to ride a horse, saying, "God created my feet for walking. That animal is a fellow-creature. I don't want him to carry me."

Saik a Datu's wisdom was legendary, and those seeking to understand the mysteries of the world would seek him out. Pindililang Piang, who was inquisitive as well as courageous, came to Saik a Datu a few years before his own death with a question no one else had been able to answer for him. He asked him, "Where is the best place to worship God? At the mosque? At home? In nature?" Saik a Datu smiled when he heard Pindililang's question and asked his own. "Datu," he said, "Do you know who you are?

"I do not," he replied, "That is why I came to you."

"You should know who you are. You are a vessel of God. God abides inside you. He is the Formless Form inside every one of us. The best place to worship him is inside yourself, by remembering him." He took Pindililang's hand and pressed it against his own chest. "Do you feel that? You worship him in there."

"How?"

Saik a Datu told him, 'Do not make a sound because the name of God is an unspoken word. If you speak his name aloud, you have sent him outside your body. But if you don't utter a sound, he is right there inside you. Remember him there always." Pindililang shed tears when he heard Saik a Datu's words. He embraced the teacher and kissed his hand, saying, "Please adopt me as your son." Then he counted out forty silver pieces as a sign of his gratitude.[4]

* * *

On October 20, 1944, the United States re-entered the fight for the Philippines. The American forces that returned to the Philippines under the command of Douglas MacArthur arrived with an armed might so powerful and so endlessly plentiful that, to both the people of the Philippines and their Japanese occupiers, it might as well have been supernatural. However, the long-suffering inhabitants of Mindanao would have to wait half a year longer for their liberation.

From the moment he escaped via Mindanao in 1942, MacArthur had planned to return to the Philippines the same way. His intended route had always been from Australia, through New Guinea to Mindanao. It was the logical choice not just for its geography but also because Mindanao had the largest and most active guerrilla movement of all the Philippine islands. Over the spring and summer of 1944, MacArthur's forces had moved steadily northwest along the Pacific coast of New Guinea—fighting at Aitape, Biak, Numfoor, and then Morotai in the Dutch East Indies, which lay directly south of Mindanao. However, his plans for Mindanao changed at the last minute when, in early September 1944, carrier-based bombing missions over the southern and central Philippines were met with only the weakest of air resistance. That discovery sparked a bold proposal by Admiral William Halsey to bypass Mindanao and land the first American troops on Leyte in the central Philippines, much closer to Manila. MacArthur immediately agreed and drew up a new invasion plan. Mindanao would wait, and wait some more, for the Americans to arrive. Instead of the launchpad for the American invasion, Mindanao became the site of its culmination—the final campaign to liberate the Philippines.

One American did return early to Mindanao. Joseph Hayden, MacArthur's point man for communications with the Mindanao guerrillas, participated in the invasion of Leyte, coming ashore at noon of the first invasion day, October 20th, an hour before MacArthur's famous walk through the surf. By noon on the 23rd, he had overseen the formal restoration of the Philippine Commonwealth and been appointed Civil Adviser to the new government. In the first days of March 1945, he flew to Mindanao in a C47, landing at an airfield in Dipolog just seized by the guerrillas from the Japanese.

The guerrillas led him through Japanese lines to Lake Lanao, where he made the rounds of Maranao communities he had first visited almost twenty years earlier. In a 1926 letter to his wife from Mindanao, he had written that traveling there was "one of the most interesting experiences that I have ever had," describing Mindanao as "America's last frontier and Lanao as the fighting edge of that land." In 1945, his mission was to meet with local leaders (some of them the same *datus* he had met in 1926) in their traditional councils and assure them "that deliverance from Japanese rule was at hand." Hayden returned to Leyte in early March and in April visited recently-liberated Manila to see old friends. He then flew to the U.S. for consultations with the War Department. By the middle of May he was dead from a heart attack at the age of 58, not having lived quite long enough to see his beloved Mindanao liberated from its Japanese occupiers and become, once again, America's westernmost frontier.[5]

Hayden, the unapologetic imperialist, was also a professional scholar of the Philippines with a particular interest in Mindanao and Sulu and, like Edward Kuder, an admirer of the Moros. He may not have loved them as Kuder did—his interactions with them had not been as intimate—but his feelings ran deeper than scholarly respect and were the reason he made his non-essential journey to the Lanao Plateau in March of 1945. It was an arduous trip for a 58-year-old man who had been working day and night for months, but he longed to be back on the shores of the crystal-blue lake and to sit once more beside the proud Maranao chieftains of Lanao.

* * *

Mohammad Adil was patrolling the cordillera when the Americans finally landed in Cotabato on April 17, 1945, almost exactly three years after the Japanese invasion force had come ashore at the same place. The American invasion of Mindanao would be the last campaign of the battle for the Philippines and one of the most difficult. More than 40,000 Japanese soldiers remained unsurrendered in Central Mindanao. They had been given orders by General Tomoyuki Yamashita, the commander of Japanese forces in the Philippines, to "pin down for as long as possible as many Allied divisions as [they] could." Acting on those orders, Lt. General Sosaku Suzuki, who led the Japanese forces in the Southern Philippines, developed plans to make a stand in central Mindanao and carve out an autonomous territory for his troops to hold indefinitely.[6]

Just two days before the landing, assault plans had been changed due to a significant victory by Wendell Fertig's guerrillas. On April 13th, Colonel Fertig radioed the Eighth Army that his guerrillas had taken the Japanese garrison at Malabang, situated on the Lanao coast at the base of the Lanao Plateau, and occupied the town. Malabang was a Moro town, and its Japanese garrison had been attacked multiple times since 1942 by the Maranao fighters of Naguib Juanday, the prewar mayor of Malabang, brother of Abak the guerrilla courier, and old friend of Hadji Adil Tambis. Fertig's guerrillas had laid siege to the garrison in earnest in March of 1945. Those guerrillas were mostly, if not entirely, Lt. Colonel Charles Hedges' elite Maranao fighters whom Edward Kuder had recruited for him at the end of 1942—the so-called Maranao Militia Force. They included Manalao Mindalanao, now a major, who commanded a regiment under Hedges at Malabang and distinguished himself, once again, in the fight.[7]

Charles Hedges (left) and Wendell Fertig at the siege of Malabang, 1945

The seizure of Malabang allowed the Eighth Army to shift its assault forces away from Malabang and further south. Two infantry divisions came ashore at Parang, near Cotabato town, and raced up both the Pulangi River and the lone highway that bisected central Mindanao, pushing east across the waist of the island toward Davao, where the bulk of Japanese forces were gathered. Further inland, ruined roads, destroyed bridges, lower water levels in the upper Pulangi River, and Japanese harassing fire slowed them only slightly. Elements of the 24th Infantry Division reached Digos on April 27th, three years to the day after the renewed Japanese assault on Digos that signaled the start of their full campaign to conquer Mindanao. This time the Japanese were *defending* Digos. And they expected the Americans to attack from the same direction *they* had three years earlier, with an amphibious assault from the sea, not an overland attack from the west. The defenders of Digos held out only until that evening when they withdrew to the volcanic slopes of Mount Apo.

The main body of Japanese forces abandoned Davao City, which had been "bombed into a shambles" by American aircraft, and set up a 25-mile-long crescent-shaped defensive line in the hills northwest of Davao. In a frontal attack as difficult and costly as any in the Philippine campaign, the 24th division assaulted the Japanese line, fighting through extremely difficult terrain. The dense jungle was bad enough, but much of the land was covered in overgrown abaca (Manila hemp) plantations, now impossibly dense with plants as tall as 20 feet growing as close as a foot apart—kelp forests on dry land, suffocating those who struggled through them. Private Lawrence Stuckenschneider, an 18-year-old replacement still in new fatigues, remembered forcing his way "through the tangled abaca leaves" feeling "dizzy, exhausted, and close to fainting."[8] For almost six weeks, through some of the worst conditions of the war, the 24th Infantry Division attacked the Japanese line until it finally collapsed and the remaining defenders withdrew into the mountains. The offensive had cost the Americans at least 350 men killed and 1615 wounded.[9]

The Mindanao operation now moved into the mopping up and pursuit phase. But thousands of Japanese soldiers remained, unsurrendered and determined, in the uplands of the island, and GIs and guerrillas faced more costly fighting. Lt. General Suzuki's strategy for an extended last stand on Mindanao seemed to be going according to plan. The inhabitants of Mindanao also knew, in June of 1945, that the battle for the island was ending but not over, and that more soldiers and civilians would die before the Japanese were fully defeated. But the punishing three-year Japanese occupation *was* over, the familiar Americans had returned, and the prospect of peace lifted their spirits.

Third Lieutenant Mohammad Adil was ordered in May to report with his platoon to Captain Gumbay Piang, who had returned upriver to his home base in Nimao. In Cotabato town, now utterly transformed by the invasion force, they marveled at the thousands of American troops bivouacked under the coconut palms on the main road into town and the dozens of heavy machine guns emplaced to protect them. An American tank guarded the ferry crossing at Tamontaka where he and his father had evaded the Japanese two months earlier.

With a travel pass from Captain Piang, Adil and his men boarded a motorized barge headed upriver. The atmosphere on the slow-moving barge was relaxed, even festive. Adil bantered with the American skipper, who admired his Browning automatic shotgun, part of his father's collection. In the bow, dressed in their best patched and ragged clothes, sat a group of six Filipino civilians returning from their excursion downriver to the newly-liberated provincial capital. Two of them were young women, and the prettier one, Adil noticed, was looking at him. He made his way forward, bringing chocolates—until a few weeks ago the rarest of treats—which he offered to her and her companions. She smiled and thanked him and told him that her name was Ignacia. Close to her now, he saw that she was older than he had imagined but no less pretty.

She lived along the riverbank in Nimao, close to his detachment, and the very next day, she brought him a gift of food. When she came again the second day with food and the same look in her eyes, he realized with surprise that she was "courting" him. He didn't understand what attracted her, but the intensity of her desire excited him. He arranged to be alone in his quarters on the third day when she came, with one of his men posted at the door for privacy. At 20 years old, he had led men and killed men, but after two years of war he was still a virgin. His virginity ended delightfully on that sultry afternoon alone with the woman from Nimao. She was almost forty and beautiful. The young Third Lieutenant, who did not remember "ever tasting the love of a mother," made love for his first time with the mother of a son nearly his age.

There were several more delightful afternoons over the next few weeks, stolen hours spent with their bodies leisurely intertwined or frantically entangled until they had, as Adil remembered, "consummated all acts." Ignacia told him she was married to a Chinese storekeeper, a cruel man who abused her and treated her like "chattel" and with whom she had four children. The afternoons with Ignacia ended when orders came for him to leave Nimao and return downriver to deploy with the Americans in their mopping-up operations.

Adil and his men had been at their new base of operations in Dalican for less than a week when a distant relative, a man as old as his father, arrived in camp accompanied by Ignacia, the woman from Nimao. "She followed me here, Datu. You need to take her now." Dumbstruck, Adil brought her quickly to his tent, where Ignacia announced through sobs that she had left her husband for him. "Do whatever you want with me. You can kill me; I don't care. I am useless. I don't have a single centavo. But I will not go back to my husband."

Nothing in his twenty years had prepared Adil for this predicament. Ignacia's overwhelming need and desperation confounded him. He was going off to fight. That, at least, was something he understood. He knew he had to send her away and only one place came to mind. He told her he had a safe place for her to wait for him. Then he penned a a short letter to his father and had one of his men escort her to his family house in Pagalamatan.

Hadji Adil Tambis was used to unannounced deliveries from his guerrilla son, but this arrival was truly unexpected. Nevertheless, he graciously accepted Ignacia into his household, where she stayed for months, eventually bringing her two youngest children to live there with her. Unsettled by his first foray into sexual maturity, young Mohammad Adil went happily back to war.

9
THE LAST RIDGE

In June of 1945, in the unmapped mountains of Mindanao, the last desperate struggle in the battle for the Philippines was being waged, with Moro guerrillas once again at the forefront. Japanese soldiers had been given their orders to disperse into the rugged highlands on the eastern and western edges of the Cotabato Basin and fight to the death, as guerrillas if necessary, to pin down American troops to protect the homeland.

In the east, Major General R.B. Woodruff of the 24th Infantry Division had given Colonel Frank McGee and his guerrillas the tough assignment of "clearing out several thousand [Japanese soldiers]" in the rugged mountains bordering the Davao Gulf. Many, if not most of his fighters were Moros, and they may have included Salipada Pendatun.[1]

In the west, 3rd Lt. Mohammad Adil was detailed in mid-June to guide an American unit pursuing Japanese holdouts in the Cotabato Cordillera—territory he knew well. The Americans needed a reliable guide. They were the soldiers of Battery B of the 222nd Antiaircraft Artillery Searchlight Battalion. They knew a great deal about spotting Japanese fighters and bombers with searchlights, much less about infantry tactics, and nothing at all about jungle warfare. On June fifth, according to the official unit history, the battery had been assigned to "seek out and destroy the enemy" in the area surrounding Mount Blit, an extinct volcano that, at 3930 feet above sea level, was the highest peak in the northern cordillera.

They numbered 100 enlisted men and three officers, and none of them had ever been under direct enemy fire. On June 17th, a scouting patrol reported to the unit's commander, Captain Dempster Drowley, that they had sighted a force of approximately 70 Japanese. That night at 2:00 A.M., 90 soldiers of Battery B set out on a night march to surprise the Japanese, and by 8:30 A.M., they had walked into a machine-gun ambush. They should have been in good hands. They were with "some guerrillas of the 119th" who were led by Captain Hamid Arashid, a Tausug and former sergeant in the Philippine Scouts and one of the most experienced and talented officers in the entire regiment. He was senior to Adil and, for that reason, had probably gotten the assignment to work with the Americans. Still, the northern cordillera was not his territory, and he was unfamiliar with it. For that reason, they had brought along a Tiruray guide who inadvertently led them into the ambush.

Caught in a heavy crossfire of machine guns, mortars, and automatic rifles commanding the high ground, the soldiers were pinned down for hours, and two of the unit's sergeants were killed. One of them, Sergeant Robert Miller, had deliberately exposed himself to draw enemy fire, which allowed his squad to assault a machine gun nest successfully. He and his men had attempted to flank the Japanese hilltop position, but when they were 50 yards from their objective, intense fire from above had stopped their advance.

Sergeant Miller, carrying only a carbine, crawled through brush and cogon grass to within 20 yards of the gun emplacement, then stood straight up and charged the position. He was shot immediately and mortally wounded, but, as his Distinguished Service Cross citation reads, his action "distracted the enemy long enough for his squad to eliminate the machine gun nest... enabling a withdrawal to a more favorable location."[2] Two enlisted men of the battery became so disoriented by the ambush that they roamed lost in the mountains for seven days until they were found, dazed from hunger and exposure, by local Tirurays and guided out of the highlands. Despite Sergeant Miller's self-sacrifice, Battery B's first significant effort to "seek out and destroy the enemy" had been calamitous.

* * *

The 222nd AAA Searchlight Battalion was organized in California in 1942 as a component of a Coast Antiaircraft Artillery force for the defense of Los Angeles and San Francisco. The members of the battalion, nearly all of them draftees, could thus have reasonably expected never to leave California during the war, let alone the U.S. But leave they eventually did, in March 1944, for New Guinea to join General MacArthur's campaign pointed at the Philippines.

Seeking the words to describe his first impressions of New Guinea, 1st Lt. Robert L. Johnson, Unit Historian for the 222nd, wrote that it was an amalgam of "atabrine tablets, salt tablets, insecticide powder, mosquito repellent, mosquito netting, malaria, Dengue, and typhus fevers; rash, foot rot, cloudbursts, dust, desert sun, mud, insects with millions of legs, flies...and half-naked natives." He hastened to add, however, that the battalion's "first taste of overseas duty was far from bitter," for they also had free tobacco, free time, "excellent showers," movies three times a week, and softball and volleyball leagues. And rumors were swirling that the battalion beer ration would soon be distributed.[3]

What they did not yet have were any Japanese planes to spot with their searchlights. They remained in Finschhafen, a staging area in eastern New Guinea, for two months while MacArthur's front lines moved west. Finally, on July 14th, 1944, they shifted west as well, to the northwest coast of New Guinea. This move, Lt. Johnson wrote, "marked the initial participation of elements of the Battalion in the 'shooting' phase of World War Number Two." It also marked the first time the battalion had been divided. Only batteries A and B were sent forward, to two different locations, while the rest of the battalion remained at Finschhafen. They would not be reunited again until the end of the war. [4]

Battery B found itself in Sansapor (alternatively spelled Sansapour) on the northwestern tip of New Guinea, much closer to the action but with still too few targets for their 60-inch searchlights and other equipment—trucks, trailers, generators, radar arrays, heat detectors, and control stations—that they had spent weeks packing and unpacking, loading onto and off liberty ships and LSTs.[5] Over the next eight months, they illuminated only 18 aircraft. They found other uses for their searchlights—to guide lost airplanes back home and to light nighttime construction at the airfield—and the men of the battery spent the rest of their time unloading ships, training, playing ball games, tending vegetable gardens, and making their "quarters and camp areas...comfortable and attractive." Summing up their time in Sansapor, Lt. Johnson noted succinctly that "everything was relatively quiet, air raids were few and far between, and there wasn't much to do."

Their one "red letter day" at Sansapor came at the very end of 1944, on December 30th, when, 30 minutes after midnight, a single

Japanese long-range reconnaissance seaplane appeared over the crowded Sansapor harbor. Almost immediately, Johnson reported, every anti-aircraft gun "on land and in the harbor" opened fire and the plane soon burst into flames and fell into the ocean. It was impossible to know who had shot the plane down "but there was no doubt in anyone's mind as to who did the illuminating! And what a picture our lights made of that plane. It was magnificent! It was colossal! It was stupendous! What a night!" Battery B received a commendation for their spotting on that memorable night. It was their only confirmed "kill" of a Japanese plane for the entire war.

With the new year, the soldiers of Battery B adopted a new motto: "The States alive in forty five." Within a few months, however, they were headed for the first time directly into harm's way, toward a future where not all of them would make it home alive. In March, "after almost eight months of sitting in one spot," they moved to Morotai in the Dutch East Indies, and then on to Mindanao in April. On May third, the unit received a commendation for "setting up the best looking camp in the area" of Parang, but the days of "attractive" camps with "excellent showers" were about to end. On May 6th, the battery was notified that they "were in for some infantry work." For the official record at least, Lt. Johnson reported the response of the battery as resolute: "Okay. We were willing to take a crack at it. At least it was something new and different, and besides, we knew we could do it." They had practiced throwing grenades and firing their weapons, including machine guns, but they had never been on patrol in the jungle or under direct fire from the enemy.

Only the soldiers from one of the three batteries in the 222nd Battalion were picking up rifles, and not even all of them. Of the 215 officers and enlisted men of Battery B, fewer than half were transferred to the infantry, specifically the 162nd Regimental Combat

Team. The rest of the men in the battery went elsewhere, on temporary duty driving trucks, handling supplies, or assisting the field artillery.

Captain Drowley and his men began their infantry duty guarding bridges and serving as MPs around Cotabato town, but by the end of May they were conducting multi-day patrols—in boats, vehicles, and on foot—with the mission to "seek information and observe any movements concerning the enemy in the Cotabato, Nuro and Dalican area." Intelligence gained from those patrols, as well as from the guerrillas, estimated that there were about 330 Japanese soldiers holding out in scattered groups of 30 to 60 men, over a wide area in the northern Cotabato Cordillera. They had likely moved south into the hills from Malabang, Parang, and Cotabato town when the Americans landed. They were equipped with mortars and heavy machine guns. Drowley's men had neither, and little experience in infantry tactics, but they had been given a mission to "find and destroy the enemy." On June 18th, 1945, "a day of great sorrow for the battery," that lack of weapons and infantry experience resulted in the deaths of two sergeants who were "personal friends of every officer and every enlisted man in the battery."

* * *

Two days after the Japanese ambush of Battery B, 3rd Lt. Mohammad Adil and his guerrilla soldiers joined the battery at their command post at the old schoolhouse in Sibutu in the foothills west of Dalican. American ammunition and other supplies arrived at Dalican by boat then were transferred to sleds pulled by carabaos for the four-hour trip overland to Sibutu. Adil and his men had been assigned to guard the supply caravan but now he had been asked to guide the Americans.

His first exchanges with the Americans did not go well. Adil looked even younger than his age and was wearing a *tubao* rather than a helmet. The Americans called him "boy" and asked, "Where is your officer?" But his men who could speak some English intervened. "He is younger than us but he is our commanding officer. You should show him respect." The Americans eventually acknowledged him and at least one became his friend.

Disappointment came again the next day. After Adil pointed out on a map to Captain Drowley a location where he knew the Japanese had a camp, the captain told him that they would follow a compass course to reach the location in addition to hiking at night. Adil asked him what that meant and in a deep, measured voice the captain replied, "You take your map, you take your compass, you draw a straight line and you follow it." When Adil understood what was being contemplated he pleaded, "Sir, I'm your guide. Believe me, I can guide you to this place safely," emphasizing his point by repeatedly tapping the spot on the map. But Captain Drowley, determined not to send one more poncho-wrapped body down the trail on a sled to Dalican, or write any more letters to parents who had assumed their sons were far from the shooting war, would not be dissuaded.

The patrol left at midnight and began hacking its way straight through the snarled jungle, over rocks and up cliffs, crossing trails but never taking them. Adil remembered that the mosquitos were terrible, the American repellent made them all smell like gasoline, and in nearly six hours they covered only six kilometers. Never had he felt so tired from such a short hike. His men were frustrated and on the verge of mutiny. "Stupid Americans! Why are they are afraid to meet the enemy?"

On this patrol, and most of the others, Adil was accompanied by three American sergeants—Clarence Barnard, Merl Burk, and

Joe Rincon, who went by the nickname Lupisto. None of them liked the compass course any more than Adil and they began to bond from their shared misery. Sergeant Lupisto Rincon was a handsome Mexican-American from New Mexico. He and Adil would talk together on their rest breaks, sharing stories of their childhoods.

Just before dawn, Adil led the patrol to a cliff overlooking a narrow ravine where his Tiruray friends had told him the Japanese had a creekside camp, and they deployed along its rim. Sergeant Rincon called the bazooka man up and Adil pointed out to him where the grass roofs of the Japanese huts could be seen tucked beneath the cliff opposite them. For the first time, Adil watched a bazooka fired and was amazed by its power. The rest of the soldiers positioned along the edge of the ridge then opened fire with their automatic weapons. He reveled at finally being among soldiers who had an endless supply of ammunition. The blind firing was also a new tactic for him but one common among American combat teams in Mindanao. In Davao, in the same month on the opposite side of the island, Private Lawrence Stuckenschneider was participating in identical maneuvers—approaching a house suspected of holding Japanese soldiers, fanning out and taking cover and then, without warning or challenge, pouring in a withering fire.

Sergeant Rincon halted the firing and ordered an advance down the rugged cliffside. The bazooka man walked a short ways, then slipped and tumbled down the steep slope, he and his bazooka landing on a sharp rock near the bottom. The man looked at his dented bazooka and swore mightily as he whipped it against the rock again and threw it into the bushes. Adil, who had just admired its power, couldn't help wondering if the bazooka might have been repairable. He made a note of where it landed, just in case.

There were no Japanese left alive or dead in the camp but

plenty of fresh signs of their presence. The bazooka man had scored a direct hit on their kitchen and bloody bits of flesh from a newly butchered cow that had been hanging there now covered every inch of what remained of the kitchen. Later, Adil led a scouting party up the creek and found six Japanese corpses lying along the creek bed, half in and out of the water. He wanted to believe they had died as a result of the American attack, but their wounds–exploded stomachs and gunshots to the head–made it more likely they had killed themselves. On one of the sprawled arms was a still-ticking wristwatch—an Omega. Adil took it and wore it until the end of the war.

Over the next two weeks, Adil and his men, along with soldiers of the 222nd, patrolled nearly every day but made no contact with the enemy, who had withdrawn further up the slopes of Mount Blit. One early morning at the command post in Sibutu, as they prepared to leave on another patrol, a Japanese soldier emerged from a nearby stand of bamboo wearing only a loincloth and a uniform cap. He was very thin and looked, to Adil's twenty-year-old eyes, very old. He also appeared to be very sick. As he walked weakly toward the command post waving a piece of red cloth, Adil could see that his stomach was covered in sores. One of Captain Drowley's officers noticed as well and shouted, "Don't go near him! He's contagious!" Less loudly he named a disease that Adil hadn't heard of and said that they would have to kill him right there. He grabbed a carbine from a nearby soldier, fired twice, and the Japanese soldier dropped his flag of surrender and fell to the ground dead. The whole encounter had taken less than a minute. The officer then ordered his soldiers to pull down an old palm-thatched hut nearby and lay the pieces carefully on the dead man. Soon a funeral pyre was burning and the slain Japanese soldier had been cremated.

It is impossible to say with certainty what illness had afflicted the Japanese soldier, but it may have been scrub typhus, a serious epidemic disease that affected both armies in the Southwest Pacific. The soldiers of Battery B were well aware of that disease. Their unit historian had reported that "the disease plagued the battery during the entire Sansapour occupation and was a serious threat to the efficiency of the battery." Scrub typhus was a deadly disease, killing up to 33% of infected soldiers in parts of New Guinea, but it was not highly contagious and could not be passed directly from human to human. [6]

At the end of June, Captain Drowley moved the Battery's command post away from Sibutu and closer to Mount Blit but still he made little progress in his mission because his patrols, most of them still following compass courses, were not making contact with the enemy. He knew approximately where on the slopes of Mount Blit the Japanese holdouts were located, but when he ordered an airstrike, the P-51 fighter-bombers sent from the Dipolog airfield did not drop their bombs because they could not see the enemy. Finally, on July 10th, he announced to his assembled officers that anyone who could hold a position within firing distance of the Japanese would be given two weeks R&R.

3rd Lt. Adil volunteered immediately. He was less interested in the R&R than he was in engaging the enemy. He was tired of compass courses and restricted patrols. He wanted to fight. He picked a squad of his best men and set off at dawn the next day with two BARs as their only automatic weapons. They headed southeast, following a Tiruray hunting trail. There would be no more straight lines and slow progress through the jungle. They climbed one ridge, then a second and a third. Just past the third ridge, Adil, leading the squad, saw a sturdy vine stretched low across the narrow trail. It looked just like a *baratik* to him–a Tiruray snare for trapping monk deer or wild pigs. He stood back and automatically raised his machete to cut the vine, as he had done on other game trails, when his uncle Maliga, a former constabulary soldier nearly as old as his father cautioned, "Don't do that, It might be a Japanese booby-trap." It was. They looked carefully and saw that the vine was attached to a wire that suspended a percussion grenade at the top of a bamboo tube. Tripping the wire would cause the grenade to fall to the bottom of the tube and detonate. They rigged a long bamboo pole, took cover, and exploded the grenade. They now knew they were on the right trail and the Japanese now knew they were coming.

They climbed another ridge, where the forest was giving way to stands of sharp cogon grass, and descended into one more still-forested valley where they found, as the trail began to ascend again, a second booby trap. Once more, they rigged a device and exploded it safely and resumed walking, but this time with even more caution because the enemy was both closer and alerted to their presence. When the trail climbed out of the forest again, Adil ordered a halt before leaving the trees. This, he knew, was where they would be, looking down on the trail and the treeline and waiting. But his mission was to make contact. He waited too, hoping to unsettle the ambushers who were anticipating them. Finally, he signaled his men off the trail and down to the ground, and they crouched and crawled forward out of the forest and into the cogon grass, he leading the way on one side of the trail and his uncle Maliga on the other.

They had advanced just a few yards when a machine gun stuttered from somewhere above them. Maliga, who was walking through tall grass in a crouch, was struck in the shoulder by a 30-caliber round and slammed to the ground. They scrambled back into the trees, pulling Maliga with them, and Adil fanned his men out along the treeline. When they located the machine-gun nest they returned fire but he could see that it was ineffective. He then sent a runner back to report to Captain Drowley that the trail between them was clear, they were holding their position under Japanese fire, and he had a wounded man in need of evacuation. Captain Drowley sent one of his junior officers, 2nd Lt. Richard Manton, forward with two 50-caliber machine guns that he had recently requisitioned from Dalican. They were brought up on a sled drawn by a carabao and Maliga was taken back on the same sled and later evacuated to an American military hospital in Leyte to try to save his arm. Adil had to convince him to go because he was afraid the Americans would feed him pork at their hospital. He not only survived the hospital but made a full recovery and lived to be a very old man who enjoyed telling the story of his adventures in far-off Leyte.

The machine gunners assembled their guns under the cover of the forest and Adil directed their fire at the Japanese position. It was the first time Adil or his men had seen a 50-caliber machine gun in action and they were astounded by the destruction it wrought. The Japanese machine gun was emplaced in a dense copse of brush, bamboo, and sturdy hardwoods halfway up the ridge. The thicket quickly disintegrated under the 50-caliber fire as brush was uprooted, bamboo shredded into splinters, and full-grown trees toppled like saplings. When the Japanese forward position was obliterated, 2nd Lt. Manton ordered the gunners to cease firing, and Adil took his men forward to the crest of the ridge from which the Japanese had fired on them.

They had reached the last ridge. From there, they could look across a steep ravine to the eastern slope of Mount Blit and the main encampment of the Japanese just a few hundred yards away. Adil returned and reported his sighting to Lieutenant Manton who first spoke on his radio to Captain Drowley and then reached into his pack and pulled out two smoke grenades–one green and one yellow–saying, "Lieutenant, throw the green grenade as close as you can to the Japanese, then take cover because our planes will attack them. When their position is destroyed, throw the yellow grenade to end the attack. Adil returned to the crest of the ridge, pulled the pin on the green grenade, then stood and heaved it as far as he could toward the Japanese position. The green smoke spread over the slope and, within minutes six P-51 Mustangs roared over their heads and swept down on the smoke-covered slope in a fury of bombing and strafing.

Despite Manton's warning to take cover, Adil excitedly leapt to his feet to watch a display of the most concentrated destructive power he had ever seen or imagined. His men followed suit and there on the crest of the ridge they jumped and shouted so loudly that they were hoarse for days afterwards. Adil felt the same awe he had experienced on that morning in the first month of the war when Japanese warplanes had attacked the airfield next to Edward Kuder's house. But now the awesome power was on his side; now the overwhelming force was being aimed at his enemies. For years the guerrillas had carefully rationed scarce ammunition and forgone attacks. Now one radio message had delivered enough firepower to destroy the enemy completely.

And the enemy *was* being destroyed. As the planes strafed, Adil could see the sparks their machine-gun rounds made when they ricocheted off the rocks of the steep mountainside. He watched the Japanese huts explode and whole pieces of the slope disappear in the bombing. When he saw no more movement on the opposite slope he threw the yellow grenade.

The next day they returned to search the main Japanese camp destroyed by the Mustangs. They found weapons and ammunition, uniforms and helmets, three "samurai swords," a radio, large sacks of Japanese occupation money, and 23 shattered bodies. The enemy threat on Mount Blit had been entirely eliminated but the enemy had not been completely destroyed. Still unaccounted for were more than 200 Japanese holdouts. The battery's mission was not yet completed.

The next morning, Adil and his men hiked two hours out of the highlands to Dalican, looking forward to their promised two week leave. But as soon as they arrived, Adil received a radio message to proceed immediately to Upi with 45 of his 100 men. He chose his men and turned around and hiked six hours back into the mountains to the terminus of Irving Edward's road in Upi. There they boarded 6X6 trucks and rode back down out of the mountains on the crushed-coral road to Tamontaka, where they were put on U.S. Navy Higgins Boats—plywood landing craft fitted out with 50-caliber machine guns—and powered down the river and out to sea.

Their destination was Meti, a tiny fishing village on Linao Bay, 30 miles south on the Cotabato coast. The official history of Battery B states that "reports of scouts and patrols in the Mt. Blit area seemed to indicate that the enemy had entirely evacuated that area and was proceeding to the Meti area." The report does not suggest why the Japanese were heading toward Meti but it may be that they were trying to link up with a larger group of 1200 Japanese holdouts concentrated north of Sarangani Bay at the southern tip of the island. A joint amphibious operation of GIs and guerrillas had just been launched against the holdouts at Sarangani Bay and the Meti landing was likely coordinated with that operation as an effort to cut off the Japanese soldiers from Mount Blit before they reached Sarangani. Although the documentation is scant, the landing at

Meti appears to have been the very last amphibious assault made in the campaign to retake the Philippines.

In the boats, Adil and his men were wholly miserable. Already tired from an entire day of hiking in the cordillera, they were now spending the whole night in an open boat in the rain on a very rough sea. No one slept and most were seasick, some terribly so, because they had not been on open water since the start of the Japanese occupation. Some of his men were also suffering malarial chills because the 119th had still not received any quinine.

At that part of the coast, the Cotabato Cordillera fell to the sea so abruptly that there was no flat unforested land to be seen at low tide. Meti was a village on stilts sitting over the water for half of every day. Arriving at dawn, the men climbed out of the boats and kept on climbing into a near-vertical rainforest so dense and trackless that they had no choice but to follow a compass course. They climbed for hours, hacking their way through the steep jungle until suddenly it thinned and they stood before a hilltop partly covered in cogon grass. As they caught their breath they saw a sight they couldn't comprehend. Coming down the hill toward them were nearly a hundred weaponless wraiths walking awkwardly with their hands above their heads. Every other hand held a sheet of white paper; some were being waved, others were tightly clenched, and a few simply shook because the Japanese soldiers holding them were trembling so badly.

Adil's men immediately raised their weapons but Captain Drowley shouted, "Hold your fire! Hold your fire! They're surrendering." As the Japanese got closer, Adil could read the English phrase written in large block letters on each piece of paper: "Attention American Soldiers: I CEASE RESISTANCE." Adil shook his head. He had just spent the most miserable and exhausting 24 hours of the war to reach this place and now there would be no fight. Hadji Hashim turned to him and asked, "Why don't we just shoot these Japanese?" It was not a thoughtless question. All of Adil's men had witnessed the enthusiasm with which their American companions had killed Japanese soldiers, including (in the case of the sick soldier waving the red cloth) those trying to surrender. Why was this situation any different?

Adil put the question to Captain Drowley and the response he received was surprisingly emphatic: "Lieutenant, they are signatories to the Geneva Convention! These soldiers are covered by the articles of war…!" Adil then understood that it was the sheets of paper that made all the difference.

* * *

It was as part of his preparations for invading the Philippine Islands that Douglas MacArthur first established the Psychological Warfare Branch, Southwest Pacific Area in mid-1944. The propaganda distributed by the branch increased in sophistication over the following months as more intelligence was received from Japanese POWs about declining morale among Japanese troops. In January 1945, for example, the wording on American "surrender pamphlets" was changed from "I Surrender" to "I Cease Resistance" because the latter wording was found to be less offensive to Japanese soldiers, many of whom could read basic English. American surrender pamphlets and other propaganda materials—focused on such topics as food shortages among Japanese troops and the overwhelming technological superiority of the American military—were dropped by the tens of millions from airplanes throughout the Philippines. One pamphlet, whose author clearly hadn't considered the accomplishments of the Bolo Battalions, was titled "You Can't Fight Tanks with Bayonets."[7]

Mass surrenders of Japanese troops in the Philippines first began in May 1945 and appear to have been directly related to the efforts of the Psychological Warfare Branch. In May and June the Americans dropped 26 million leaflets in the Philippines and processed 6,450 Japanese POWs—more than five times the number of surrenderees as in the first months of the campaign. MacArthur and his staff had good reason both to attempt to provoke mass surrenders and to treat Japanese soldiers humanely when they did surrender. Every Japanese soldier who did not fight to the death saved American lives and shortened the road to Tokyo. And it was hoped that news of the humane treatment of Japanese POWs would help protect the interests of American prisoners still in Japanese hands.

The Japanese soldiers attempting to surrender on the hilltop above Meti also had good reason to tremble. For most of the Pacific War, American GIs had been averse to taking Japanese prisoners. It was an aversion based on firsthand stories disseminated in the American press as well as in military intelligence bulletins that Japanese soldiers regularly feigned surrender in order to kill Americans more easily. It was also due more generally to the no-holds-barred nature of the fighting in the Pacific. But when MacArthur, in New Guinea in May 1944, heard "numerous reports" of American troops shooting Japanese soldiers who were holding surrender passes and attempting to surrender, he demanded an investigation in order to stop the practice. As a result, the Psychological Warfare Branch, which had long been aware of the problem, distributed hundreds of instructional kits to intelligence and education officers in combat units, focused on the susceptibility of Japanese soldiers to American propaganda and the value of Japanese prisoners. One year later, their efforts seem to have borne fruit.[8]

* * *

Down off the hilltop and back through the dense jungle the soldiers hiked with their 90 Japanese prisoners, this time on a Tirurary trail a mile or two south of Meti—a longer route, but less steep. At the narrow beach at the southern shore of Linao Bay, Captain Drowley, just to be safe, placed Adil and his guerrillas on a separate boat from the ones carrying the Japanese. Back finally in Cotabato town, at the huge 12-acre stockade the Americans had constructed at its outskirts, Adil and his men were astonished once again when the Japanese prisoners were given brand new fatigue uniforms along with boots, underwear, and even towels. Adil shook his head and swore again. "Goddamn fools!" He looked at his men and himself, dressed in scraps of uniforms and cast-off American boots. All his men wore too-big boots with rags stuffed in their toes to make them fit. A few even had mismatched pairs with two left or right boots.

His men were so outraged that the Japanese POWs were being treated better than they were that they clenched their rifles and suggested shooting them again. Some began throwing rocks at the POWs when the American officers weren't looking. Adil approached Captain Drowley for the second time that day. To his credit, Drowley quickly recognized and remedied the unjust situation. He immediately requisitioned new uniforms and boots for the guerrillas, allowed them to draw their pay, and sent them off, exhausted but now happy, on their two-week R&R leave.

Not surprisingly, the unit historian for Battery B of the 222nd described June and July of 1945 as the hardest months in the battery's history. "In these months the greater part of the battery learned the dirty part of war. They slept in the jungles, went without food and rest, and were wet almost constantly. They killed—and were killed." Mohammad Adil and his guerrillas of the 119th had known "the dirty part of war" for nearly two years, although there was one experience they had not shared with Battery B, which had "two of the best liked boys in the battery …cut down in battle [just as]…the war was nearing its end." Third Lieutenant Adil had not lost a single soldier in nearly two years of engaging the enemy, and that included the weeks he spent guiding the American soldiers of the 222nd.

* * *

I was not able to enjoy the peaceful interior of the Eisenhower Presidential Library in Abilene, Kansas. The Covid pandemic kept it, and so many other libraries, closed for well over a year. It was thanks to a compassionate and resourceful archivist at the library, Michelle Kopfer, that I was able to obtain photocopies of the official history and roster of the 222nd AAA Searchlight Battalion. Those materials were far more engaging, and affecting than I had imagined.

I had sought them out, as I had other historical documents, to validate Mohammad Adil's recollections, and they did not disappoint. There in the narrative history and on the roster I found the exact names of the men he had mentioned so often in his stories—Captain Drowley, Sergeant Burk, and Sergeant Lupisto Rincon (whose last name Adil thought was "Lincoln," probably because the Magindanaon language has no "R" sound). One name missing from the historical narrative is Mohammad Adil's, which came as little surprise to me. For American soldiers in the Pacific War, including soldier-historians, the social universe was divided into Americans (and their occasional Australian or British allies), "Japs," and "natives." All members of a local populace—whether "half-naked" tribeswomen in New Guinea or college-educated lawyers in the Philippines—were "natives." As such, their names were not recorded, and their activities were not considered worthy of mention. The battalion history does, however mention on multiple occasions the assistance provided by the 119th Guerrilla Regiment, Adil's unit.

For the unit historian of Battery B, who, until June 1945, had only experienced the clean part of war, the last two full months of the Pacific War were so filled with unfamiliar strain and sorrow that his anguish spills onto the pages of his otherwise dry recounting of the unit's monthly activities. As recently as April 1945, the soldiers of Battery B had been handling radar units, generators, and searchlights at well-defended airfields. Suddenly in June, half of them they were holding rifles and slashing their way through deep jungle, seeking out an enemy at his most desperate. They had spent almost the entire war either in Southern California or at the South Pacific equivalent of a Boy Scout Jamboree, receiving commendations for tidy campsites. For almost the entire war there had been no enemy planes to spot and no one shooting at them. Now, in the last weeks of the war, they were killing and being killed at close range.

Due to the vagaries of war, while the members of Battery B patrolled on Mount Blit, the entire rest of the battalion enjoyed an uneventful June and July, with "negative" enemy air activity and time spent mostly on equipment maintenance and classroom study. The particular "dirty part of war" that Battery B experienced was also the forgotten part. The operation in the Mount Blit area, apparently because of its relatively small scale, is not mentioned in any of the general histories of the Mindanao Campaign and, as far as I know, exists only in the 222nd unit history and in the stories of Mohammad Adil. Thanks to the initiative of 3rd Lt. Adil, the man they had called "boy," the soldiers of the 222nd accomplished their mission on Mount Blit. If they hadn't had him as their guide and comrade, more of them may well have died in the process. If they had found him a few days earlier, all of them might have made it home alive.

10
REUNION

The wide streets of Cotabato town, running up from the riverside wharves, bustled even more than they had two months earlier. Adil and his men, with money in the pockets of their crisp new khakis, proudly walked the reinvigorated town. Shops and restaurants had reopened and there were goods for sale that hadn't been seen in years. With public transportation once more available, civilians arrived on boats and trucks from villages they hadn't left in years to stroll the provincial capital and celebrate their liberation.

On a corner near the public market, Adil saw four young women standing together talking. One of them was so exceptionally pretty that everyone was watching her. He noticed that they were speaking Illongo, so he asked two of his soldiers, Illongo brothers, who she was. They told him that she was "Miss Maganoy of 1941, the beauty queen of Maganoy." "They added that the girl, Teofila Lubaton, was their second cousin, and Adil asked them to introduce him.

The four girls looked up as they neared. Although the men wore new uniforms, they still had the unshorn hair that marked them as guerrillas, and Adil's long hair was wrapped in a colorful *tubao*. Although still younger than any of the men he commanded, he was no longer the smiling youth of 1943. Years of hardship had carved the boyish face into sharper contours and his once wide and twinkling eyes now surveyed the world around him with a penetrating glint. Resculpted by war, he had become an impressively handsome young man.

In a group portrait in late 1945, Mohammad Adil, transformed by war, stands far right. His father stands next to him with Hadji Hashim on the far left. Their wives are seated in front of them.

One of the brothers, Benigno, approached his cousin and greeted her in Illongo. She told him that she and her friends had come to town for the day to visit. Before he could introduce Adil she asked him in Illongo, "Who is this Moro with you?" Adil quickly spoke up in Illongo, surprising her. "Yes, I am a Moro. My name is Mohammad Adil, and I am pleased to meet you." Benigno formally introduced Lieutenant Adil to Miss Teofila Lubaton, and then they parted, but Adil would remember their brief exchange.

Later that afternoon, as they strolled near the Matampay bridge, Adil suddenly recognized a familiar enemy riding in an open jeep being driven across the bridge by an American officer. He jumped into the road with his rifle raised, and halted the jeep, then told his men to seize the passenger and tie him up. The man was Pangan, a sergeant in the pre-war Philippine Army before joining the Japanese-formed Bureau of Constabulary (BC). Pangan, who was wearing his sergeant's chevrons today but without the red BC armband, was one of the ambushers who had nearly succeeded in killing Adil at the Talayan River and then boasted about it afterwards.

The American officer, shocked at the disruption, demanded to know what was going on. "Sir," Adil said, "I am an officer of the guerrillas and this man is a well-known Japanese collaborator. If you had been here during the occupation, this man would have been the first to kill you."

"Oh, that's good to know, Lieutenant." And he drove on alone.

While they decided what to do with Pangan, five of his fellow BC constables moved in to free him. Adil and his men quickly disarmed them and tied them up as well. By now a crowd had gathered and Adil invited any civilian who so desired to come forward and slap the BC men left and right, in the same way that Japanese soldiers had regularly slapped civilians in the street during the occupation. A number of them now stepped up swinging, seeking some small retribution for years of forced privation and humiliation. Adil recognized one of Pangan's constables as the informer who had him arrested by Japanese soldiers in 1943. They hung Pangan by his heels and decided to exact vengeance then and there on the man who had tried to kill them. Adil told one of his men to hurry to his quarters and return with his kris and he told Hadji Hashim to prepare himself for his job. The kris had belonged to his grandfather,

Pangilamen, and it had a name, *Dilumukung*, or Soundless. In Magindanaon, "*lukung*" is the sound a wooden paddle makes when it strikes the side of a dugout canoe while paddling. "*Dilumukung*" is when the paddle makes no sound as it slices smoothly through the water. His grandfather's kris seemed the appropriate weapon to dispatch this traitor.

As they waited for the arrival of the executioner's sword, four jeeps filled with American military police roared across the bridge and pulled up in front of them. The informer's sister had seen him taken and was afraid for his life, so she ran to tell her boyfriend, an American Military Police officer, about a summary execution in progress. Adil and his men were now surrounded by more than a dozen M.P.s, all pointing Thompson submachine guns. "Lieutenant, tell your men to drop their weapons!" Adil's men held tight to their guns and began muttering in Magindanaon. They had had enough of Americans and were ready to fight. Adil unslung his rifle and lowered it to the ground, then raised his hands slowly and told his men to do the same. The officer of the M.P.s, Lt. Blair, took Adil's pistol from its holster and escorted him to his jeep. Then the Americans drove off as fast as they had arrived, leaving Adil's men standing in the street with their hands still raised and their weapons at their feet.

The MPs took him back to where he had just deposited the Japanese prisoners. The American stockade was a full-scale prison camp with guard towers, searchlights, and machine guns. As the only guerrilla officer in the entire stockade, he was given his own tent in a small enclosure. He noticed that the tent and everything in it—cot, pillow, blanket, water pitcher—was brand new. He breathed in the newness, a smell he hadn't experienced in three years until being issued his new uniform a day earlier.

He sat on the pristine cot surrounded by the scent of clean

canvas and shuddered from the shame of it. Once again, he had been captured and imprisoned, but this time it was even worse. This time he had been disarmed and detained in front of his men. This time he had been arrested by his own army and locked up alongside his enemies. Ashamed and despondent, he spent a day and night on the cot, never leaving his tent. Eventually, though, he stirred himself to explore his surroundings. The Japanese prisoners of war, more than a thousand in all, were held at one end of the camp, separated from the other prisoners by "barbed wire not even a cat could pass through." At the other end were the common criminals—rapists, murderers, thieves, the drunk and disorderly. Toward the center of the camp was a fenced compound for political prisoners—active Japanese collaborators. And in the very center of the camp, next to the political prisoners, stood his enclosure, holding just a single inmate in a category all his own.

The compound for political prisoners held more than 200 members of the Bureau of Constabulary. One large tent was reserved for senior BC officers from Cotabato. They included Datu Sinsuat Balabaran, his son, Odin Sinsuat, and Usman Baraguir, the chief of police of Cotabato Town, who had gotten Adil released from the Japanese stockade. As the most prominent and active collaborator in the province, Datu Sinsuat had used the local Bureau of Constabulary as his private police force.

As he paced the perimeter of his small section of the camp one evening, Adil saw Datu Sinsuat waiting on the other side of the wire to speak with him. He greeted him, and Datu Sinsuat asked after Adil's father, his second cousin. Sinsuat, slight of build, bespectacled, and now elderly, did not project physical power, but Adil knew better. The old man told the young man that he had information he wanted to share. Word had spread about the reason Adil was in prison, about his vendetta against the BC. Sinsuat told him that two BC officers had just come to him asking his permission to kill Adil there in the camp. "I refused their request, but be very careful young man, I can't guarantee that they won't still try to harm you."

Adil returned to his tent that night and did not sleep. He had neither weapons nor companions, and the fence between his compound and the next, unlike the one separating off the Japanese prisoners, could be easily, and silently, breached. He needed out of the stockade immediately, but an escape attempt would be difficult. If it failed, he would be shot at the fence and even if it succeeded it would make him an outlaw to the Americans. He decided to try writing his way out of prison first. The next morning, he asked his guard for a pencil and paper and began to write a petition for his release. By early afternoon it was ready to submit to the prison commandant. The multi-page petition included selections from the Declaration of Independence, the Preamble to the U.S. Constitution, and the Gettysburg Address that he had memorized as a schoolboy.

Two days later, he had visitors to his enclosure—Lt. Fallon, the prison commandant, was accompanied by another officer and two armed guards. Lt. Fallon introduced Captain Spencer, who, he said, had some questions for him. Captain Spencer held Adil's handwritten petition. "Lt. Adil, did you write this?"

"Yes sir, I did."

"Are you sure you're the sole author, or did you hire someone to help you?

"No sir, I wrote it myself."

"If I tore this up, could you write me another one right now?"

"Yes, sir, I could."

Colonel Spencer tore the petition in half, stuffed it in his pocket, and left with the commandant, telling one guard to remain behind in the enclosure. In two hours they returned and Adil handed him the new petition, which he had improved on second writing. Colonel Spencer looked it over quickly then tucked it under his arm. He told Adil that he worked for the C.I.C, the U.S. Counter-Intelligence Corps. He offered to have him released from prison on the condition that he would come work for him to identify and investigate local wartime collaborators. Mohammad Adil, delighted at this turn of fortune, readily agreed.

A short while later, he was released from the stockade. Most of his two week leave had been spent behind barbed wire. For the few days remaining, he went home to Pagalamatan. He wanted to see his family but he wanted more to visit Ignacia, to feel her warmth and taste her passion again. He then returned to Cotabato town to begin his detached service with the CIC, writing reports for Captain Spencer.

Adil approached his new job with enthusiasm, reporting on the wartime activities of the BC men who had informed on him, ambushed him, and sought to kill him in the prison camp. But when it came to the most senior leaders of the Cotabato BC he found himself less eager. Datu Usman Baraguir, the BC Chief of Police for Cotabato town, had given him his freedom and most likely saved his life by arranging his release from the Japanese stockade in 1943. *Maratabat* would not allow him to report Baraguir to the Americans.

Datu Sinsuat Balabaran presented a more difficult decision. It is true that he had warned Adil of the threat against his life in prison, but he was also the leading Japanese collaborator in the province. Men under his control had killed guerrillas and burned the homes of their civilian supporters. And his son Odin directly led these efforts. At home, when he asked whether or not he should report the Sinsuats, his father replied, "It would be better not to. Datu Sinsuat is your uncle." His grandmother, Bai Tambis, a woman of the high nobility accustomed to being obeyed, was more direct. "I forbid it!" In the end, he reported to the Americans that Datu Sinsuat and his son were passive collaborators, reluctantly leaving out almost everything he knew about their actual activities during the war.

Between writing reports, Adil created a document of his own on CIC letterhead. It was a Certificate of Good Conduct in the form of a short formal letter in English composed by Adil:

> I know the bearer of this note to be a peaceful,
> law-abiding citizen. He has never collaborated in any
> way with the Japanese. I request every American soldier
> to give him due respect. If he has committed some minor
> infraction of the law, please consult me first.

Each certificate was signed with Adil's name and rank, and he mimeographed more than a hundred of them and distributed them widely. His father, who knew his son was aiding the Sinsuats unwillingly and against his better judgment, had suggested that he do something for his own Tampakanen kinsmen, who had been asking for assistance in dealing with the new military authorities. Thirty years later, a few of the certificates could still be found in the lower delta, their owners treasuring them like prized talismans, which in a sense they were.

Within a few weeks, tired of the desk work and the moral predicaments, Adil asked Captain Spencer to let him rejoin the 119th. When Spencer agreed, Adil was on his way immediately to Davao, where Gumbay Piang and the 119th guerrilla regiment were preparing to take part in Operation Downfall, the invasion of the Japanese home islands. Bivouacked along with thousands of American soldiers on Talomo Beach on the Davao Gulf, Adil had time to contemplate fighting on foreign soil as part of a massive invasion force and how different that would be from defending his own homeland from foreign invaders.

The announcement of the Japanese surrender on August 15th brought an end to the war, to Operation Downfall, and to his contemplation. Just two days prior to that joy-filled day, the news had been sad. Colonel Frank McGee, who since June had been leading his guerrillas against one of the last significant groups of Japanese holdouts north of Davao City, had been shot and killed. He was on the front line with a small patrol, moving between two of his units when a single shot from a Japanese sniper sent them seeking cover. When there was no further firing after a long interval, McGee started to get up to continue advancing, and a second shot severed an artery in his hip. He died a short while later. He was 56 years old. Grievously wounded in the last war, he had a long list of reasons to stay out of this one, or at the very least away from the front lines. But he was exactly where he wanted to be. Thirty years after graduating from West Point he had recreated his career as a field officer—a role that had been cruelly taken from him by his early war injury.

Later that year, Frank McGee was posthumously awarded the Silver Star for conspicuous gallantry. It was his second world war, his second wound, and his second medal, but the injury had proved quickly fatal this time. McGee was not the only Mindanao guerrilla to receive a citation for valor. The guerrilla chief of Mindanao, Wendell Fertig, was awarded the Distinguished Service Cross by Douglas MacArthur in August 1943 for his actions in May, June, and July of 1943—the period in which Misamis, his "Capital of the Free Philippines," was overrun and his guerrilla forces scattered. It appears to have been an effort by MacArthur's headquarters to bolster his authority at a time when his position had been so weakened that local guerrilla leaders, such as Salipada Pendatun and Luis Morgan, were more inclined to challenge it. Charles Hedges, who with his elite Moro fighters rescued Fertig from Japanese-held Misamis, did not receive a citation from MacArthur.

One Moro guerrilla under Wendell Fertig's command did receive an American citation. Manalao Mindalano, whose deeds during the war were extraordinary even by the standards of the Moros, was awarded the Silver Star belatedly in 1951. His citation commends him for leading an ambush in September 1943 against a Japanese patrol outside Ganassi "which destroyed 10 hostile soldiers" and for exceptional gallantry during the battle for Malabang in April 1945. Mindalano had of course been attacking Japanese soldiers in Lanao since the first days of the occupation, but his remarkable successes as a freedom fighter against the Japanese occupiers of Lanao throughout 1942 were accomplished before the American-led guerrilla movement had fully gotten underway. It is not clear how he came to receive the Silver Star or why it was only awarded to him in 1951. He was, it seems, the only Moro guerrilla in Mindanao to receive official American recognition for his contribution to the defeat of Japan.

* * *

Two months before the Japanese surrender, on June 13th, 1945, Edward Kuder sat at his typewriter in his cousin's Washington apartment to compose a letter to James Forrestal, the Secretary of the Navy. The city outside his window was in a victorious mood. The war in Europe had been won, Manila had fallen, and the total defeat of Japan was just a matter of time, although how many months and American lives would be required for victory over Japan was, in June, still unknown. The soon-to-be capital of the postwar world had begun to focus its attention beyond the current conflict, and so had Edward Kuder.

In his letter, Kuder tells Forrestal that he has seen him quoted in the New York Times stating that the U.S. Navy will retain and establish bases in the Philippines after the end of the war. He then suggests Mindanao-Sulu as an excellent location for such a base and offers himself as the ideal candidate to provide "educational services" for both naval dependents and the "native inhabitants" of any "security area" established around such a base. The letter concludes with a detailed listing of his qualifications.

Kuder's letter to Forrestal reveals a man anxious to return to the Philippines and afraid that the place he most wants to be no longer has need of him. He is aware that the world swept away by the Japanese invasion will never return, and he has known for a decade that Philippine independence would eventually arrive and end his colonial career. But he is hoping to recreate a small slice of the old colonial world in a new "security area"—a part of the Philippines the United States might hold back when it returned formal control of the Philippines to its people, as promised, in 1946.

Edward Kuder was not being pushed from the United States by a shortage of success. Given the condition in which he arrived home in 1944, his achievements had been remarkable. In June of 1945, he did not hold a regular job, but his bank account stood at $4000, enough funds to live comfortably in D.C. for two more years. He had garnered public recognition with his Saturday Evening Post series and his social network included prominent government officials. His letter to Forrestal listed as references a U.S. senator, Thomas C. Hart of Connecticut, and J. Weldon Jones, Assistant Director of the Bureau of the Budget (the predecessor of the federal Office of Management and Budget).[1]

He had also acquired a scholarly reputation with his writing and was universally acknowledged as the leading American authority on the Moros and on the Southern Philippines. With the end of the war, a suitable stateside position—at a federal agency, a college, or a large public school district—would likely have been available to him. But Kuder's sights were set solely on the newly-liberated Philippines. He was a 49-year-old man unsure of his role in the coming post-war world. The Philippines was where he felt most at home and where he wanted to spend the rest of his life, even though he knew that his opportunities to make a living there would now be severely constrained.

At the end of July, Kuder received a polite but noncommittal one-page reply from Admiral John L. McCrea, the Deputy Chief of Naval Operations. A few weeks later, a temporary solution to his problem appeared with the surrender of Japan and a request by the Commonwealth of the Philippines for him to return to the islands to reopen the schools of Lanao. The job would be temporary but the return would not. After he stepped onto the airplane to take him back across the Pacific, Edward Kuder never set foot in the country of his birth again.

* * *

One morning in late August, Mohammad Adil, now serving as a transportation officer overseeing the movement of American soldiers and materiel from Cotabato to Davao on their way to returning home to the U.S., was interrupted at his work by an orderly and told to report immediately to Colonel Senate at the Philippine Civil Affairs Unit (PCAU) located in a large tent in front of City Hall. Adil assumed he had gotten himself in trouble again and asked why. "Some civilian over there is looking for you. Bader? Gruder?" Adil hurried to Colonel Senate's office to find Edward Kuder, dressed in a khaki uniform with no insignia, sitting in a chair chatting with the colonel and two other American officers. Kuder smiled and rose to embrace him, and they both cried right there to see each other again.

They conversed excitedly in fragments. "When did you arrive?"

"I was in Manila for a week to get approval to travel south. I came to Cotabato purposely to see you. I was evacuated to Australia and then California. I waited for you but you didn't arrive."

"My sister died."

"They operated on me. They even removed my rib." And he lifted his shirt to show Adil the still-bright scar and deep hollow on his ribcage. Kuder then turned proudly to Colonel Senate. "This is my boy!"

Colonel Senate headed the Cotabato PCAU detachment, one of the last of the 30 PCAU teams still operating in the Philippines. Douglas MacArthur, intent on avoiding post-invasion chaos, had chosen Joseph Hayden to solve the problems of administering civilian affairs under military government. Hayden and his team invented the concept of self-contained civil affairs teams designed to quickly revitalize areas damaged by the Japanese occupation and the American invasion. The teams had specialists in medicine, law enforcement, agriculture, and administration and they brought with them tons of supplies intended solely for civilians. Working from Australia just prior to the invasion, Hayden had only had weeks to put the program together and assemble the teams. It was his last major planning project before his untimely death, and the PCAU teams that he created became a universal success. It was Colonel Senate's team that was responsible for shops reopening and public transportation resuming so quickly in Cotabato.[2]

The colonel was impressed with young Lieutenant Adil and

when Adil told him that the Moros of the lower delta, who lived along rivers and away from the main roads, had not received any PCAU supplies he immediately arranged for two loaded cargo trucks and drivers to arrive by barge at the Tamontaka ferry landing, the place where Adil had escaped death a few months earlier. Adil hopped aboard one of the trucks and off they drove down the narrow trails to the riverside communities where he distributed an unimaginable bounty of American goods to his relatives and neighbors. Off the backs of the trucks came bolts of cloth, fatigues, blankets, mosquito nets, and shoes (most of them too big). They handed out rice, sugar, dried milk, dehydrated eggs, corned beef, canned goods, and c-rations—chicken and rice, oatmeal, but nothing containing the prohibited pork. Everyone received American supplies, everyone ate American food for months afterwards, and everyone remembered that it was young Datu Adil who had obtained this windfall for them.

In a few weeks, Adil was transferred east again with the rest of the 119th Battalion to patrol the rugged mountains of Davao from Kisante to Mati. Intelligence indicated that bands of Japanese holdouts were about to sweep down from the slopes of Mount Apo and slaughter as many civilians as they could. Once again, it seemed, Moro guerrillas and Japanese troops would be facing off in the deeply forested uplands west of Digos. For three months, Adil and his men chased ghosts along the sharp ridges and deep green ravines that fanned out from the majestic volcano, never encountering a living Japanese soldier despite the many excited reports of sightings by local villagers. In early November of 1945, the 119th was officially transferred from the U.S. guerrilla forces to the reconstituted Philippine Army and Adil was promoted to second lieutenant. The new Philippine Army was fully independent and no longer was Douglas MacArthur its Field Marshall, having been already installed in his new position as Supreme Commander of the Allied Powers, super-vising the occupation of Japan from Tokyo.

That same early November, Edward Kuder penned a letter from Lanao, where he was reopening the schools, to his foster son, replying to an October letter from Adil asking about the things he had left at their shared house in Marawi in late 1941. Kuder had sent Adil quickly home to his parents after the first Japanese bombing and most of his belongings had been left in the rush. Kuder wrote him that everything was gone, his bicycle, books, and clothes. Some had been stolen, along with Kuder's cameras, by one of the two boys from Sulu, Marajuni, before he left to go back home. Kuder added, "I am sorry he turned out that way...but perhaps God punished him, for the Japanese killed him."

Adil had also apparently asked Kuder about a "pension." Adil's original letter has been lost but he was almost certainly referring to one of the Philippine Commonwealth-funded college scholarships available for war veterans. Kuder replies that he is "writing Salipada to help you..." Salipada Pendatun had already been appointed sen-ator for the soon-to-be republic, fulfilling one of Kuder's wishes for his foster sons. Despite agreeing to help, however, Kuder was clearly not pleased with Adil's request. Kuder's "boy" had grown into an exceptional young man over four wartime years, only a few weeks of which the two had spent together. Nevertheless, Kuder's writing slips quickly into quasi-parental disapproval when he feels his stan-dards aren't being met.

"...but why do you spend all your money on that woman of the *Lanang*...and then ask the government for a pension?" "That woman" was Ignacia (*Lanang* being the Magindanaon term for the Chinese), and Kuder had learned of the relationship. In the letter, he advises his grown foster son that it is time to prioritize. "One...must select what he wants *most*: woman or love or education."

Kuder is telling his foster son to select how he wants to spend his time and money; on the "woman of the Lanang," on the "love" of a wife (for Kuder knew that Adil was of the age when most young Moro men marry), or on the "education" that Kuder wants most for him. Adil was not, however, ready to choose. He was a young man, energetic and ambitious, and ready to have it all at once. Four months later, in March 1946, he was about to return to civilian life along with hundreds of other World War II veterans whom the Philippine government was reverting to inactive status. He was still spending delightful time alone with Ignacia whenever he could. He was scheduled to start college in a few months at the University of the Philippines in Manila on a government scholarship as a "student-veteran *pensionado.*" And he had recently realized that he was in love, but not with the "woman of the Lanang."

Teofila Lubaton, the beauty queen of Maganoy, had captivated him since their first brief meeting. She now had a small dress shop with two sewing machines in Cotabato town, and he had contrived reasons to stop by and see her as often as he could over the past months. They talked about their lives before and during the war and about the people they knew in common. He learned that everyone called her by her nickname, Nene, and that she had been a primary school teacher before the war and had been crowned as a beauty queen just before her life was frozen in place for almost four years during the occupation as her parents tried to keep her and her sisters safe from Japanese soldiers and roving bandits. Adil told her he regretted never patrolling in her area as his Illongo soldiers had urged him to do in order to get a glimpse of Miss Maganoy.

This pretty young woman with modern looks and modern attitudes quickly stole his heart. She attracted him far more than the aristocratic young Moro women his father had in mind for him, who were poorly educated but haughty, skilled only in traditional etiquette and in managing great houses crowded with servants. Adil knew he wanted to marry Nene and he knew he had to propose soon, before someone beat him to it, but he also knew the odds against him. As with many Christian settlers to Cotabato, her parents regarded Moros as uncivilized, dangerous, and deceitful. After sheltering her from years of wartime hazards, they would never, under any circumstance, allow their daughter to marry a Moro. He decided he would have to steal her.

* * *

Stealing a bride was something young Moro men knew how to do. The Moros regarded women so highly that they required a man who wanted to marry to provide a significant amount of wealth to the family of the bride. This "bridewealth" was mostly controlled by the father of the bride but a significant portion went directly to her. The frustrations brought about by high bridewealth requirements led to predictable consequences. When they could not produce the bridewealth they needed to marry, some men resorted to bride theft.

These abductions were almost always in fact elopements, with the brides agreeing to and sometimes initiating the escape plan. The runaway couple would flee to the house of a neutral chieftain who would then adjudicate the case to resolve the crisis, usually by a quick marriage and the payment of a fine that was significantly lower than the bridewealth would have been.

* * *

As far as Adil knew, no Moro in Cotabato had ever stolen a Christian bride. Muslim-Christian marriages were extremely rare in 1946. Adil's foster brother, Salipada Pendatun, was the only Moro he knew personally who had married a Christian. He had shocked his community during the war by divorcing his first wife, the highly-regarded Bai Matabay Plang, to marry Aida Farrales, the daughter of a Christian family in Cotabato. But Pendatun had not stolen his Christian wife—Aida was a free-spirited woman already independent from her parents. Adil would have to steal his.

His bride theft would be more an actual abduction than an elopement. He had decided not to tell Nene in advance to avoid scaring her away. He was confident she wanted to marry him, but the costs to her for doing so would be so significant that he didn't want her to spend too much time thinking about them. He planned the escapade as carefully as he had the ambush of the Japanese detachment at Salebu. It was, after all, a sort of ambush.

First, he invited her for a romantic boat trip upriver to his birthplace to meet his family. Next, he arranged for his two former soldiers, her Illongo cousins, to accompany them as chaperones. Then, without telling him of his plans, he contacted his father to ask him to send Ignacia away to her parents' house. Both he and Ignacia knew this day would come. It had just arrived sooner than expected.

They left Cotabato town in two dugouts on a Saturday morning with his former soldiers, some of them still in uniform, paddling. Nene had never been in a Moro dugout, carved from a single immense mountain hardwood and able to hold twenty or more people. She had also never travelled on the thoroughfares of the Moros—the interlaced waterways that linked the two great rivers of the broad delta. They glided in silence except for the occasional thunk of a paddle against the hollowed hull, Adil pointing out egrets and stilts on the muddy banks. Before noon they had arrived in Pagalamatan.

Adil helped her from the boat onto the riverbank, the same beach he had gone to war from in 1943. When his father came from the house to meet them he spoke to him in Magindanaon. "Father, I'm going to marry this woman today. Please send for the *pandita*." Hearing the tone of his voice and the look on his father's face, Nene turned to him and asked, "Why did you bring me here?" Adil replied, "To marry you." Her eyes widened with surprise and her voice caught with fear. "I didn't know. Why didn't you tell me?"

"It doesn't have to be today, but I *will* marry you." He pointed to her cousins. "They are leaving now. If you want, they will take you home. Do you want to go with them?"

"No," she replied softly, "I will stay," then she began to cry quietly as the full significance of what she was about to do settled on her. Adil told her cousins to return to town in one of the dugouts then to go to her parents' house, collect her things, and tell her parents that she was marrying him that day.

Ama ni Sansu, the senior *pandita* of Pagalamatan, soon arrived, and the community gathered as word spread. He greeted Adil's father and asked, "Hadji Datu, why did you call for me?"

"My son here has found a woman that he has decided to marry."

"Where is this woman?" Hadji Adil pointed her out, and the *pandita* saw that she was wearing a Christian dress, one she had made herself especially for the visit. Ama ni Sansu, turned to Adil. "Datu, I cannot wed you to this woman because she is a Christian."

"Is that the only reason we can't be married?"

"Yes."

"Then we'll fix the problem." He told his sister to bring a *malong* from the house. She put it on Nene, tying it over her dress. The *pandita* asked for rainwater to be obtained from the tank. He then poured a small amount of water on the back of her head and whispered the *Shahada*, the Muslim declaration of faith, in her ear. Then he turned to Adil. "Datu, she is now a Muslim. You may marry her." And so they were married by the *pandita* there at the riverside as the community looked on.[3]

Because the bride he had stolen was not a Moro, there would be no adjudication, no fine, and no settlement. Her parents simply disowned her for the sin of marrying a Moro. They shunned her completely, not speaking to her for years, and her siblings turned away from her just as thoroughly, except a single younger sister who would visit her on occasion. All of that she knew, or could have predicted, when she made the instantaneous and extraordinarily brave decision to stay in that unfamiliar place and marry that intriguing young man.

That young man had far fewer costs to pay. His father and Edward Kuder were upset at the marriage—his father because he had not married a Moro and Kuder because he had not prioritized education over love. The elders could not understand why he had chosen to marry a Christian but his younger kinsmen understood the appeal, and within ten years, Muslim-Christian marriages were becoming common in Cotabato. He had survived a guerrilla war, a Japanese stockade, and an American prison camp, and now he had succeeded in marrying the woman of his dreams. He felt ready to face any challenge the new postwar world held in store for him.

* * *

In the end, I did not fulfill the responsibilities of an honorary kinsman, at least not in time. My failure started with a decision that would have had Mohammad Adil's approval, had I asked for it. After ten years living and working in a place geographically and culturally distant from my own, I wanted to take myself and my family back to our home land, where we were born and where our relatives and friends still lived, the place where we longed to be. But that required that I leave anthropology, at least temporarily, and start a new career. Magically thinking that I could do it all, I told him, and myself, that the move would cause only a short delay in finishing the book. Mohammad Adil, who had been given the secret knowledge, may have had the magic to accomplish that, but I didn't.

Though overwhelmed from the start, I did not abandon Mohammad Adil or the Moros. I continued writing to him and writing about them in occasional articles, but something had to give and I gradually put the book project aside. As year followed upon year, the emotional tension of disappointing him became too hard to sustain and I let the lines of communication between us fray and then break. I could no longer face him with the fact that I hadn't finished the book because I couldn't face myself with that same fact.

I spent a decade and a half unable to write a word of this book. For all those years, however, I also felt a quiet but insistent sense of obligation, even inevitability. The foremost obligation was to Mohammad Adil, of course, but I also felt an obligation to the stories themselves. For fifteen years they were never far from me; most had been imprinted on cassette tapes that were growing more anachronistic by the year, some had been scribbled in notebooks and then typed onto sheets of paper using an Olivetti portable typewriter, and as many as possible had been digitized and transferred to a thumb drive that I carried with me.

When it came time to tell my honorary uncle that this book was finally finished and ready to publish, it was too late. I had been away for too long and he was gone. I had failed to say goodbye to him or to thank him or to reassure him that his story would be told before he died. This book, the first of two planned books about Mohammad Adil, Edward Kuder, and the Moros in the twentieth century, is a belated tribute—a posthumous citation, as it were—to Mohammad Adil and his fellow Moro guerrillas.

EPILOGUE

Manila, July 4th, 1946

In sharp contrast to the other postwar colonial powers in Asia—Britain, France, and the Netherlands—the United States transferred sovereignty to its former colony quickly and peacefully. It should perhaps be forgiven, then, for failing to recognize the historical irony in the day it had chosen to grant independence to the Philippines in 1946. July 4th, the day that America celebrated its successful fight for independence from foreign rule, would now, awkwardly, also commemorate Imperial America's release of the overseas colony it had fought hard to possess for almost 50 years.[1] It was, nonetheless, a day of celebration in Manila, the war-shattered capital of the new nation, and Edward Kuder, Salipada Pendatun, and Mohammad Adil, all now living in Manila, were there to share in the festivities. Pendatun, now an elected member of the Philippine Senate, would almost certainly have joined the massive celebration in the heart of the city. Kuder and Adil were also likely attendees, especially as Douglas MacArthur, their former supreme commander, had flown in from Tokyo to speak at the gathering. The wet season had started and the skies poured rain for most of the day but neither MacArthur nor the jubilant crowd was deterred.

Adopting the same self-congratulatory approach to the turn-over that had prompted the choice of July 4th, MacArthur declared that "America buried Imperialism here today."[2] As he looked out over the crowd that filled the Luneta, the broad park in the center of the city, he could not have helped seeing the still-ruined public buildings that surrounded that open space—dark and hollow reminders that it was his artillery that had destroyed so much of the city he loved. Manila was the closest equivalent to a hometown that MacArthur, a military brat, had ever known, and 16 months after the battle for Manila, his hometown was still mostly in ruins, with endless acres reduced to ashes or rubble. In a global war defined by its colossal tragedies, the destruction of Manila was one of the worst, and remains one of the least known.

It was a tragedy in the classical sense as well, in that the supreme commanders of the two opposing armies had each tried hard to spare the city, and still it was destroyed. Douglas MacArthur had long hoped to avoid the ruination of Manila. On December 26th, 1941, as he withdrew into the Bataan Peninsula, he declared Manila an "open city" to save it from destruction. Three years later, in February 1945, he both forbade American airstrikes in the battle to retake Manila and strictly limited artillery use in order to protect the city and its population.

General Tomoyuki Yamashita, who had defeated the British on the Malay Peninsula and conquered Singapore, earning the nickname "Tiger of Malaya," was the commander of Japanese forces in the Philippines. Yamashita, built more like a bull than a tiger, had been appointed to the position in late September 1944 and knew immediately upon setting foot in the country in October that he had inherited a disaster. Although later hanged after being found guilty of the war crime of failing to prevent the destruction of Manila and its associated atrocities, Yamashita was not primarily responsible for the calamity that befell Manila and had instead attempted to prevent it.

By mid-December 1945, Yamashita had decided not to defend Manila. Instead, he withdrew almost all his 260,000 troops to mountain strongholds throughout the island of Luzon, leaving only a contingent of 17,000 Naval Defense Force troops in Manila whose orders were to destroy its ports and bridges before the Americans' arrival and then abandon the city once their work was completed. On December 26th, Yamashita evacuated Manila just as MacArthur had done almost exactly three years earlier, but stopped short of declaring it an open city.

The commander of the Manila Naval Defense Force, Rear Admiral Sanji Iwabuchi, had made a very different decision, which caused him to ignore the orders of General Yamashita. He had decided to stop the Americans at all costs, even if that meant destroying Manila. Admiral Iwabushi's nihilistically stubborn stand was likely prompted by his personal history. Iwabushi had lost the battleship he skippered in a sea battle at Guadalcanal but, to his shame (and to the detriment of his naval career) he was rescued and survived. As historian James M. Scott notes, "Iwabuchi...saw Manila as his redemption...This time...he had no intention of abandoning his ship. He would go down with it."[3] Iwabuchi justified his failure to withdraw from the city to his immediate superior by claiming that he had not yet completed his mission to destroy Manila's port, harbor, and bridges. His army commander, General Yokoyama, trying to avoid creating more friction between the army and navy, did not push him to leave the city until it was too late.

As American forces tightened their noose around the city, the Japanese naval troops fortified its center, building barricades and bunkers, emplacing guns, planting mines, and setting booby traps. They then began blowing up bridges but did not stop there. Admiral Iwabuchi adopted a scorched-earth policy, ordering his troops to demolish every building in the north of the city that could be useful to their attackers. Soon the entire business district was ablaze, with flames shooting 200 feet into the sky. The firestorm in the city's northern half lasted for days, destroying entire neighborhoods and killing thousands of civilians. Then, with a ferocity matched only by the 1937 Rape of Nanking, Iwabuchi's marines began to rape, murder, and terrorize the city's civilians in a string of atrocities that were both frenzied and systematic, combining random barbarities with highly organized mass executions of men, women, and children.

The naval troops made their final stand in southern Manila, where they had dug in with heavy guns salvaged from their damaged ships. So difficult were they to dislodge that MacArthur eventually lifted his restrictions on field artillery fire which, when fully unleashed, was astonishingly destructive but not consistently accurate. The Japanese had burned much of the northern half of the city. Now the Americans pulverized most of the south. The surviving residents of Manila, caught between the opposing forces, died by the thousands from American and Japanese shellfire. Of the more than 100,000 civilians (at least 10 percent of the city's population) who died in the battle for Manila, most were casualties of those artillery exchanges. [4]

After almost four weeks of brutal fighting, Admiral Iwabuchi, who had directed one of the most devastating and pointless battles of the entire war and had allowed, if not ordered, some of its very worst outrages, made his very last stand in the American-designed

Agriculture and Commerce Building at the edge of the Luneta and, as American artillery shells pulverized the building around him, took his own life. Within two days the Battle of Manila was over, but the cost of victory, the surviving residents of Manila realized as they emerged from their hiding places into a ravaged hellscape, had been unimaginably high. Other than Warsaw—which Adolf Hitler had ordered razed to the ground in 1944 as punishment for the Warsaw Uprising—no other allied city paid a higher price for its liberation.

The desolation visited on Manila in February of 1945 still defined the city in mid-1946. The "Pearl of the Orient" had been irreparably damaged. More than 11,000 buildings, including nearly all those in the business district, had been flattened or burnt to the ground. The city's extensive streetcar network had been shelled out of existence, and three-quarters of its factories had been obliterated. Seventy percent of the public water and electrical systems had been destroyed and only partly repaired. Housing was almost impossible to find and the cost of living was far higher (as much as five times higher, according to Edward Kuder) than before the war. And the civilian survivors of the Battle of Manila, still suffering the crushing effects of total war—the severe physical and psychic injuries, the loss of their loved-ones, their homes, and livelihoods— remained overwhelmed with shock, sorrow, and anger at the death of their city.

The Agriculture and Commerce Building, the Legislature Building, the Finance Building, the General Post Office Building, the University of the Philippines— Iwabuchi's troops had fortified each of those American structures, and MacArthur's artillery had systematically demolished them. The neoclassical icons of American colonialism that had stood proudly in central Manila for decades were handed over to the government of the Philippine Republic as derelicts or rubble piles. With their 155 mm howitzers sometimes

firing at point-blank range, MacArthur's artillery had unintention-
ally but effectively dismantled nearly every symbol of American
imperial power in the Philippine capital. The field artillery that had
defeated the Filipino insurgents and massacred the Moros in the
first decade of American rule had now, in the fifth, turned its guns
on the colonial edifices that were raised in the capital following
those lopsided victories.

Mohammad Adil, newly-enrolled at the University of the Philippines as a student-veteran *pensionado* on a meager government
grant, started college on a campus in ruins. Admiral Iwabuchi's
troops had strongly fortified the university's main buildings in the
south-central part of the city, and a combination of American shelling and Japanese demolitions had wreaked tremendous damage. The
country's premier university, founded shortly after the imposition of
American rule, was, like the city that surrounded it, barely recogniz-
able to those who knew it before February 1945.

Mohammad Adil had not known it before. He was in a new city
attempting to begin his postwar life. But walking to his classroom in
one of the few intact buildings on campus, passing charred remains
of houses, piles of rubble, and mass gravesites on the way invariably pulled his mind back to the war. He had decided not to bring
his new bride with him to Manila right away because they could
not yet afford even a room of their own there. His father had been
made a poorer man by the war and could no longer help him finan-
cially as much as he had planned. But his father did help in another
way. Nene stayed in Pagalamatan at his father's house and, as Adil
remembered, was happy despite the separation because Hadji Adil
Tambis had taken a particular shine to his new daughter-in-law and
"would give her anything she wanted." Though far removed from her
new husband, she had found a new supportive family.

Adil lived first with Edward Kuder on General Solano Street, in a neighborhood just north of the Pasig River that had been mostly burned to the ground. Once again he found himself in a house filled with young men, this time mostly Indonesian college students studying at a local university. On the day after the July Fourth celebration of Philippine Independence, Edward Kuder began his new position at the United States Veterans Administration overseeing education and training assistance to eligible veterans under the G.I. Bill of Rights of 1944, which provided a range of benefits for returning World War II veterans.

Kuder had found a U.S. agency—a civil-service holdover of the old regime in the new independent nation—to employ him. For the lifelong educator, the position would have been both personally fulfilling and societally significant. Once again, he would be providing American educational resources to students in the Philippines—this time primarily to former guerrilla soldiers under General MacArthur's command who had helped the U.S. win the war. The position seemed a perfect fit but for one last-minute twist.

As the consequence of U.S. legislation passed a few months earlier, the vast majority of Philippine veterans who had fought under MacArthur, including Kuder's own two foster sons, had been declared ineligible for any American veterans benefits by the time Kuder started his job on July 5th, 1946. The U.S. Rescission Act of February 1946 retroactively annulled nearly all of the benefits promised to Philippine veterans as recently as September 1945 by declaring that service either in the Philippine Commonwealth Army under MacArthur or in the organized guerrilla forces recognized by MacArthur "shall not be deemed to have been active...military service for the purposes of...conferring benefits by reason of service in the...[U.S.] Armed Forces."[5] It had been decided that, because of the estimated price tag of $1.5 billion over 50 years for extending it, the G.I. Bill, which famously lifted millions of U.S. veterans into the middle class, would be denied to Philippine veterans who, in the words of U.S. President Harry Truman, had "fought as American nationals, under the American flag, and under the direction of our military leaders."[6]

In his position, which he held for most of the next 15 years, Kuder administered education benefits for the few Philippine veterans who still qualified for them under the new rules. Mohammad Adil would receive no American veterans' scholarship and, for a while, struggled to finance his education and support his new family. Edward Kuder's surviving letters don't reveal what he felt about the Rescission Act. Was he of two minds about it? In his November 1945 letter to Adil he expressed the opinion that his foster son should learn to conserve his money rather than "ask the government for a pension." It was an opinion certainly in keeping with his own strict Presbyterian upbringing but also a curious one given that, for most of his adult life, he had been borrowing money from family and friends and rarely paying it back. Edward Kuder was an undeniably generous man with what money he had, but, at least since his failed land venture with Salipada Pendatun, he had never quite managed to stand on his own two feet economically and would continue to have money problems for the rest of his life. As for his now-delimited position, he may have consoled himself with the knowledge that, among the very few veterans in the Philippines eligible for the American benefits were the Philippine Scouts, a regular component of the U.S. Army since early in the century, and the Moros, long considered a "martial race" by the American colonizers, were overrepresented among the Philippine Scouts.

Kuder's postwar life had changed even more than Adil's. He

was in a new city with a new job, and was now living in a country that was no longer an American colony. His wartime health problems, however, were still with him. He was still infected with the "organism" (likely an amoeba) that had caused his liver abscess and nearly killed him. He was receiving treatment for it when, late in 1946, he felt a familiar severe pain in his right flank. It was diagnosed as a recurrence of the liver abscess, and he underwent a fourth operation. His greatest fear was of losing his Veterans Administration job for health reasons, but he was able to recover once more and resume his position.

Salipada Pendatun lived a bit further north on Maria Natividad Street, and his house was somewhat less crowded, so when invited to live there, Adil jumped at the chance. As the Legislature Building had also been mostly destroyed, the Philippine Congress and Senate met, in 1946, in a schoolhouse on Lepanto Street, not far from Pendatun's house. The Senate convened in the Manila City Hall the following year, which was damaged but usable, its concrete exterior still heavily pockmarked with bullet holes. Mohammad Adil remembered the excitement of riding to school in Pendatun's official car and spending time with him in his Senate office.

In 1946, Senator Pendatun sponsored the Republic Act 65, which created the Philippine Veterans Board, intended to provide the benefits to Philippine veterans that the U.S. had denied them. When the bill passed (albeit with meager funding) Pendatun helped his foster brother obtain a job in the employment office of the Veterans Board. Adil began to save money to bring his wife to Manila to live with him. In the meantime, he made regular trips home on school breaks.

Another source of funds arrived in 1946. The provision denying Philippine veterans G.I. Bill benefits was attached to a budget item appropriating $200 million for back pay due veterans of the

Philippine Army and recognized Philippine guerrilla units. Mohammad Adil collected affidavits from his superior officers in March of
1946 to apply for his back pay. He also helped the men who served
under him to collect theirs. Suddenly, the Philippines—and particularly Mindanao, which had the largest guerrilla movement—was
flush with an infusion of U.S. dollars. Moros who had fought in
the Bolo Battalions or with the guerrillas used their payments to
buy food and clothes for their families, but also boats and outboard
motors, and gold jewelry for their wives or sisters to replace jewelry
stolen by the Japanese or sold to feed families. Young men used the
money to pay bridewealth in order to marry and older men made the
pilgrimage to Mecca. And many of the former guerrillas also took
the opportunity to buy guns.

When the American liberators departed Mindanao, they left a
mountain of equipment behind, including an extraordinary number
of guns. After assiduously restricting the supply of firearms to Moros
for 40 years, to the point of denying firearms to Moro volunteers at
the outset of the war, the Americans left Mindanao awash in guns
and ammunition. American guns were lost, sold, stolen, or simply
abandoned. When the Americans attempted to "condemn" hundreds of rifles by dumping them in the sea, the Moros went fishing
for them. By 1946, firearms were so plentiful and inexpensive to
acquire that every Moro who wanted a gun possessed one, and most
owned more than one. Browning Automatic Rifles (BARs), which
had been exotic rarities at the start of the war, were now common-
place. With the war over, the Moros had finally received the arms
they had been refused in 1941. They used those arms, among other
ways, to fight traditional feuds with new weapons.

The war they had just fought had brought modern modes of
killing to the Philippines as well as modern weapons. Traditional
Moro feuding featured combat so intimate that killings were usually

accomplished at arms' length. The war, by contrast, had been won with artillery barrages and automatic weapons that dealt anonymous and indiscriminate death. Before the war, Moros mainly had fought one another with their swords, primarily the short and sinuous kris. But by the end of the war, an offended party would be more likely to bring a BAR to a fight, and Mindanao became a deadlier place.

* * *

The last duel in the Cotabato delta that included a kris was fought by Mohammad Adil's uncle, Bayan, in 1945. Bayan fought with a kris, his opponent with a .45 revolver. The kris won. Twenty years earlier in the 1920s, when he was still a teenager, Bayan had nearly had his arm severed from his body when he found himself in a sword duel with the two most notorious pirates of the Cotabato coast, Lanao and Pulindao. The pirates had been sauntering through the weekly market at Lumbay na Gi (Flower of the Cogon), Adil's birthplace, with their hands on their sword hilts and their long hair swinging behind them. When they demanded that he step aside to let them pass, Bayan refused as any young datu would. Pulindao then pulled his kris and, with one sudden sweep of his arm, buried it deep in Bayan's left shoulder. Bayan's father, Pangilamen, and his uncle, Saik a Datu, the Sufi warrior, were at the other end of the market, heard the commotion, and ran to Bayan's defense. They battled the pirates so fiercely that Lanao and Pulindao withdrew to their boat and later died of their wounds.

Bayan recovered from his gashed shoulder, but his wounded pride never fully healed. Then one day in June of 1945, shortly after the Americans' arrival in Cotabato, he was gambling with Datu Baman, the younger brother of Datu Sinsuat, the patriarch of the Sinsuat clan. Baman, who had spent time in prison for murder, was cheating. Bayan caught him at it and made his accusation. Both men pushed back from the table and stood, and Baman reached for his holstered .45. Bayan, who had been practicing his sword draw since the day he lost the duel with the pirate, drew his kris and swung it backhanded across the table, slicing through Baman's carotid artery just below his jawline. Datu Baman bled to death, still gripping his .45. Datu Sinsuat was enraged at his brother's killing and would have sought retribution, but within a week, he was arrested by the Americans for collaboration.

* * *

The U.S. also appropriated $620 million in rehabilitation funds to the Philippines—$220 million for the repair of public property and $400 million for war damage claims. Those funds, however, came at a great cost. The U.S. Congress extorted the new republic by refusing to provide any aid whatsoever to the Philippines until its congress accepted the terms of a 1946 U.S. Bill, the Bell Trade Act, that gave more rights to U.S. businesses in the Philippine Republic than they had during the colonial period. At the same time, the Philippines was pressured into granting the U.S. 99-year leases on 22 military bases throughout the country—bases that did indeed have "security areas" around them where the U.S. maintained its control.

The availability of the war damage funds encouraged individuals to file claims for a variety of losses. Adil filed a loss claim on behalf of his father, who had provided rice and other foodstuffs to his guerrilla company during the war and received receipts from Captain Gumbay Piang promising eventual payment. A significant number of the reparation claims were paid and, after the long years of hardship during the war, the people of Mindanao had a few years of comparative plenty.

The large majority of the damage claims filed were both modest and genuine. More than 60 percent of all approved claims were for less than $500, and investigators for the U.S. War Damages Commission "disclosed few cases of willful attempts to defraud through falsification of claims."[7] A few individuals, however, filed entirely fictitious claims, and the most audacious of all may have been the claim filed by young Ferdinand Marcos, who in 1946 was a special assistant to Manuel Roxas, the first president of the Philippine Republic. Adil was in Pendatun's senate office one day when Marcos entered breezily without knocking, talked with Pendatun for a while about the guerrilla days, then took a manila folder from under his arm and opened it, saying, "Sali, I have here a claim against the United States Government for 1500 head of cattle in Bukidnon." Pendatun took the affidavit that Marcos had prepared for his signature, looked it over, and told Marcos that he knew nothing about the cattle he claimed.

Adil remembered Marcos's reply: "That's not important. All you need to know is that the U.S. government has a rehabilitation fund with hundreds of millions of dollars to pay to Filipinos. I'm just trying to collect my share." Pendatun told Marcos he would think about it. After Marcos had left, Pendatun told Adil, "That was Ferdinand Marcos, the man who shot Julio Nalundasan. He was my cadet in ROTC at U.P. (the University of the Philippines)."[8] Marcos returned the next day to try again to obtain Pendatun's signature. When Pendatun told him he could not sign the claim, Marcos said that he would look for someone else to help him. A week later, Marcos stopped by Pendatun's office to show him that another senator had signed his claim.[9]

Was Salipada Pendatun's refusal to support Marcos's fraudulent scheme the result of *maratabat*, the influence of his American foster father, or simply personal dislike of the brash and larcenous young Marcos? Or, more likely, was it some combination of the three? From this far away, it is impossible to know. What is known, is that this first encounter with Ferdinand Marcos would not be the last for either of Edward Kuder's foster sons.

In 1946, Salipada Pendatun and Mohammad Adil, who had distinguished themselves in the war, were on the verge of even more impressive accomplishments. Later in that year, Pendatun, the Moro boy from an actual backwater—roadless Pagalungan, the Mirrored Place, where the great Pulangi flattened and widened and became so still that it perfectly mirrored the cloud-framed sky above it—travelled with his new wife to New York and Paris to attend the inaugural conference of the United Nations Educational, Scientific, and Cultural Organization (UNESCO) as an official representative of the Philippines. The trip announced his arrival as a political figure worth watching and marked another milestone in the fulfillment of Edward Kuder's aspirations for him. Within a decade, he had become the most politically prominent and powerful Moro of his generation.

Mohammad Adil remained in Manila and law school until a personal tragedy led him to abandon the legal career that both his father and Edward Kuder wanted for him and return to the military, the place he felt most at home. By 1960, he had become one of the most decorated officers in the Philippine military and the subject of newspaper headlines and magazine articles. He had also cheated death on at least half-a-dozen more occasions.

The Japanese war had formed the two men and primed them for their subsequent accomplishments, but it would not be the greatest challenge of their lives. That would come when Ferdinand Marcos, soon after declaring himself dictator in September of 1972, once again turned his attention to Mindanao and the Moros, this time with deadly intent. With the tacit support and active financial assistance of the country that their American foster father had taught them to admire—the country they had fought for, the country of Douglas MacArthur—Ferdinand Marcos, in 1973, invaded their homeland and attacked the Moros. Once again a hostile occupying army was hunting guerrillas, confiscating guns, and driving civilians from their homes. Once again, Moros were being strafed by airplanes and assaulted by tanks. Edward Kuder, blessedly deceased, did not have to witness the desecration of his lifelong dream of Moro integration into a multi-ethnic Philippine democracy. His Moro foster sons, their lives uprooted for a second time by a military occupation of their homeland, once more chose resistance.

ACKNOWLEDGMENTS

As a book project begun in the last century, *Moro Warrior* has accumulated a long list of benefactors whose assistance and encouragement made its completion possible. Esmael A. Abdula and Zamin K. Unti, my friends and research assistants from Cotabato, first told me about Mohammad Adil and then introduced me to him. Esmael Abdula, educator, writer, researcher, public speaker, translator, community activist, and expert authority on the Bangsamoro—the Moro people—helped me over the years in innumerable ways despite his always busy schedule. Both were individuals I was proud to call brother and both are gone today, having tragically died too young. It is my hope that this book honors their memory.

A research grant from the American Council of Learned Societies provided early support, enabling multiple return visits to the Philippines to record the stories of Mohammad Adil. I appreciate the council's early faith in the project and am happy to report that their investment has finally borne fruit. I am indebted, as always, to the Mindanao-Sulu scholars and journalists whose work has guided my way. They include Patricio Abinales, Jeremy Beckett, Reynaldo

Ileto, Kawashima Midori, Lela Noble, Stuart Schlegel, Larry S. Schmidt, James Warren, and Criselda Yabes.

My former U.S. research assistant and longtime friend, Jennifer St. John, provided invaluable assistance early on as a tireless transcriber and again recently as a thoughtful and gentle reader of multiple chapter drafts. My old friend and mentor, Dr. William G. Davis, who has been providing me with dependably good advice for a shocking 40 years, offered key insights and suggestions at various points on the path. Dr. Paul Watsky, poet-counselor, has aided this project in innumerable ways, from occasional line editing to advising about the book's overall concept. Most crucially, however, he was the first to encourage me to pick up the long-abandoned manuscript and make the book a reality.

I have benefitted from the generous assistance of multiple librarians and archivists, including James Zobel and Michelle Kopfer. I wish to thank especially Patrick Shannon of the University of California at Berkeley for going out of his way to help me. I am also grateful to the additional readers of various chapter drafts who gave generously of their time and attention, including Anne McKenna, Sheila McKenna, and Kermit Patton. I was also fortunate to have the assistance of editors along the way. Wyn Cooper provided early organizational help. Hilary Hinzmann gave the book the basic form it has today, including the critical addition of Edward Kuder as a central character.

In my quest to have the book published, I collected my full share of rejections but also received a considerable amount of encouragement and valuable advice. My thanks in particular to Peter Bernstein, Lisa DiMona, Timothy Mennel, Aaron Sachs, and Keith Wallman. I am deeply indebted to my good friend, author and analyst Martin Schwirn, for offering to introduce me, out of the kindness of his heart, to Maryann Karinch, and I am especially grateful to Maryann for believing in this book and helping me every step of the way in publishing it.

With a sharp and sensitive eye, Vince Lupiano edited the final manuscript, streamlining my writing to make it flow more sweetly. With impressive artistry, Najla Kay took my raw ideas and turned them into beautiful maps for the book.

Only one person, my wife Patti, had to live with me and without me, listen to me, and put up with me during the entire course of this project. She is the same person who, with extraordinary generosity and forbearance, gave me the support and assistance as well as the time and the space I needed to complete this book. I have dedicated it to her as a small token of all that I owe her. I first conceived the idea for this book with my twelve-year-old son Matthew in mind. I hope he enjoys this adventure story just as much today as a young thirty-something father of his own.

It remains to thank the individuals closest to this book, the family of Mohammad Adil. I am grateful to his surviving children, Bai Ruth (named after Edward Kuder's sister), Bai Grace, and Datu Arthur Adil (named after Douglas MacArthur) for their trust and support. I would especially like to thank his widow, Bai Zainab Dolores Lubaton Adil, for her extraordinary hospitality, her kindness, and her patience.

Needless to say, this book owes its existence to Mohammad Adil, the man who was both its main subject and main source. What does need saying is that I am especially grateful to him for telling me more than once, in an oblique but unmistakable reference to our work together, that "There is no greater sin in the eyes of God than nonfulfillment of a promise." That declaration—part statement of belief, part threat of supernatural punishment—gave me the extra ounce of motivation I needed to return to the project and complete it after such a long hiatus. I offer this book to him and his family as a posthumous fulfillment of a promise made long ago.

A BRIEF NOTE ON SOURCES AND METHODS

In addition to the historical documents and other materials generously provided by the families of Mohammad Adil and Edward Kuder, I relied on a few key archives and online sources for primary materials. The Joseph Ralston Hayden Papers collection at the Bentley Historical Library was a rich source of material by and about Edward Kuder and Joseph R. Hayden. From the Eisenhower Presidential Library I received the official unit history of the 222nd AAA Searchlight Battalion. And from the MacArthur Memorial Archives and the Australian War Memorial I obtained copies of rare World War II photographs of Mindanao.

The online Philippine Diary Project (https://philippinediaryproject.com) was a rich source of historical details and offered excerpts from Wendell Fertig's wartime diary (the original is available at the MacArthur Memorial Archives). The Chan Robles Virtual Law Library (https://www.chanrobles.com/index1.htm) provided online access to Philippine Supreme Court cases, including the one that Edward Kuder and Salipada Pendatun lost. The

Hathi Trust Digital Library (https://babel.hathitrust.org) was also an invaluable source, particularly for U.S. government reports.

Moro Warrior is a work of narrative history based on the recorded memories of Mohammad Adil and on a wide range of primary and secondary written sources about the Philippines in World War II. No characters have been fictionalized, and no events have been invented or dates rearranged. The quoted dialogue in the book, unless otherwise noted, comes directly from Mohammad Adil with only slight modifications for grammar and readability in English. All translations from Magindanaon are my own. On occasion, where the historical record or Mohammad Adil's recollections have lacked details, I have imagined them based either on my firsthand anthropological knowledge of Mindanao or on inferences drawn from other people, periods, and places. Any factual errors or inaccuracies found here are mine alone.

ENDNOTES

Prologue

1   Louis Morton, *United States Army in World War II: The War in the Pacific, The Fall of the Philippines* (Washington, D.C.: Center of Military History, 1989), 57.

2   Brigadier General John Hugh McGee, *Rice and Salt: A History of the Defense and Occupation of Mindanao During World War II* (San Antonio: The Naylor Company, 1962), 44.

3   Colonel Hiram W. Tarkington, "There Were Others," (Unpublished Manuscript), Military History Institute, Carlisle Barracks, Pennsylvania, 125, 129.

4   Brigadier General John Hugh McGee, *Rice and Salt: A History of the Defense and Occupation of Mindanao During World War II* (San Antonio: The Naylor Company, 1962), 43.

5   General Sir William Slim, *Defeat into Victory: Battling Japan in Burma and India*, 1942-1945 (New York: Cooper Square Press, 2000), 539.

6   In this book I use the term "Filipino" rather than "Christian" or "Christian Filipino" to refer to the majority population of the Philippines that became Hispanicized and Christianized as the result of Spanish colonialism. I avoid the term "Christian" because the key distinction between Filipinos and Moros is their different experiences of Western colonialism, not their religious identities. Both Christian Moros and Muslim Filipinos can be found throughout Philippine history and at present. By distinguishing Moros from Filipinos I am not, however, making

a statement about their status vis-à-vis the Philippine Republic. The Moros have been negotiating that status themselves for nearly half a century.

7   Jose D. Fermin, *1904 World's Fair: The Filipino Experience* (West Conshohocken, PA: Infinity Publishing, 2004), 109. As with the discipline in general, American cultural anthropology has deep colonial roots. It was an American anthropologist working for the U.S. government, Albert Jenks, who arranged for the Moros and other Philippine groups to travel to St. Louis and be put on exhibit at the fair. See Carmen Nelson Richards, ed., *Death Stalks the Philippine Wilds: Letters of Maud Huntley Jenks* (Minneapolis: The Lund Press, Inc., 1951).

8   Peter Gordon Gowing, *Mandate in Moroland: The American Government of Muslim Filipinos 1899-1920* (Quezon City, Philippines: New Day Publishers, 1983), 88-94.

9   Leonard Wood quoted in Gowing, *Mandate in Moroland*, 165.

10   J. Ralston Hayden, "What Next for the Moros?," *Foreign Affairs* 6, (1928), 633-644.

11   Lt. Jesse Gaston to Bliss, January 8, 1909, cited in Gowing, *Mandate in Moroland*, 177.

12   John J. Pershing quoted in Gowing, *Mandate in Moroland*, 240.

13   William McKinley quoted in Stanley Karnow, *In Our Image: America's Empire in the Philippines* (New York: Ballantine Books, 1989), 197.

Chapter One: Invitation to War

1   Edward M. Kuder, "Statement, 1943, of Edward M. Kuder to Hayden on events and conditions in Lanao immediately preceding the war and from 1941-1943" (Hereafter, "Statement of Kuder"), Box 41, Joseph Ralston Hayden Papers, Bentley Historical Library, University of Michigan, Ann Arbor, Michigan.

2   Richard Connaughton, *MacArthur and Defeat in the Philippines* (New York: Abrams Press, 2001), 287.

3   John H. McGee notes that the Moros at Digos also suffered "other inequalities" in addition to the ones listed. McGee, *Rice and Salt*, 44.

4   John Keats, *They Fought Alone: Wendell Fertig and his WWII Guerrilla Campaign in the Philippines* (Brattleboro Vermont: Echo Point Books, 2014), 171. Wendell Fertig's 1963 authorized biography, *They Fought Alone*, is an odd hybrid work—a third-person account written in a hard-

boiled prose style that is, in fact, an autobiography. Although John Keats is the author of record, it is, in all essentials, a third-person autobiography authored by Fertig, a fact that Keats acknowledges in the Preface. Because it is based entirely on his diaries, memoirs, and a 600-page rough draft of a manuscript that he wrote, I refer to it from now on as his autobiography.

5   Edward M. Kuder, "The Moros in the Philippines," *Far Eastern Quarterly* 4, no. 2 (1945): 126. Kuder, "The Philippines Never Surrendered" Part III. Saturday Evening Post (February 24, 1945): 22.

6   Keats, *They Fought Alone*, 307.

7   Scott Walker, T*he Edge of Terror: The Heroic Story of American Families Trapped in the Japanese-occupied Philippines* (New York: St. Martin's Press, 2009), 81.

8   Detailed accounts by passengers and crew of the last two American evacuation flights from Corregidor and Mindanao may be found in Elizabeth M. Norman's *We Band of Angels: The Untold Story of the American Women Trapped on Bataan* (New York: Random House, 1999), and in Roscoe Creed's PBY: *The Catalina Flying Boat* (Annapolis: The United States Naval Institute, 1985).

9   According to Keats (presumably based on Fertig's memories), in the first meeting between MacArthur's emissary, Chick Parsons, and Wendell Fertig, Parsons suggested to Fertig that MacArthur "blew up" when he heard of Fertig's self-promotion to brigadier general because he considered himself the only one in charge of the Philippines. Keats, *They Fought Alone*, 194-5.

10   Kuder, "The Philippines Never Surrendered" Part IV, *Saturday Evening Post*, March 3, 1945.

Chapter Two: The Journey North

1   In its original Magindanaon: *Sakali makauma su mga Amerikanu na amayka kaputi su kakuak na u kaitum su talaung.*

2   Kuder, "The Philippines Never Surrendered," Part V, (March 10, 1945): 20.

3   Kent Holmes, *Wendell Fertig and his Guerrilla Forces in the Philippines: Fighting the Japanese Occupation*, 1942-1945 (Jefferson, North Carolina: McFarland and Company, 2015).

4   Kuder, "The Philippines Never Surrendered" Part V, *Saturday Evening Post* (March 10, 1945): 20.

5   Kuder, "Statement of Kuder," 18. In his autobiography, *They Fought Alone*, Fertig contradicts his own diary and the contemporary account of Edward Kuder to claim that he had ordered William Tait to Misamis Occidental and was present for the action in September of 1942. It is one of multiple such examples of self-aggrandizing fantasy in the book. For other examples see Clyde Childress, "Wendell Fertig's Fictional 'Autobiography': a Critical Review of They Fought Alone," *Bulletin of the American Historical Collection*, Vol. 31 No. 1(123), January 2003.

Chapter Three: Total Resistance

1   Kuder, "Statement of Kuder," 7.

2   Kuder, "The Philippines Never Surrendered" Part I, *Saturday Evening Post* (February 10, 1945): 58.

3   Kuder, "Statement of Kuder," 16.

4   Ibid., 16.

5   Kuder, "The Philippines Never Surrendered" Part II, *Saturday Evening Post*, (Feb. 17. 1945): 82.

6   Kuder, "The Philippines Never Surrendered" Part III, *Saturday Evening Post* (February 24, 1945): 22.

7   Kuder to Calvin Kuder, February 27, 1935, private collection.

8   Kuder, "The Philippines Never Surrendered" Part III, *Saturday Evening Post* (February 24, 1945): 90.

9   Ibid., 90.

10   Kawashima Midori, "The Battle of Tamparan," in Paul H. Kratoska, ed., *Southeast Asian Minorities in the Wartime Japanese Empire* (London: Routledge Curzon, 2002), 234. Dr. Midori's chapter is based on historical and field research, including interviews of Maranao survivors of the battle. It is, to my knowledge, the only account in English of the battle other than Edward Kuder's relatively brief description in his *Saturday Evening Post* article.

11   "United States of America vs. Yoshinari Tanaka," Headquarters Eighth Army, Review of the Staff Judge Advocate, Yokohama, Japan, (22 November 1948): 5. https://www.online.uni-marburg.de/icwc/yokohama/Yokohama%20No.%20T347.pdf.

12   John L. Ginn was a prison guard at Sugamo Prison. His 1992 book,

Sugamo Prison, Tokyo: An Account of the Trial and Sentencing of Japanese War Criminals in 1948, by a U.S. Participant (Jefferson, North Carolina: McFarland, 1992), contains impressive detail, some of which (particularly the descriptions of war crimes) is horrifying. At the same time, the book is infused with great humanity as all involved—prisoners, judges, and guards—come to terms with the terrible costs of all-out war. My account of Yoshinari Tanaka's execution is based on Ginn's general description of the process, which, he notes, was carried out in every case without any "mishaps or mistakes."

13   Kawashima Midori, "Japanese Administrative Policy towards the Moros in Lanao," in Ikehata Setsuho and Ricardo Trota Jose, eds., *The Philippines Under Japan*, (Manila: Ateneo de Manila University Press, 1999), 113.

Chapter Four: "A Good Moro Boy"

1   John R. White, *Bullets and Bolos: Thirteen Years in the Philippine Islands* (New York: The Century Co., 1928), 232.

2   Florence Horn, *Orphans of the Pacific: The Philippines* (New York: Reynal and Hitchcock, 1941), 92.

3   Joseph Ralston Hayden to Elizabeth ("Betty") Hayden, September 17, 1926, Box 35, Joseph Ralston Hayden Papers, Bentley Historical Library, University of Michigan, Ann Arbor.

4   Edward Haggerty, *Guerrilla Padre in Mindanao* (New York: Longmans, Green & Co., 1946), 147.

5   This is an excerpt from a draft manuscript) for an article, "Forest Marksmen in Mindanao," that Kuder submitted to the Roanoke College alumni magazine, *The Collegian*, in April, 1945.

6   Philippines Free Press article, August 5, 1939, quoted in Lewis E. Gleeck, Jr., *Americans on the Philippine Frontiers* (Manila: Carmelo and Bauermann, 1974), 78.

7   Kuder to Calvin Kuder, April 11, 1932, Private Collection.

8   Heirs of Datu Pendatun v. Director of Lands et al., Philippine Supreme Court Jurisprudence, G.R. No. 36699, March 3, 1934. https://www.chanrobles.com/index1.htm.

9   Kuder to J. R. Hayden, May 1, 1934, Box 29, Joseph Ralston Hayden Papers, Bentley Historical Library, University of Michigan, Ann Arbor, Michigan.

10   Dorothy Dore Dowlen, *"Enduring What Cannot Be Endured: Memoir of a Woman Medical Aide in the Philippines in World War II"* (Jefferson, North Carolina: McFarland & Company, 2001), 107, 110-112.

11   Haggerty, *Guerrilla Padre in Mindanao*, 147. Mohammad Adil had also met the couple's adopted child and told me her name. I have been unable to discover any more about her. Her parents may have been killed or interned by the Japanese.

12   Samuel C. Grashio and Bernard Norling, *Return to Freedom: The War Memoirs of Col. Samuel C. Grashio USAF (Ret.)* (Tulsa: MCN Press, 1982), 132.

13   Haggerty, *Guerrilla Padre in Mindanao*, 87.

14   Ibid., 153.

15   Haggerty, *Guerrilla Padre in Mindanao*, 144-145.

16   Chick Parsons was a larger than life figure and multiple books recounting his exploits were published in the decades following the war. A more recent work by Peter Eisner—*MacArthur's Spies: The Soldier, The Singer, and the Spymaster who Defied the Japanese in World War II* (New York: Penguin Books, 2017)—is the first to portray him as a fully three-dimensional, and even more fascinating, character.

17   Carlos Quirino, *Chick Parsons: America's Master Spy in the Philippines* (Quezon City, Philippines: New Day Publishers, 1984), 47. Wendell Fertig, who considered both Pendatun and Andrews to be troublemakers, noted in his diary on May 3rd, 1943 that Andrews "is violently anti-American, is largely responsible for Pendatun's attitude." Diary of Wendell Fertig, Philippine Diary Project.

18   Keats, *They Fought Alone*, 161-162.

Chapter Five: "Dig Up Your Guns"

1   Joseph Ralston Hayden to Dr. Barr, September 21, 1926, Joseph Ralston Hayden Papers, Box 21, Folder 30, Michigan Historical Collections, Bentley Historical Library, University of Michigan, Ann Arbor.

2   White, *Bullets and Bolos*, 219.

3   Gumbay Piang, "The Treason and Courtship of Bamboo Ear," *Philippine Free Press*, 9 July 1932, 49.

4   Lt. Col W.W. Fertig to Datu Gumbay Piang, Correspondence File No. 65, drawer No. 4, Philippine Archives, National Personnel Records Center, St. Louis, originally cited in Larry S. Schmidt, "American Involvement in the Filipino Resistance Movement on Mindanao during the Japanese Occupation, 1942-1945," Master's Thesis, U.S. Army Command and General Staff College, 1982: 172.

5   In the U.S. military, the third lieutenant rank has been used at various times as a cadet or training commission. In the American colonial Philippines the rank was first widely used in the Philippine Constabulary and reserved for Filipino junior officers, assuring that they would never outrank their American counterparts.

6   Odin Sinsuat's execution of Abu Dimatinkal was unlawful even according to Moro customary law. The Luwaran, the code of Moro customary laws prescribes a fine and (usually) a forced marriage for a single man caught having sexual intercourse with an unmarried woman, not death.

7   Dorothy Dore Dowlen, whose father was a U.S. Army veteran of the Moro Wars and a close friend of Frank McGee, describes in her memoir of the Japanese occupation how in 1942 she gathered medicine and food for McGee and his fellow guerrillas in response to his urgent request to her father. *Enduring What Cannot Be Endured*, 90.

8   The concept of *palabas* is key for understanding public discourse in the Philippines. Palabas (literally "for the outside") is best translated as "for public consumption." While a non-Filipino might see it as simply exaggeration or overdramatization on the part of a speaker, it a far more subtle and interesting than that. It is a tacit cultural agreement between a speaker and her or his listeners that they will be told a compelling story— one in which the drama and excitement is emphasized—and that they will in turn discount any overstatement or exaggeration in its telling. One way for a listener to control for *palabas* when trying to get "just the facts" is simply to recognize *palabas* when it occurs and do the discounting. Another way is to become enough of an insider (as I did over time with Mohammad Adil) that *palabas* no longer comes into play because the stories are no longer being told "for public consumption."

Chapter Six: War in the Cordillera

1   Simeon F. Millan, ed., *1952 Cotabato Guidebook* (Cotabato City: Simeon F. Millan, 1952), 93.

2   The (unofficial) American colonial prohibition on Christian proselytizing missions only applied to the Moros, who practiced Islam, a world religion. In areas of Mindanao inhabited by "pagans," Christian missionaries were encouraged and supported. The anthropologist Stuart Schlegel worked for decades among the Tiruray of the Cotabato Cordillera. It is only through his dedicated research that we know about the traditional Tiruray of the upland forests as well as about the career of Irving Edwards. See Schlegel's *Wisdom from a Rainforest: The Spiritual Journey of an Anthropologist* (Athens Georgia: University of Georgia Press, 1998). In this, one of his later works, Schlegel uses the spelling "Teduray" rather than "Tiruray," the name he employed in his previous books. While "Teduray" is the more accurate transliteration, I have chosen to use "Tiruray" which was the name by which Mohammad Adil referred to them and the name most commonly used for them in the 1940s.

3   Stuart A. Schlegel, *Children of Tulus: Essays on the Tiruray People* (Quezon City, Philippines: Giraffe Books, 1994), 173, 177.

4   Schlegel, *Children of Tulus*, 20-21.

5   A casualty roster for the 119th compiled in 1945 and signed by Wendell Fertig lists a Private Baguio Moro as killed in action on December 24, 1943. This could be the same person because "Moro" was the surname given to any Moro recruit who did not quickly volunteer a family name. If so, the reason for the discrepancy in dates is unclear.

6   Casualty Roster, 119th Infantry, 106th Division, 10th MD.

7   Oral accounts of the date of Pinidililang Piang's death differ. The casualty roster for the 119th lists him as killed in action on December 25, 1943, more than a month before the Japanese attack on the 119th headquarters.

8   Open Letter: Gumbay Piang to His Parents and Relatives, The Moros of _____:, November 20, 1934, Hayden Papers, Bentley Historical Library, University of Michigan, Box 27, Folder 30, File 2.

Chapter Seven: Escape

1   Kuder, "The Philippines Never Surrendered." part V, Saturday Evening Post, March 10, 1945, 58.

2   Diary of Wendell Fertig, Philippine Diary Project: Diary entries from Philippine History, https://philippinediaryproject.com/1943/09/29/september-29-1943-2/. See also MacArthur to Fertig, September 28th, 1943, Memos concerning evacuees from the Philippines September

1943-August 1944, Box 42, Folder 31, Joseph Ralston Hayden Papers, Bentley Historical Library, University of Michigan, Ann Arbor, Michigan.

3   Grashio and Norling, *Return to Freedom*, 137.

4   Grashio and Norling, *Return to Freedom*, 138.

5   Claudine Ferguson to Mattie Kuder July 8, 1942, private collection.

6   Edward Kuder's ability to think like an intelligence agent was apparently not an unusual quality in America's Philippine colony. In *Policing America's Empire: The United States, the Philippines, and the Rise of the Surveillance State* (Madison: University of Wisconsin Press, 2009), Alfred McCoy marshals extensive evidence to make the argument that the colonial apparatus imposed by the Americans, including the education bureaucracy, was remarkably efficient at surveilling the populations under its control in order to suppress dissent.

7   Kuder, Statement of Kuder, Appendix 1-A.

8   Horn, *Orphans of the Pacific*, 90-91.

9   Kuder to Auditor General of the Philippine Commonwealth, May 29, 1944, private collection.

10   George Drach and Calvin F. Kuder, *The Telugu Mission of the General Council of the Evangelical Lutheran Church in North America: Containing a Biography of the Rev. Christian Frederick Heyer, M. D.* (Reading, Pennsylvania: General Council Publication House, 1914), 317.

11   Drach and Kuder, *The Telegu Mission*, 156-161.

12   Edward Kuder to Mattie Kuder, October 14, 1935, private collection.

13   Edward Kuder to Jorge Bocobo, August 19, 1935, Box 29, Folder 24, Joseph Ralston Hayden Papers, Bentley Historical Library, University of Michigan, Ann Arbor, Michigan.

14   Claudine Ferguson to Mattie Kuder July 8, 1942, private collection.

15   MacArthur to Fertig, October 4, 10, 1943, Memos concerning evacuees from the Philippines September 1943-August 1944, Box 42, Folder 31, Joseph Ralston Hayden Papers, Bentley Historical Library, University of Michigan, Ann Arbor, Michigan.

16   Edward Dissette and H.C. Adamson, *Guerrilla Submarines: The Never-before-told True Story of the Secret Action that Changed the Course of the War in the Pacific* (New York: Ballantine Books, 1972), 80.

17   Travis Ingham, *Rendezvous by Submarine: The Story of Charles Parsons and the Guerrilla-Soldiers in the Philippines* (Garden City, New York: Doubleday, Doran and Company, 1945) 182.

18   Walker, *The Edge of Terror*, 204-206.

19   Dissette and Adamson, *Guerrilla Submarines*, 115-116.

20   Louise Spencer had lived in the same hamlet as the Baptist missionaries on Panay but escaped their fate and made her way with her husband, as well as Claude Fertig and his wife, to a submarine rendezvous in March of 1944. She told the story of her years as a fugitive in a popular book published early in 1945—*Guerrilla Wife* (New York: Thomas Y. Crowell Company, 1945).

21   In an introductory column—"Keeping Posted"—in the February 10th, 1945 issue of the Saturday Evening Post, an unnamed editor informally introduces Edward Kuder to the magazine's readers by relating his conversation with the author. In it, Kuder telegraphs his approach to the series by relating a set of amusing, self-deprecating stories about his misadventures in Mindanao as a younger man.

Chapter Eight: Bulletproof

1   Kuder, "Statement of Kuder," 38.

2   The M2 carbine was a rare weapon in the Second World War, used only in a few engagements, primarily in the Pacific, including in the Philippines. It was clearly an inefficient weapon for guerrillas in an environment where ammunition was an extremely rare resource.

3   The Seven Sleepers of Ephesus is an ancient tale shared by Muslims and Christians. It tells of a group of young men from the Greek city of Ephesus who hide in a cave to escape an evil emperor. They fall magically asleep and do not wake for hundreds of years. See Gabriel Said Reynolds, "Seven Sleepers" in *Medieval Islamic Civilization*, Josef W. Meri, ed., (London: Routledge, 2004), 720.

4   In his advice to worship silently in the heart, Saik a Datu Barat, unlettered though he may have been, was eloquently describing a central Sufi practice—silent recollection in order to fill the heart with nothing but God. The oldest surviving written treatise on the silent form of recollection (or *dhikr* in Arabic) is from the 14th century Egyptian Sufi, Ibn 'Ata' Allah, who describes silent *dhikr* as "purification from heedlessness and forgetfulness by the constant presence of the heart with God." That silent recollection is also known as "remembrance of the

heart." Sufi Sheikhs have been called "masters of the heart." Saik a Datu Barat was clearly one of those. Carl W. Ernst, *The Shambhala Guide to Sufism* (Boston: Shambhala Publications, 1997), 29, 92-93.

5 Memorial, Joseph Ralston Hayden, Faculty History Project, The Millenium Project, University of Michigan, 2011. http://faculty-history. dc.umich.edu/faculty/joseph-ralston-hayden/memorial.

6 Robert Ross Smith, *Triumph in the Philippines: The United States in World War II, the War in the Pacific* (Washington, D.C.: Center of Military History, United States Army, 1963), 587.

7 Smith, *Triumph in the Philippines*, 621.

8 Brother Placid Stuckenschneider, "The Last Campaign: Mindanao," HistoryNet.com, March, 1999. www.historynet.com/the-last-campaign-mindanao-march-99-world-war-ii-feature.htm.

9 Smith, *Triumph in the Philippines*, 635.

Chapter Nine: The Last Ridge

1 Major General R. B. Woodruff, "Colonel Frank McGee," *The Taro Leaf: Newsletter of the 24th Infantry Division Veterans Association*, Volume II, Number 2, June 1949, 3.

2 The Hall of Valor Project, Distinguished Service Cross, Robert L. Miller, https://valor.militarytimes.com/hero/32088.

3 Robert L. Johnson, Overseas History: 222d Anti-Aircraft Artillery, Searchlight Battalion, Box 279, U.S. Army Unit Records, Dwight D. Eisenhower Library, Abilene, Kansas.

4 Johnson, Overseas History, 8.

5 LST is an abbreviation for Landing Ship, Tank—a naval vessel that could carry troops, vehicles, or cargo directly onto shore without the need for docks or piers.

6 Robert K.D. Petersen, "The Real Enemy: Scrub Typhus and the Invasion of Sansapour," *American Entomologist*, Volume 5, Number 2, Summer 2009, 91-94.

7 For information on the work of the Psychological Warfare Branch in the Philippines, I've relied on Allison B. Gilmore's finely detailed work, also titled *You Can't Fight Tanks with Bayonets: Psychological Warfare Against the Japanese Army in the Southwest Pacific* (Lincoln, Nebraska: University of Nebraska Press, 1998).

8   Gilmore, *You Can't Fight Tanks with Bayonets*, 60, 63.

Chapter Ten: Reunion

1   Hart and Jones were also acquaintances that Kuder had made in the Philippines. Senator Thomas Hart had been Admiral Hart before the war and commander in Chief of the U.S. Asiatic Fleet, headquartered in the Philippines. Kuder presumably entertained Hart at his home when he visited Jolo. J. Weldon Jones was High Commissioner to the Philippines from 1934 to 1940.

2   Memorial, Joseph Ralston Hayden, Faculty History Project, The Millenium Project, University of Michigan, 2011. http://faculty-history. dc.umich.edu/faculty/joseph-ralston-hayden/memorial. See also David Smollar, "Hard, Bitter, Unpleasantly Necessary Duty: a Little Known World War II Story of the Philippines," *Prologue* (Summer 2015): 6-15, https://www.archives.gov/files/publications/prologue/2015/summer/pcau. pdf.

3   Ama ni Sansu had likely never conducted a ritual to convert an adult to Islam before. It appears that he improvised by adapting a haircutting ritual for infants, where the baby's hair is wetted, a small piece of hair is cut, and the Shahada, the Islamic declaration of faith, is whispered in the child's ear.

Epilogue

1   The historical irony ran deeper still, for it was also on July 4th, in 1902, that U.S. President Teddy Roosevelt declared victory over Philippine independence fighters seeking to establish their own republic. The Philippines has since changed its Independence Day to June 12th, a date which commemorates the declaration of Philippine independence from Spain in 1898.

2   MacArthur quoted in Karnow, *In Our Image*, 324.

3   James M. Scott, *Rampage: MacArthur, Yamashita, and the Battle of Manila* (New York: W.W. Norton & Co., 2018), 93. My account of the Battle of Manila is drawn primarily from Scott's finely researched and exceptionally powerful 2018 book.

4   American soldiers killed in the Battle of Manila numbered 1010, just over 1% of civilian deaths. At least 16,000 Japanese troops died in the fighting. Smith, *Triumph in the Philippines*, 306-307.

5   Title 38 U.S. Code § 107. Certain service deemed not to be active service. Legal Information Institute, Cornell Law School. https://www. law.cornell.edu/uscode/text/38/107.

6   Harry S. Truman, "Statement by the President Concerning Provisions in Bill Affecting Philippine Army Veterans," February 20, 1946, Harry S. Truman Library and Museum, https://www.trumanlibrary. gov/library/public-papers/38/statement-president-concerning-provisions-bill-affecting-philippine-army. Truman vetoed the first Rescission Act for reasons unrelated to the Philippines. When Congress passed it a second time he considered vetoing it but signed it while attaching a statement intended to reassure Philippine veterans that he "considered it a moral obligation of the United States to look after the Welfare of Philippine Army veterans." Then he designated a committee to study the problem. See also "The Seventh and Final Report of the United States High Commissioner to the Philippine Islands Covering the Period from September 14, 1945 to July 4, 1946, House Document Number 389 (Washington D.C.: United States Government Printing Office, 1947, https://babel.hathitrust.org.

7   Fifth Semiannual Report of the United State Philippine War Damages Commission, Manila Philippines, For Period Ending December 31st, 1948 (Washington: United States Government Printing Office, 1949), 4. https://babel.hathitrust.org.

8   In 1939, Ferdinand Marcos was convicted of murdering his father's political rival, Julio Nalundasan in 1935 while still a student at the University of the Philippines. The conviction was overturned by the Philippine Supreme Court in 1940 after Marcos argued the appeal in front of the justices himself. Raymond Bonner, *Waltzing with a Dictator: The Marcoses and the Making of American Policy* (New York: Times Books, 1987), 11-14.

9   Marcos's war damage claim was rejected. Given that Pendatun was the commander of the Bukidnon guerrillas for much of the occupation, his signature may well halve carried more weight. Primitivo Mijares, Marcos' former publicist, also relates the story of the false claim "demanding payment for cattle he claimed he supplied starving American and Filipino troops…" Mijares states that it was a "multimillion-dollar" claim. That amount seems high, even for someone as audacious as Marcos, but I have not searched for the original war damage claim in the U.S. National Archives. *The Conjugal Dictatorship of Ferdinand and Imelda Marcos* (Quezon City, Philippines: Bughaw, 2017), 372.

GLOSSARY AND PRONUNCIATION GUIDE

Adil (AH-deel)

Bai (Buy): Lady, princess

Balabaran, Sinsuat (SIN-soo-aht Ball-ah-BAR-ahn)

Bapa (BAH-pah): Uncle

Carabao (car-a-BOUGH): water buffalo

Datu (DAH-too): a chieftain, a male member of the traditional nobility

Gandamasir (gahn-da-mah-SEER): a guerrilla courier

Jolo (HOE-low)

Kadungan (kah-DOONG-ahn): servant of Hadji Adil

Kampilan (kahm-PEE-lahn): a long single-edged sword

Kanduli (kahn-DOO-lee): a ritual feast

Kota (KOH-tah): a wooden palisaded fort

Kulintang (koo-LEEN-tahng): a musical instrument composed of a set of five to nine graduated bronze pot gongs laid on a decorated wooden frame and played with two wooden sticks.

Magindanaon (Mah-guin-dah-NOUN)

Malong (MAH-long): a sarong. A long cotton wrap-around skirt worn by women and men.

Maranao (Mah-rah-NOW)

Maratabat (mah-rah-tah-BAHT): a central cultural ideal of the Moros most directly translated as dignity or self-worth

Pagalamatan (Pahg-ah-la-MAH-tahn)

Pangilamen (Pong-EE-lah-men)

Hadji Adil Tambis (HAHD-gee AH-deel TAHM-beese): Father of Mohammad Adil_

Panabas (pah-nah-BAHS): a bladed weapon or farm implement with a rattan-wrapped hardwood handle just as long as its two to three foot curved blade.

Pendatun, Salipada (Sah-lee-PAH-dah Pen-DAH-toon): Foster brother of Mohammad Adil

Piang, Gumbay (GOOM-buy Pee-AHNG): Mohammad Adil's commander, son of Datu Piang

Piang, Pindililang (Pin-DEE-lee-lahng Pee-AHNG): Commander of Bolo Battalion, brother of Gumbay Piang

Sinsuat, Odin (OH-din SIN-soo-aht): Son of Sinsuat Balabaran

Tausug (Tao-SOOG)

Tubao (two-BAO): a cotton kerchief tied around the head like a turban.

Umbus a Bai (Oom-boose a BUY)

SELECT BIBLIOGRAPHY

Bonner, Raymond. *Waltzing with a Dictator: The Marcoses and the Making of American Policy.* New York: Times Books, 1987.

Childress, Clyde. "Wendell Fertig's Fictional 'Autobiography': a Critical Review of They Fought Alone." *Bulletin of the American Historical Collection* Vol. 31 No. 1 (January 2003): 1-24.

Connaughton, Richard. *MacArthur and Defeat in the Philippines.* New York: Abrams Press, 2001.

Creed, Roscoe. *PBY: The Catalina Flying Boat.* Annapolis: The United States Naval Institute, 1985.

Dissette, Edward and H.C. Adamson, *Guerrilla Submarines: The Never-before-told True Story of the Secret Action that Changed the Course of the War in the Pacific.* New York: Ballantine Books, 1972.

Dowlen, Dorothy Dore. *Enduring What Cannot Be Endured: Memoir of a Woman Medical Aide in the Philippines in World War II.* Jefferson, North Carolina: McFarland & Company, 2001.

Drach, George and Calvin F. Kuder, *The Telugu Mission of the General Council of the Evangelical Lutheran Church in North America: Containing a Biography of the Rev. Christian Frederick Heyer, M. D.* Reading, Pennsylvania: General Council Publication House, 1914.

Eisner, Peter. *MacArthur's Spies: The Soldier, The Singer, and the Spymaster who Defied the Japanese in World War II.* New York: Penguin Books, 2017.

Fermin, Jose D. *1904 World's Fair: The Filipino Experience.* West Conshohocken, PA: Infinity Publishing, 2004.

Gabriel Said Reynolds, "Seven Sleepers" in *Medieval Islamic Civilization,* Josef W. Meri, ed.. London: Routledge, 2004.

Gilmore, Allison B. *You Can't Fight Tanks with Bayonets: Psychological Warfare Against the Japanese Army in the Southwest Pacific.* Lincoln, Nebraska: University of Nebraska Press, 1998.

Ginn, John L. *Sugamo Prison, Tokyo: An Account of the Trial and Sentencing of Japanese War Criminals in 1948, by a U.S. Participant.* Jefferson, North Carolina: McFarland, 1992.

Gleeck, Lewis E. Jr. *Americans on the Philippine Frontiers.* Manila: Carmelo and Bauermann, 1974.

Gowing, Peter Gordon. *Mandate in Moroland: The American Government of Muslim Filipinos 1899-1920.* Quezon City, Philippines: New Day Publishers, 1983.

Grashio, Samuel C. and Bernard Norling, *Return to Freedom: The War Memoirs of Col. Samuel C. Grashio USAF. Ret.* Tulsa: MCN Press, 1981.

Haggerty, Edward. *Guerrilla Padre in Mindanao*. New York: Longmans, Green & Co., 1946.

Hayden, Joseph Ralston. "What Next for the Moros?" *Foreign Affairs* 6,1928. 633-644.

Holmes, Kent. *Wendell Fertig and his Guerrilla Forces in the Philippines: Fighting the Japanese Occupation, 1942-1945*. Jefferson, North Carolina: McFarland and Company, 2015).

Horn, Florence. *Orphans of the Pacific: The Philippines*. New York: Reynal and Hitchcock, 1941.

Ingham, Travis. *Rendezvous by Submarine: The Story of Charles Parsons and the Guerrilla-Soldiers in the Philippines*. Garden City, New York: Doubleday, Doran and Company, 1945.

Johnson, Robert L. "Overseas History: 222d Anti-Aircraft Artillery, Searchlight Battalion, 1942-1945." Box 279, U.S. Army Unit Records, Dwight D. Eisenhower Library, Abilene, Kansas.

Karnow, Stanley. *In Our Image: America's Empire in the Philippines*. New York: Ballantine Books, 1989.

Kawashima Midori, "Japanese Administrative Policy towards the Moros in Lanao." In Ikehata Setsuho and Ricardo Trota Jose, eds., *The Philippines Under Japan*. Manila: Ateneo de Manila University Press, 1999. 113.

Kawashima Midori. "The Battle of Tamparan." in Paul H. Kratoska, ed., *Southeast Asian Minorities in the Wartime Japanese Empire*. London: Routledge Curzon, 2002.

Keats, John. *They Fought Alone: Wendell Fertig and his WWII Guerrilla Campaign in the Philippines.* Brattleboro Vermont: Echo Point Books, 2015.

Kuder, Edward M. "The Philippines Never Surrendered." Parts I-V, *Saturday Evening Post.* February 10th to March 10th, 1945.

Kuder, Edward M. "The Moros in the Philippines." *Far Eastern Quarterly* 4, no. 2 (1945): 119-126.

Kuder, Edward M.. "Statement, 1943, of Edward M. Kuder to Hayden on events and conditions in Lanao immediately preceding the war and from 1941-1943," Box 41, Joseph Ralston Hayden Papers, Bentley Historical Library, University of Michigan, Ann Arbor, Michigan.

McCoy, Alfred W. *Policing America's Empire: The United States, the Philippines, and the Rise of the Surveillance State.* Madison: University of Wisconsin Press, 2009.

McGee, Brigadier General John Hugh. *Rice and Salt: A History of the Defense and Occupation of Mindanao During World War II.* San Antonio: The Naylor Company, 1962.

"Memorial, Joseph Ralston Hayden." Faculty History Project, The Millenium Project, University of Michigan, 2011. http://faculty-history.dc.umich.edu/faculty/joseph-ralston-hayden/memorial.

Mijares, Primitivo. *The Conjugal Dictatorship of Ferdinand and Imelda Marcos.* Quezon City, Philippines: Bughaw, 2017.

Millan, Simeon F. ed., 1952 Cotabato Guidebook. Cotabato City: Simeon F. Millan, 1952.

Morton, Louis. *United States Army in World War II: The War in the Pacific, The Fall of the Philippines.* Washington, D.C.: Center of Military History, 1989.

Norman, Elizabeth M. *We Band of Angels: The Untold Story of the American Women Trapped on Bataan.* New York: Random House, 1999.

Petersen, Robert K.D. "The Real Enemy: Scrub Typhus and the Invasion of Sansapour." *American Entomologist,* Volume 5, Number 2 (Summer 2009): 91-94.

Piang, Gumbay. "The Treason and Courtship of Bamboo Ear." *Philippines Free Press,* 9 July 1932, 48.

Quirino, Carlos. *Chick Parsons: America's Master Spy in the Philippines.* Quezon City, Philippines: New Day Publishers, 1984.

Richards, Carmen Nelson ed. *Death Stalks the Philippine Wilds: Letters of Maud Huntley Jenks.* Minneapolis: The Lund Press, Inc., 1951.

Schlegel, Stuart A. *Children of Tulus: Essays on the Tiruray People.* Quezon City, Philippines: Giraffe Books, 1994.

Schlegel, Stuart. A. *Wisdom from a Rainforest: The Spiritual Journey of an Anthropologist.* Athens Georgia: University of Georgia Press, 1998.

Schmidt, Larry S. "American Involvement in the Filipino Resistance Movement on Mindanao during the Japanese Occupation, 1942-1945." Master's Thesis, U.S. Army Command and General Staff College, 1982.

Scott, James M. *Rampage: MacArthur, Yamashita, and the Battle of Manila.* New York: W.W. Norton & Co., 2018.

Slim, General Sir William. *Defeat into Victory: Battling Japan in Burma and India.* New York: Cooper Square Press, 2000.

Smith, Robert Ross. *Triumph in the Philippines: The United States in World War II, the War in the Pacific.* Washington, D.C.: Center of Military History, United States Army, 1963.

Smollar, David. "Hard, Bitter, Unpleasantly Necessary Duty: a Little Known World War II Story of the Philippines." *Prologue* (Summer 2015): 6-15. https://www.archives.gov/files/publications/prologue/2015/summer/pcau.pdf.

Spencer, Louise. *Guerrilla Wife.* New York: Thomas Y. Crowell Company, 1945.

Stuckenschneider, Brother Placid. "The Last Campaign: Mindanao." HistoryNet.com, March, 1999. www.historynet.com/the-last-campaign-mindanao-march-99-world-war-ii-feature.htm.

Truman, Harry S. "Statement by the President Concerning Provisions in Bill Affecting Philippine Army Veterans," February 20, 1946, Harry S. Truman Library and Museum, https://www.trumanlibrary.gov/library/public-papers/38/statement-president-concerning-provisions-bill-affecting-philippine-army.

Walker, Scott. *The Edge of Terror: The Heroic Story of American Families Trapped in the Japanese-occupied Philippines.* New York: St. Martin's Press, 2009.

White, John R. Bullets and Bolos: Thirteen Years in the Philippine Islands. New York: The Century Co., 1928.

Woodruff, Major General R. B. "Colonel Frank McGee." *The Taro Leaf: Newsletter of the 24th Infantry Division Veterans Association* Volume II, Number 2, June 1949, 3.

ILLUSTRATION CREDITS

- Lt. Col. Charles Hedges and his elite Maranao fighters displaying Browning Automatic Rifles (BARs) recently delivered by an American submarine, circa 1943 (*The MacArthur Memorial*)

- Life on the Pulangi River, 1933 (*American Geographical Society Library (AGSL), University of Wisconsin-Milwaukee*)

- Alun and Adil, 1938 (*Adil Family*)

- Mohammad Adil, age 13, at Edward Kuder's house in Jolo (*Adil Family*)

- Jolo Harbor with Chinese Pier and, in the background, Bud Dajo, 1933 (*AGSL, University of Wisconsin-Milwaukee*)

- Adil in Boy Scout Uniform at Sulu High School, (*Adil Family*)

- Edward Kuder with the young Salipada Pendatun, 1927 (*Philippines Free Press*)

- Robert Bowler, Salipada Pendatun, and Chick Parsons, Bukidnon, 1943 (*The MacArthur Memorial*)

- Datu Piang with visiting American officers, 1899 (*B.W. Kilburn, Public Domain*)

- Datu Piang with the young Gumbay Piang, 1933 (*Joseph Ralston Hayden Papers, Bentley Historical Library, University of Michigan*)

- Magindanaon dugout canoe on the Pulangi River, 1933 (*AGSL, University of Wisconsin-Milwaukee*)

- Adil, seated far left, is still the smiling schoolboy on the eve of being commissioned as a guerrilla officer in 1943. In this studio photo he poses with the older fighters who will accompany him to the hills, including, seated next to him, the well-armed Hadji Hashim Ali and his wife. (*Adil Family*)

- A young Magindanaon man wearing a *tubao* and carrying a *panabas* stands on Irving Edwards' road to Upi, 1933 (*AGSL, University of Wisconsin-Milwaukee*)

- Charles Hedges and Wendell Fertig at the siege of Malabang, 1945 (*Australian War Memorial*)

- In a postwar group portrait in 1945, Mohammad Adil, transformed by war, stands far right. His father stands next to him with Hadji Hashim on the far left. Their wives are seated in front of them.(*Adil Family*)

INDEX